R U S K I N
as
LITERARY CRITIC

SELECTIONS

R USKIN
as
LITERARY CRITIC

SELECTIONS

Edited by

A. H. R. BALL, M.A.

Senior English Master
Liverpool Collegiate
School

GREENWOOD PRESS, PUBLISHERS
NEW YORK

First published in 1928
by Cambridge University Press, London

Reprinted with the permission
of Cambridge University Press

First Greenwood Reprinting, 1969

SBN 8371-1149-8

PRINTED IN UNITED STATES OF AMERICA

PREFACE

Most previous editions of extracts from Ruskin have been intended to illustrate his work as a prose artist, a project which Ruskin himself regarded with particular dislike. The aim of this volume is to collect in continuous and readable form the thoughts of Ruskin on two topics of special interest to-day—literature and aesthetics. The attention which has been given to Ruskin's other subjects makes the neglect of this branch of his work more striking, for there is here much of permanent value. Interesting themes, original treatment, suggestive ideas which warm and stimulate the mind, are set out in a more easily readable form than is usual in Ruskin's works; and always there is the incomparable beauty of his prose style. These provide a general background of culture not accessible elsewhere in so small a compass.

The arrangement of the extracts requires little explanation; it is intended to indicate both the character and range of Ruskin's literary criticism. The well-known passages on the value and study of books, from *Sesame and Lilies*, are placed first. The most representative sections on the broad general principles which underlie all his criticism, both of literature and of art,—the "moralistic theory," the treatises on aesthetics, and the study of the grotesque —are next grouped together. The survey of landscape in literature, including the chapter on the "Pathetic Fallacy," and the extracts on style, are among Ruskin's most useful criticisms, and deserve careful study. It is regretted that it is impossible to make any suitable short extract from the *Elements of English Prosody*. The criticisms of individual authors are chiefly on Dante, Shakespeare, Scott, Byron, and Wordsworth, but a few others are included

where the expression is particularly happy. Exigencies of space require somewhat ruthless excision in a few cases, but the selection includes representative and valuable essays. Lastly there are grouped together a few of Ruskin's definitions and aphorisms.

The Introduction indicates the early influences on Ruskin's critical faculty, attempts a brief estimate of the merits and demerits of his work, and gives a summary of the most important topics in this book, bridging over the inevitable gaps in the selections by reference to passages not quoted in the text. The life of Ruskin is not pursued in detail, as this is fully treated in the Introduction to A. C. Benson's *Selections from Ruskin*. For convenience a list of proper names, giving the allocation of characters to the books in which they occur, and brief notes where necessary, is appended. Textual references are indicated by footnotes.

Few readers have easy access to the Library Edition, and the references in this volume are to the numbered sections, which are alike in all editions.

I am indebted to my friends Dr H. A. Needham, of the University of Bristol, and Mr W. Holdgate, of Liverpool, for their valuable advice and criticism during the preparation of this volume, and my thanks are due to Messrs George Allen and Unwin, Limited, and to the Ruskin Trustees, for permission to include extracts from books which are still in copyright.

A. H. R. B.

Wallasey
1928

CONTENTS

CONTENTS

INTRODUCTION

(i) EARLY INFLUENCES

To understand Ruskin's literary criticism, almost all that need be known of his life is in his childhood and youth. His characteristic powers of genius had already ripened in 1843 when he began the publication of *Modern Painters*. There were changes after that—the setting-in of sobriety and restraint, and the mental depression of later years—but all his chief powers had flowed in by 1843. Subsequent changes were against the current. The making of his mind, which is reflected in *Praeterita*, was determined largely by the unusual combination in his father of artistic temperament and business efficiency; and the main factor in its development was a quiet and refined home, stored with culture and untroubled by care, presided over by two devoted parents whose interests in life were focussed on the genius of their only son.

He was born in London in the year 1819, and was educated mainly at home by his father and mother. John Ruskin, Senior, was a strange mixture of man of romance and man of business. During the day he was an honest and industrious wine merchant, but his nights he devoted to the poets and painters, and read every evening to his wife and child, usually in the garden. He had good taste, in literature as in sherry, and he put before his son only the best models. Both father and son, however, had a sense of being "profane and rebellious characters" compared with Mrs Ruskin, a stern Scotch Puritan, a woman of great power, indomitable will, and almost saturnine religious faith, who considered contact with the world a desecration and chil-

dren's toys a sinful frivolity. It is easily seen whence the boy derived that peculiar combination of the Greek and the Hebrew spirit, the puritan attitude towards art mingled with intense appreciation of beauty, the capacity for careful and patient work, piercing analysis, and the all-pervading poetic gift.

Mrs Ruskin had qualities which endeared her to the boy. He owed to her his grounding in that model of models—the English Authorised Version. Together they read the whole book once every year, his mother "watching every intonation, allowing not so much as a syllable to be misplaced, until every word slipped into its place unnoticed as a familiar guest, unchallenged as a household friend". The discipline was hard, but Ruskin was ever after grateful for it. "These readings", he said, "established my soul in life, and were the one essential part in all my education." At the same time, his father, whom he described as "an absolutely beautiful reader of the best poetry and prose", was reading to him "all Shakespeare, comedy and historical plays, again and again, all Scott and all Don Quixote, Pope, Spenser, Byron, Goldsmith, Addison and Johnson". A little later with his cousin Mary he "got through the evenings over 'Pilgrim's Progress', Bunyan's 'Holy War', Foxe's 'Book of Martyrs', Mrs Sherwood's 'Lady of the Manor', and Bingley's 'Natural History'". All this in the first decade of his life! At first he showed little inclination towards the classics, and after a few incursions into light literature, he turned all the more seriously to Scott and Wordsworth, Miss Edgeworth, Marryat, Isaac Walton, and Fenimore Cooper. Thus commenced "forty years of desultory yet careful reading", which covered all the best of ancient and modern literature.

At the same time another equally important part of his education was being carried on. His parents loved travelling, and his father's business took him from one end of the

country to another. They travelled by coach, visiting all the old country houses, stored in those days with the spoils of Italy, and his father took care that he should see every good picture, and no bad ones. Once a year also for thirty years they journeyed to the continent and visited most of the picture galleries of Europe. These tours not only cultivated Ruskin's aesthetic tastes, but they first revealed to him the beauty and spiritual qualities of nature, and gave him that sympathy and intimacy with the greatest source of all poetry, which is his peculiar gift.

Such a training seems suitable for the work Ruskin was to do, but it had its disadvantages. The strictness of the home discipline, the lack of toys and playmates, produced the "dangerous and lonely pride", which he acknowledged himself. The restraining force of early associations remained long with him, and his views were always conservative. Moreover, the comparative luxury of his life left him out of sympathy with those brute facts and forces that make up so much of the average experience. He noted later his inability to regard life with the gross relish of Chaucer, Shakespeare, Fielding, and Hogarth.

Ruskin early embarked on his literary career, both in poetry and prose. His poetry, large in bulk, and modelled upon Scott, Byron, and Wordsworth, is good imitative work, but nowhere reaches a very high level. As juvenilia, however, it shows merit, and his parents believed that he would write "poetry as good as Byron's, only pious". The hope was vain. He won the Newdigate, and acquired a certain facility and accuracy in the use of verse; but he himself was the first to perceive that he was on the wrong track, coming to "the extremely wholesome conclusion that in poetry I could express nothing rightly that I had to say". He turned his attention all the more seriously to prose, and at once proved that he had found his natural medium. It is interesting to note that among his

early essays for his tutor was one comprising a glowing defence of Scott and Byron, and an attempt to set out the comparative advantages of music and painting. In 1837 he went to Oxford, where he was a fellow-commoner of Christ Church. The life here brought him into contact with his fellows, and broadened his mind. He worked quietly and well, not confining his interests to literature, but spending much time on sciences, botany, geology, and mathematics. After he left the university his life is the story of increasing concentration, now on this study, now on that; but always with the same thoroughness and care. At the age of twenty-four he presented to the world a book giving ample evidence of the richness of his mind, attacking boldly the most universally established reputations, and reasoning acutely on subjects which usually take a lifetime to master.

The remainder of his career does not concern us in its details. His criticisms of books are scattered over the whole of his literary work, and whatever the subject, he usually found occasion for a few remarks on literature. A chronological list of his books is given on page 35. Up to 1860 they comprise the great works on art and architecture, with a gradually increasing concentration on moral and social issues. From 1860 to 1870 he was occupied with disputes on political economy, from which he emerged tinged with considerable bitterness, "an old man, always impatient and often tired". From 1869 to 1885 he divided his activities between the publication of his lectures and addresses on art and kindred subjects, and the issue of *Fors Clavigera*, a kind of prose *Don Juan*, but this differs from its predecessor in that it records the journey of a great and bitter mind through Vanity Fair. In 1885 he began *Praeterita*, which has taken its place among the few really great autobiographies of the world. He shakes off his cares, his sorrows, and his disappointments, and broods, still sadly,

but serenely, over a life in which he had done what he could.

(ii) RUSKIN AS A LITERARY CRITIC

The multiplex products of the many-faceted genius of Ruskin have aroused storms of controversy. On any subject that interested him he let his mind stream out in all its great variety of moods and thought, and it flows with the energy and caprices of a rippling brook. He wrote on art, architecture, political economy, natural history, morals and ethics, geology, mineralogy, biography, fairy tales, military tactics, and all kinds of literature. The comprehensive mind of a Goethe could not have dealt infallibly with them all. And yet it is hardly an exaggeration to say that the tendency of recent years has been to justify many of the main issues of his writings, especially in political economy and art. His minor themes, however, have received less attention than they deserve, and particularly is this evident with regard to his work on education, theology, and literature. Most critics and biographers of Ruskin find room for a few lines of praise, usually with reservations, of his views on books, regarding them as a rule as more or less interesting diversions from more important themes. But a careful reading of his books reveals a mass of literary criticism by no means inconsiderable in itself, and which, when collected, merits more than a few passing remarks.

"Ruskin's remarks on books", says Professor Saintsbury, "are delightful literature, but they are never criticism." Modern criticism is less conservative, and tends to modify this judgment. In the latest and best balanced appreciation of Ruskin, the author speaks enthusiastically of his incursions into literature. "A small volume might with profit be put together containing his criticism of books.

His dislikes are not always interesting or safe, but safety is
not everything in a critic. Where he is at home with his
author, his critical judgments are among the best to be
found anywhere."[1] Professor Saintsbury's attitude is somewhat difficult to understand, and good criticism may be a
more literary thing than he seems to make out. Ruskin's
life was "persistently literary"; he trained himself to that
end with infinite industry and assiduity. The views of such
a man on literature at any time deserve attention, and, when
sufficiently extensive, may even claim a place in the history
of criticism. However much we may disagree with particular judgments or deductions, it is always valuable to
study the opinions of a highly cultured man on his con-
temporaries, and on those spheres of literature which he is
particularly qualified to discuss. Moreover, Ruskin's
critical equipment was by no means inadequate. Practice
was not its least feature, and if we define criticism simply
as the faculty of passing a judgment on anything, then
Ruskin possessed the faculty in the highest degree. His own
age complained chiefly of his summary methods of passing
judgment on everything. Nothing less than definite assertion ever satisfied him, and it often proved a matter for
lamentation when, as *Punch* had it, "savage Ruskin dug
his tusk in". But his criticism was based on more than this.
In analysis, interpretation, and description, the power to
awaken fresh and vivid currents of ideas and emotions,
his genius was unequalled; and he imparted to all his works
something personal and distinctive. It is dogmatic to say
that any criticism is right or wrong; there are degrees
of right, and degrees of wrong. Points of view must vary;
and it is particularly necessary in Ruskin's case to look at
things from his standpoint and in complete realisation of his
standard of judgment, before we can fully appreciate his
criticisms. He made mistakes, as did others before him.

[1] Oliver Elton, *Survey of English Literature*, 1830–70.

Blindnesses and antipathies have marred the judgments of greater critics. We cannot judge Sainte-Beuve by his attitude to Balzac, Landor by his dislike of Shelley, Emerson by his distaste of Poe and Shelley, or Matthew Arnold by his antipathy to Victor Hugo's poetry. Where great ends are reached we overlook minor defects.

Whatever his achievement, Ruskin had a never-swerving nobility of aim. He wrote "neither for fame, nor for money, but of necessity". He felt that he had a message for mankind, and he delivered it to the best of his ability. At the close of his life he could speak honestly of his books as "the thoughts of a man, who, from youth up, and during a life persistently literary, has never written a word either for money, or for vanity, nor even in the careless incontinence of the instinct for self-expression, but resolutely spoke only to teach, and to praise others". The rare and superb gift of absolute sincerity is stamped on every sentence he wrote. He wrote exactly what he thought, extenuating nothing and setting down nought in malice. He spent the whole of his life in the spirit of devotion to great men, and in endeavouring to communicate this love to others. His mission in an iron age, and to a materialistic nation, was "to declare and to demonstrate, wherever they exist, the essence and authority of the beautiful and the true". All his work was an effort to hold men to the things which are lovely and of good report.

"Not one word of any book is readable", he wrote in *Fors Clavigera*, "except so far as your mind is at one with the author, and not merely his words like your words, but his thoughts like your thoughts." Sympathy, the soul of criticism, Ruskin possessed in a peculiar degree: a deep, sensitive and imaginative sympathy, which naturally became more intimate as he grew older. The writers he loved entered into his life; he knew their works by heart; he studied even the single words they wrote; and above all he

practised their principles. He looked at them from every side with a range of sympathies almost unequalled in literature, accepting their weaknesses and their faults, but so placing and harmonising them with their merits as to form one noble whole. This is the origin of the invaluable chapters on Dante, Shakespeare and Scott.

For breadth of vision and comprehensiveness of knowledge Ruskin is rarely equalled among literary critics. He hardly ever wrote of what he did not know. His opinions came from a mind stored with varied and curious knowledge. Behind every judgment was "much thought and much strong emotion, brought to the subject by years of thinking over subjects full of pain. It constantly needed examination and thought, prolonged during many days, to form opinions which the reader may suppose to be dictated by caprice, and will hear only to dispute". Thoroughness was the very essence of his method. He never spared himself in his analyses; no detail was too inconsiderate, no labour too great, to get at the truth. His reading of literature, if not wide beyond that of the average man of his class, was sound and deep. Moreover his learning extended to all the fine arts, and while the close correlation of the arts is not always safe, Ruskin saw them all as the expression of the order and sweetness which make life beautiful. Thus he was unusually successful in indicating the relation of the fine arts to one another and to life.

To the gift of long and patient study Ruskin added an inherited power of keen insight and observation, and the combination made his intuitions, both on books and on life, deep and piercing. "Ruskin", said Mazzini, "possesses the most analytical mind in Europe." In *Praeterita*, the author modestly disclaimed any special power or capacity except "that patience in looking, and precision in feeling, which afterwards, with due industry, formed my analytical power". And this analysis is often set out in words with

a keen eye for effect. It is usual to deny him the power of close and logical presentation of facts, what Arnold calls the "ordo concatenatioque veri", and it must be admitted that at times his habit of digression causes confusion; but Ruskin can always rise to the occasion and at times advances his views with scientific precision. No proposition of a great argument could be more close in presentation or more subtle than the second volume of *Modern Painters*; no technical matters could be treated with greater simplicity of argument than the essays on the pathetic fallacy and landscape in literature; and his definitions are often masterly.

If Ruskin's treatment of literature were destitute of any other qualities, it would be studied for these alone. But when we add to the interest of subject matter and skill in exposition a gift of language unsurpassed in an age of great stylists, Ruskin occupies almost a unique position in literary criticism. Even those who thought he wrote nonsense admitted that he wrote it beautifully. His judgments are those of a man who knew what it was to write, both in prose and verse. He was a master of literary swordsmanship, and this served him well or ill according as he applied it to fields of reality which were or were not congenial. Nowhere is this more apparent than in his criticism of literature and of art. When he deals with a great subject his style is distinguished by eloquence and imaginative richness; at times it catches the note of prophetic authority and spiritual glow; elsewhere he dons the whole armour of controversy, and supports calm and unimpassioned reasoning with clear-cut, incisive sentences, and shattering epigram. The style varies with the matter in hand; but there is always the same abundance of picturesque illustrations and powerful metaphors, the same melodious cadence of words. And it is all couched in a diction stately and plain; characterised by a fine lucidity of expression. We never have to read a paragraph

twice to ascertain its meaning. The eloquence is perfectly combined with the body of critical and expository matter. Ruskin's limitations are well known. Professor Saintsbury has accomplished the somewhat easy task of extracting from their context in Ruskin's work various contradictory remarks, and by placing them in juxtaposition has proved that he was no critic. There is no doubt that Ruskin's enthusiasm and earnestness often led him to assert what he thought and felt at the moment, chance preferences and dislikes, irrespective of what had gone before. That he was "continually learning" made this worse. "True taste", he says, "is for ever growing, learning, reading, worshipping, laying its hand upon its mouth because it is astonished." One might answer that change should at least be from variety to unity of opinion. But there is less inconsistency in Ruskin's literary criticism than is usually alleged, and the rash assertions are usually inconsequent sentences. In fact, this department of his work is peculiarly free from hasty and unthinking apportionment of praise and blame, and the important passages are careful and considered statements of settled opinions.

Goethe once said that a loving interest in the person and works of an author, amounting to a certain one-sided enthusiasm, alone leads to reality in criticism; all else is vanity. In this sense Ruskin is a very real critic, for he is always in danger of personal absorption in his subject. He makes a cult of certain authors, approaches them with humility and free giving of himself, and takes up their work and characters as bits of nature. Such a view is penetrating and valuable, but it is only a partial one. His sympathies are intense, but narrow. And the natural corollary is the tendency to condemn petulantly and sometimes unfairly those who are not acceptable to Ruskin the man, or who fail to satisfy Ruskinian values. So Ruskin does not rank with the great impartial historians and critics. He lacks the distinctive power

of the finest criticism, the faculty of seeing a thing steadily and seeing it whole.

The most just accusation brought against Ruskin is that he does not know where to stop. In him we have a combination of the theorist, the logician, and the enthusiast, with the result that he is tempted to carry good and accepted principles beyond the limits of truth and reason. His actual opinions and theories are usually simple and sensible, but they are sometimes pressed to the complex and absurd. This is why we have that strange mixture of common sense and eccentricity, acute deduction followed by chains of error, confusion of mind following the most systematic reasoning. His gift of imaginative interpretation often led him to interpret too far, and to read himself into his subjects. Shakespeare would probably have resented the interpretation of the *Tempest* as an allegorical representation of true liberty and slavery. Ruskin is often in an ecstasy of admiration. He saw as few others have seen, but, as his biographer remarked, "he looked at times through a halo of sentiment and out of eyes deep set with genius and with poetry".

In spite of all this, Ruskin's work retains for us a peculiar fascination, for it possesses to a remarkable degree the rare power of kindling our thoughts and inspiring our critical faculties. All his reasoning on literature may not add much to our knowledge, but it illuminates what we do know. "Hitherto", wrote Miss Brontë of *Modern Painters*, "I have only had instinct to guide me in judging of art; I feel as if I had been walking blindfold; this book seems to give me eyes." "He gave the seeing eye and thought and feeling a practical reality which they will never lose, but never had before", wrote another admirer. And this is what he still does for us. "He puts us into a new world of observation, beauty, power, and progressive thought."[1]

[1] G. R. Parkin, *Life of Edward Thring*, 1898.

(iii) THE "MORALISTIC THEORY"

"Poetry", says Ruskin, "is the suggestion, by the imagination, of noble grounds for the noble emotions." This definition suggests the key to all Ruskin's criticism, his intense operation on moral and practical issues. Here was Ruskin's debt to, or perhaps affinity with, Plato. Both adopted the moralistic attitude towards the fine arts. Plato would banish from his republic all poets who are not edifying; his test of good music is its effect upon the moral character. Ruskin carried the idea still further, making the arts an exponent of the social and political virtues of a nation, and of the writers themselves. This reciprocity of art and morals in the state was not a new discovery. It had been discussed by other writers before 1850; Hume, Burke, Reynolds, Kant, Ballanche, Madame de Staël, Chateaubriand, and Carlyle, all touch on the subject, and in some cases develop it. But Ruskin made the idea so peculiarly his own that in England, at least, it is always associated with him. Whether the theory is entirely sound or not, it is difficult to tell with our insufficient data, but the case Ruskin makes out for himself in the *Stones of Venice*, in *Lectures on Art*, and in his social teaching, is at least plausible, and substantially convincing. It is true that the efflorescence of art seems always to accompany corruption in society, but this may be because the evil is a challenge which brings out the good. It does not alter the fact that art comes from goodness. The literature of the English Restoration is an obvious example. The books which were the products of the vice and license of fashionable society are easily distinguished from those which sprang from the natural purity of the country at large. The origins of the Restoration drama and of the *Pilgrim's Progress* are clearly marked.

Ruskin never swerved from this belief, that no great art was ever created by a bad man. Within limits the theory would need little argument, but when he applies it to individuals Ruskin is inclined to carry his ideas too far. This is more obvious in the application of the theory to painting and to architecture than in its relation to literature, for a great literary work is usually the product of one man whose life is well known, whereas it is difficult to generalise on the lives of all those who contribute to the building, say, of a Gothic cathedral. Literature in general supports the theory that there is a correspondence between moral elevation and imaginative work. Ruskin's case is best presented in the Rede lecture, "The Relation of National Ethics to National Arts", on which the passages quoted from *Lectures on Art* were largely based. In general, he seeks to show what absolute goodness is in the art, and what absolute goodness is in the spirit, and to see how far the one is the product of the other. He acknowledges at once the inextricable mixture of good and evil in man, and admits that nobility may include, or even require, some exhibition of moral decadence, the better part of art being obliged not only to work in companionship with, but in some sort to work down through the evil, using it as its instrument. This corollary is pursued in the study of the grotesque—that constant outcrop of animal coarseness in literature and art, a delight in those forms of burlesque which are connected in some way with the foulness of evil. Good art, Ruskin says, is balanced, reserved, constructive, inventive, complete, pure, and lovely, as opposed to the unsymmetrical, intemperate, unconstructive, unimaginative, incomplete, sensual, and undelightful; and it requires little demonstration to show that each of these attaches itself to a quality of the soul which produces them all. The best artist is he who exhibits the most of these qualities. By the sacrifice of all the others for any one quality, an intensity

of achievement is obtainable, but absolute rightness comes only from the perfect balance of these higher faculties. Ruskin is able to draw from this theory various inferences as to the elements of character necessary for the production of true formative art. These are, first, brightness of physical life and the manly virtues belonging to it; then the broad scope of reflection and purpose; then the distinctive gift of imagination, together with the innocent perception of beauty; and to crown all, the perfect peace of an honest and living faith. Finally, Ruskin works out the relationship between the artist and the ethical state of his age. The finest artists live entirely within their own age, in it they find their characters and their themes. Thus all the qualities of the artist will be rendered useless if the condition of persons and things around him is degraded. It is only in a nation unselfish and generous, seeking truth, loving goodness and hating falsehood, that the artist will find the subjects necessary to make him great.

(iv) AESTHETICS

Like Coleridge, Ruskin was from the first determined to investigate the "faculty or source from which the pleasure given by any poem or passage was derived", and by his twenty-seventh year he had worked out for himself elaborate theories of the Beautiful, and of the Imagination. The subject was popular in the nineteenth century, and many ingenious results had been attained, among which Ruskin's work has a unique place. He read very little of other treatises in the same field, and his essays are fresh in tone and thought, amply illustrated from his own knowledge of literature and art. He was attracted to the subject, not by any delight in abstract philosophising, but by an attempt to find a criterion which would enable him to interpret the merits of any great work of art. His state-

ments are often novel and suggestive, and they are all
stamped indelibly with the mark of his personal genius.
Moreover, rarely afterwards did he propound his theories
so carefully as in the second volume of *Modern Painters*.
There they are set out clearly and lucidly, elaborately yet
consistently, and all in the most simple and limpid prose.

Ideas on Beauty are elusive, and few writers have em-
bodied them successfully. Ruskin's treatise in its day was
one of the most elaborate since the Greek attempts during,
and immediately following, the age of Pericles. Modern
scholarship has not followed on the lines of Ruskin's work,
and his theory is still almost unique in the history of English
aesthetics, but it is consistent with itself, and, as Sir Edward
Cook points out, it "explains many of the phenomena, and
harmonises better than any other philosophy, with a
system of natural religion". Ruskin's aesthetic writings
have a permanent value of their own. One who is perhaps
best qualified to give an opinion on the subject writes: "It
is not too much to say that Ruskin, like Winkelmann, has
given the mind a new organ for the appreciation of
Beauty."[1]

Burke had been concerned with the physiological aspect
of beauty, finding its manifestation in those objects which
produce in us a feeling of pleasure, languor, or repose. The
elements of beauty, he states, are smallness of size, delicacy
suggesting fragility, smoothness of surface, variety of outline in curves, and brightness or softness of colour. Coleridge found beauty in the harmonious relation of the parts
of a thing each to each, and of all of them to the whole.
Ruskin begins by denying that impressions of beauty are in
any way sensual or intellectual. Beauty is not the true, or
the customary, neither does it depend upon emotion.
Ruskin's ideas go back to Plato and Plotinus, who taught
that beauty was "an emanation from the Infinite, and a

[1] Bosanquet, *History of Aesthetics*.

disclosure of it". Every beautiful object, says Plato, consists of sensible phenomena or form, but it also embodies an idea, a reflection of the infinite and perfect, which underlies the form; and it is the function of the form to lead us to the idea. The first part of Ruskin's analysis differs little from this, christianised, though the immediate suggestion probably came from the chapter on "Symbols" in *Sartor Resartus*. All Ruskin's aesthetic philosophy is permeated with religious spirit; it is indeed part of his religion. He finds all over nature certain external qualities which are typical of divine attributes, and it is these qualities which constitute beauty. This beauty, therefore, exists everywhere, and it is absolutely identical whether found in man, beast, or stone.

These typical qualities which Ruskin finds in nature are six. The first is Infinity, for which we have an instinctive yearning as we look at nature, and which is a type of the Divine Incomprehensibility. The second is Unity, which is a type of Divine Comprehensiveness. Then there is the "Universal instinct of repose", which is a type of Divine Permanence. Symmetry similarly is typical of Divine Justice, Purity of Divine Energy, and Moderation of Divine Government by law. This class of Beauty Ruskin calls "Typical Beauty". It is the stamp of God's image on whatever he has created, the "expression of the creating power of the universe".

There is, however, a second class of Beauty, which is seen in the "felicitous fulfilment of function in living things, more especially the joyful and right exertion of perfect life in man". This class of Beauty Ruskin distinguishes as "Vital Beauty", and it can be either relative or generic: relative when an organic creature exhibits appearances or evidences of happiness, and generic when our impressions are connected with the more or less perfect fulfilment of the appointed function by different individuals

of the same species. Why is the skylark beautiful? Because it so happily fulfils its function as "songster of the skies". It fulfils our bird ideal.

There are deficiencies in this theory and it can easily be attacked on the philosophical side. The conclusions are cleverly worked out and amply illustrated, but they are not always convincing. The division and classification, too, are somewhat overdone, for Ruskin's mind naturally broke up a general proposition into details, and he abounds in particular proposals, some shrewd, some not. The distinction between the two classes of Beauty, for instance, is open to objection. Neither is his definition very conclusive— "There is no other definition of Beauty than that it is what one noble spirit has created, seen or felt by another of similar or equal nobility." Yet, in spite of its faults, the treatment is well and admirably carried out, in method single and clear, and marvellously eloquent. The argument is sustained to the end, and he never loses sight of the object. Few philosophical treatises have such power to induce serious and solemn reflection. Moreover Ruskin's ideas of Beauty lead on naturally to his theory of "the distinctive gift of the Imagination".

(V) THE "IMAGINATION"

Ruskin's analysis of the "Imagination", though arrived at independently, differs little from that of Coleridge. It is more analytic, more elaborate, and furnished with more examples, but it comes to the same thing. "Imagination," says Ruskin, "is the result of a common and vital, but not therefore less divine spirit, of which some portion is given to all living creatures in such a manner as may be adapted to their rank in creation." It is the possession of this faculty which distinguishes man from the rest of the brute creation, and, when possessed in a high degree, distinguishes the poet

or the artist from the ordinary man. Like Wordsworth, Ruskin saw the imagination as the link between man and God; it is only by the imagination that he can recognise the divine qualities in nature, and see what is before him as the symbol of something greater than itself.

In art we see the operation of this faculty in various ways. When the sources of beauty are presented in any great work, it is not in the form of a pure transcript. They invariably receive the reflection of the mind under whose influence they have passed, and they are modified or coloured by its image. This modification is the work of the imagination. Moreover, the imagination has three distinct functions. The great artist, seeing a landscape, breaks it up, accepts this and rejects that, and finally brings the pieces together again to make a new whole. This is the theory of the *Biographia Literaria*, the conception of genius as putting out in art the same creative power that God used when He made the world. The artist, however, must not merely rearrange the objects, as a watchmaker fits together the parts of a watch; he must fuse all into one consistent whole, and put life into his work. The result of this will not be false to nature, for it is a close and clear reproduction of facts. All will be true to the actual world, for the artist neither alters nor improves nature, but seeks in it for whatsoever things are pure and lovely, and directs attention to them. To do this he must not deprive beauty of her foils. The theoretic faculty takes out of anything only that which is beautiful, but the imagination takes hold of the very imperfections which are thus rejected and fuses all into complete harmony. So Shakespeare places Caliban beside Miranda, and Autolycus beside Perdita, that the whole may be a more perfect vision. This is the first function of the imagination—it combines, and by combination creates new forms. Ruskin therefore calls it the Imagination Associative.

The imagination, however, treats and regards both images and combinations in peculiar ways. The poet sees a landscape permeated by a single mood, of joy or of sorrow, and he either lends this mood to the landscape from himself, or he draws it from the landscape. Thus again he is a creator and life giver. So Wordsworth talks of the auxiliar light shed by the poet on nature, "the light that never was on land or sea", and Coleridge in the *Ode to France* speaks of the poet's own spirit, which

> Shoots its being through earth, sea, and air,
> Possessing all things with intensest love.

Similarly Shakespeare did not describe Hamlet—he became Hamlet. The poet must draw from the life of the world, identify it with his own, and put his own heart in the centre of it. This function Ruskin calls the Imagination Contemplative.

The last peculiar function of the imagination is that it penetrates, analyses, and reaches truths discoverable by no other faculty. It always seizes the innermost point, ploughs all externals aside, and nothing contents its spirituality but getting down to the "very central fiery heart of things". This is evident in the conceptions of all great poets and painters. "Every character that is so much as touched by men like Aeschylus, Homer, Dante, or Shakespeare is by them held by the heart. . . every circumstance or sentence of their being, speaking or seeming, opens for us a way down to the heart, leads us to the centre, and there leaves us to gather what more we may." Moreover this power of looking closest, piercing deepest and holding most securely gives to its possessors the most intense passion and gentleness of sympathy: "Power of imagination may always be tested by accompanying tenderness of emotion, hence there is no tenderness like Dante's, neither any intensity nor seriousness like his." This type is the Imagination Pene-

trative—it reaches by intuition and intensity of gaze a more essential truth than is seen at the surface of things.

Like Coleridge, Ruskin distinguishes the Imagination and Fancy as two different mental faculties. He looks on the imagination as the source of all that is great in the poetic arts, and fancy as merely decorative and entertaining. Fancy, he says, has three distinct functions, one subordinate to each of the functions of the imagination. It can call up images from nature in multitudes, and may render them so truthfully as to be impressive and instructive, but the images are correlated, not fused. Secondly, the poet does not infuse his own spirit into the work. And lastly, Fancy sees the outside, and is able to give a picture of the outside, clear, brilliant, and full of detail, but staying at the externals it can never feel, it contains no passion, and is purely and simply an intellectual faculty. The whole distinction is worked out in detail, with appropriate examples.

Whether we regard Ruskin's aesthetic teaching as part of his critical equipment or as a contribution to the history of thought, there is no doubt that it deserves to rank with the work of more famous investigators in the same field. His analyses are subtle and delicate, highly suggestive and illuminating. His work abounds, as Matthew Arnold remarked, in "brilliant aperçus". Every paragraph is crammed with information and inferences drawn often from the most obscure and unlikely places. And there is a great deal of hard, matter-of-fact, logical reasoning. He seems able to account for every difficulty in a subtle way of his own. Sir Leslie Stephen, writing of the passages on the imaginative faculty, says, "I never read anything which seemed to me to do more to make clear the true characteristics of good poetry." And Mr Eliot Norton, Ruskin's American friend and editor, paid an equally generous tribute: "The treatises of Ruskin and Wordsworth are mutually complementary, and they afford a body of doctrine admirably

fitted to enlighten, enlarge, and elevate the understanding
of the reader in its appreciation of the worth and work of
the most precious and loftiest of the human powers." The
second volume of *Modern Painters* marks the culmination
of the English School of Aesthetics begun by Coleridge.
It was continued by William Morris and his school, but
subsequent aesthetic criticism in the nineteenth century
developed on different lines. John Addington Symonds,
Walter Pater, and Oscar Wilde all came under the influence of Ruskin, and carried on the movement in its
various phases, but they abandoned the emphasis on ethics
which is the mark of Ruskin's aesthetics.

(vi) RUSKIN AND NATURE

That part of Ruskin's literary criticism which is best known
and least assailed is undoubtedly the essay on landscape
which forms part of the third volume of *Modern Painters*.
He was here at home with his subject, and critics who denied
his qualifications in other directions, could not but admit
his claims to be heard on nature and its reproduction in art.
From earliest years Ruskin had been a close observer of
nature, and the home discipline of his solitary boyhood had
forced him into the keenest sympathy with her. He studied
nature in the fine garden at Herne Hill, in the family tours
through England and Scotland, and found its full revelation
in the Alps and European scenery. He loved nature in its
great masses; he studied it in its minutest forms. Like
Wordsworth, he found in nature a teacher and a friend; he
saw in it a divine import and a solemn meaning. The nineteenth century, in contrast to the eighteenth, made much of
nature as a subject of literature. The Romantics, the Pre-
Raphaelites, Tennyson, Matthew Arnold, all loved her
and described her in different ways. It was left to Ruskin
to write the first considered and elaborate summary of the

extent to which the influence of nature has entered into books.

(vii) THE PATHETIC FALLACY

The greatest difference between ancient and modern art, according to Ruskin, lies in our use of what he felicitously terms the "Pathetic Fallacy". In general, this is the application to the forms of nature of terms which should only be used to describe human emotion—the imputation to inanimate objects of powers and characters which they cannot truly possess. Much of our modern poetry is saturated with this fallacy, and we regard it as an added beauty. The question, therefore, is of vital importance to Ruskin, who throughout his teaching insists on the association of goodness and truth. It should be noted that Ruskin's views on the subject go a little further than is usually supposed. He distinguishes two distinct types of the fallacy: one in which it is used wilfully, and with no real expectation that it will be believed; this is mere prettiness, and should be condemned; and a second form, which is caused by an excited state of the feelings, making us for the time more or less irrational. The emotions are then, apparently, true.

Ruskin applies the theory to literature, and classifies poets according to their indulgence in this feeling; the greatest are those who can receive impressions strongly and yet stand serene, watching the feeling, as it were, from afar off. The classification is ingenious and amply illustrated, but it is unconvincing. Ruskin places Homer in the highest class because his use of the fallacy is justified by the strength of its cause. But even Homer was not above skilful poetic artifice. And when Tennyson and other great modern poets are relegated to an inferior class, we suspect that the theory, or its application, is somewhere going wrong. The state of mind which regards nature in this way may be far from irrational. It may be intelligently modifying ordinary

impressions by the use of the imagination, in the way Ruskin himself has indicated. The great artist is an interpreter rather than an imitator. He gets to the "very central fiery heart of things", and to interpret their hidden meaning and impart it to others, terms of emotion may be the only ones possible. Aristotle, the master of realists, explains that, in his definition of poetry as "mimesis", he does not mean what we should call photographic reproduction, but that actions must be represented with "more rareness than is found in nature".

The association of nature and emotion has, too, a certain traditional basis in human nature. Most people feel at some time the correspondence between the spiritual and material worlds, and this apparent connection between nature and human life has been recognised and utilised by the greatest poets since the beginning of literature. In Shakespeare it was more of a wilful fancy than with the Greeks. There are moments in life when natural images impress themselves on our minds in terms of human emotion. Many felt the foam to be "cruel" and "crawling" before Kingsley found words for the feeling. Even where the fallacy is used in wilful fancy one may assume that the average intelligence can appreciate the metaphor, and condemn it if it is not sufficiently suggestive to convey dramatic propriety. When it does so, the metaphorical epithet is more effective than any number of vaguer, if truer, descriptions. It is most often when the poet succeeds in focussing his meaning into a single epithet of emotion that he achieves the unforgettable line.

The application of the theory to literature is highly coloured by Ruskin's preferences and dislikes. Homer does not say that the sea rages; it is a god in the sea which rages: therefore his faith is stronger than that, say, of Keats, for he can separate in his mind the material and living qualities of the sea, and embody them as a god. A critic justly asked

why Homer should be ranked higher in this respect than Keats, because he was labouring under one delusion which prevented him falling into another. Aeschylus and Aristophanes, the truest representatives of the greatest period of Greek art and literature, have much of this love of picturesque form; therefore they are not truly Greek, or this is the part of their activities which is not representative of the national spirit. No word of how these national characteristics are to be distinguished! And what of *Lycidas* and Shakespeare's *Sonnets*? The theory goes wrong in application, but not in argument. Ruskin reasons throughout with the same conclusiveness, and his logic, always his bright sword, never reinforces his eloquence better than in this essay. It is honestly and unawares that he moulds the theory to the wants of his own imagination; he spoke the truth as it defined itself to his mind and feelings. We cannot accept all his views, but they deserve careful study both as a warning against disconnected trains of luxuriant and fanciful images, and for their suggestion of new and illuminating lines of research.

(viii) LANDSCAPE IN LITERATURE

The historical portion of the essay on landscape is more accurate in its conclusions and happier in its illustrations. It forms, says Professor Elton, "one of Ruskin's most delightful, coherent and trustworthy studies, all the more trustworthy that he is here safe on his own territory of rock and valley, and lowland." Ruskin does not go far wrong in this sketch, and it affords ample opportunity for his knowledge and power of analysis. He chooses three salient points in the history of literature and art, and by analysing a typical poet of each age he attempts, with considerable ingenuity, to detect the dominant features of the feelings of the writers of that age towards external nature. The three periods are the Greek, the Medieval, and the Modern;

and for his examples he draws upon Homer, Dante, and Scott. Objections to these easily suggest themselves, but they answer the purpose with sufficient precision.

The Greeks had no right regard for natural scenery. They were too superstitious, too materialistic, and too familiar with the grandeur of nature to appreciate it. In any case it was a different type of beauty that they admired and strove to attain: the beauty of the human countenance and form. In so far as it is introduced into literature by the Greeks, nature is merely a conventional background for the human comedy, and the more agreeable its aspect, the better it is suited for that purpose. Ruskin's illustrations are confined to Homer, generally to the *Odyssey*, to which belongs more naturally the landscape of cultivated nature. Contrary examples can easily be found in the choral lyrics of the drama, and in the later lyrical and idyllic poetry, but those Ruskin selects serve their purpose.

To the medieval mind, a thousand years later, the external world is more precious for its own sake, but it is still subordinate to human life. The medieval is more perceptive, and he realises something of the moral of nature, especially of mountains; but his attitude is sensuous, giving evidence of idleness and a more sentimental enjoyment of scenery. The essential change from the ancients is that the medieval has learnt to regard with a deep love the flowers and the grass, not as a means of life, but as sources of pleasure. The examples from the *Divina Commedia* illustrate Dante's intense definition, his fine portraiture of mountains, his deep dislike of woods, his love for the grass, and keen sense of colour. Ruskin's analysis is impartial and penetrating.

The modern mind differs considerably from these two in its attitude to nature. The range of vision has extended, and we can appreciate freely and intensely, but the prevailing note is cloudiness, darkness, and mutability. The landscapes

are vaster, but they lack the sense of solemnity; and this has led to a general profanity of temper, a total absence of faith in the presence of any deity in nature. Connected with this is the strong tendency in all but a few to deny the sacred element of colour, and the loss of delight in human beauty. But in spite of all this, nature is loved for its own sake, and united with human emotion. Scott is chosen as the representative of the spirit of this age, and these characteristics are illustrated from his mind and books. Whatever objection may be taken to particular inferences, this essay undoubtedly contains a great deal of truth and illuminating detail. In conjunction with it the essay on the sea in literature (a subject hitherto practically untouched), from the *Harbours of England*, and the chapters on mountains in *Modern Painters*, volume IV, should be read. These represent the high water mark of Ruskin's literary criticism. The argument rarely goes wrong, and is distinguished by sanity and restraint. Clearness of intellect, power of observation, love of truth, and independence of character are combined with a beauty of style and delicacy and splendour of description not yet surpassed.

(ix) STYLE

The "grand style" is a favourite subject in these days, and Ruskin has much to say about it. His own literary workshop was a place of infinite labour, and it is characteristic of the breadth of knowledge which he brought to his criticism, that one who had stressed so much the aesthetic side of the poet's equipment should lay equal emphasis on the value and necessity of style and technique. In the third volume of *Modern Painters* he analyses the elements of the "grand style" in fine art. Greatness of style, he says, consists, first, in the habitual and sincere choice of noble subjects; and the choice is seen as much in the treatment of the subject as in

its selection, the artist seeking chiefly to represent what makes the subject noble. The second characteristic is the introduction in the conception of the subject of as much beauty as possible, consistent with truth. Beauty, however, must not be deprived of her foils: Shakespeare places Caliban beside Miranda and Autolycus beside Perdita; and often beauty and ugliness must be enjoyed together to learn truly what is beautiful. Next, since it is not possible to give all the truths of nature, the largest possible quantity should be given in the most perfect possible harmony. Thus greatness is shown largely in the choice of the facts represented or omitted. Lastly, great art is produced by the imagination, that is, it not only presents grounds for noble emotion, but it furnishes these grounds by imaginative power. Imaginative art includes historical or simply narrative art, but history and narrative are never great in themselves until the poetical or imaginative power touches them. The word "great" can truly be used of art embodying all these characteristics, for the sum of them is the sum of the human soul; such art compasses and calls forth the entire human spirit. In the third article of *Fiction, Fair and Foul*, Ruskin returns to consider the elements of the "grand style" in literature, deducing them from two passages of Shakespeare, the first an expression of anger from *Henry V*, and the second of love from *Coriolanus*. The essential requirement again is "nobility". This alone gives the sweetness, simplicity, and melody of expression which are characteristic of master song. The passage is quoted in full in the text of this volume.

(x) PERSONAL CRITICISM

In turning to the consideration of Ruskin's views on individual authors we are on more arbitrary ground. The main difficulty is to separate what we may call pure exposition

from criticism, for in his works, especially the later ones, there are readings from many authors, some comparatively unknown, and explanations of particular books. To embody all these would require many volumes. The actual criticism may generally be divided into two classes. In the first we may place the elaborate and detailed studies of those authors who formed his earliest studies, and to whom he remained faithful to the end—Shakespeare, Scott, Byron, Wordsworth, and later, Dante. Secondly, there are, scattered through the whole of his works, numerous critical remarks on authors whom he was at the time reading, or on whom he was drawing for illustrations. Many of these are highly discriminating; some are founded upon insufficient knowledge or upon personal prejudice. It seems hardly fair to hold up a man's passing judgments as evidence of his taste, but a few of them have permanent value in the felicity of their expression, and some examples are included here.

These remarks in general are appreciative. Ruskin's fault, if it may be called so, was that he encouraged too freely. He always tends to overestimate rather than depreciate, particularly where the theme is congenial. Just occasionally an excessive contempt for those who fail to appreciate the noble and the beautiful creeps in, and there are caustic remarks on the taste of those who "prefer to live among snipes and widgeons". The criticism often interprets the critic rather than his author, and the personal element is always clear. It is all the more charming for that, for we are coming more and more to demand that the critic shall be present in his work, not as mere intelligence, but as a distinct personality. The most striking feature of these appreciations is their range. Like Carlyle's, Ruskin's judgments were limited, but they were never insular. From his childhood he had known the continent almost as well as England, and this kept him in touch with the literature of

Europe. There are also frequent references to the classics. "We are constantly struck", says Frederick Harrison of Ruskin's work, "with the range of reading, the subtle comments, and the force of sympathy with which he had realised the inmost soul of so many classical writers, both prose and verse, Latin as well as Greek. Nor has any Professor of Greek, of Poetry, or of Philosophy, touched with a wand of such magic power so many inimitable passages of Homer, Hesiod, Aeschylus, Pindar, Aristophanes, Aristotle, Xenophon, Lucian; or again of Virgil, Horace, and Catullus." To make this list complete we should have to add Herodotus, Thucydides, Sophocles, Euripides, Anacreon, Callimachus, Juvenal, Livy, and Tacitus.

The object of this volume precludes the introduction of most of these classical studies, and limits the selection from Ruskin's great achievement, the revelation of the ages of faith. To Ruskin, Dante was "the central man of all the world as representing in perfect balance the imaginative, moral, and intellectual faculties, all at their highest." These were the qualities which appealed to Ruskin: his power of seeing to the heart of things, the "imagination penetrative", the minute presentation of faithfully observed imagery, and words pregnant with spiritual significance. References to Dante occur in almost every one of Ruskin's books, sometimes in the most peculiar places, and they form a detailed commentary on the *Divina Commedia*, scattered and irregular, but of peculiar interest.

Ruskin wrote no definite treatise on Shakespeare, but his careful study of the dramatist is evident in many of the essays in this volume. He was the only dramatist Ruskin really loved, for the words of Theseus were to him a "faultless and complete epitome of mimetic art":

The best of this kind are but shadows.

A portion of the Dublin lecture on "The Mystery of Life

and its Arts", with its deeply suggestive criticism of Shakespeare's message for humanity, and also the appreciation of his feminine characters, are quoted in full. They are finely critical passages, and give a valuable estimate of the poet's power.

There was a trait in Ruskin's character which seems strangely allied with the eighteenth century; yet he wrote little about the literature of that period. The projected life of Pope was never completed, and Johnson was the only prose writer for whom he cared. The fine tribute from *Praeterita* is given here. His most extensive criticism was reserved for his own age, and he is foremost among the exponents of Sir Walter Scott. His enthusiastic belief in the supreme genius of that author is constantly asserted, and its expression deserves comparison with Carlyle's more famous essay. Both critics were men highly endowed with literary gifts: fine imagination, high poetic power, keen insight and discrimination; but their views diverge widely. If Carlyle admits any genius in the novelist it is with many qualifications. As he contrasts the popular enthusiasm for Scott with the neglect of Burns, he speaks of the poet with the heart of Scotland behind his words, but in his treatment of the novelist he almost does dishonour to the greatest of Scotland's sons. Carlyle was a Puritan to the end, and he came to art with a great suspicion of the imagination. So he asked more of Scott than the author intended, or was prepared, to give. Ruskin had a clear idea of the field in which Scott laboured, and of what he did in the world, and he judged him for what he was—a story-teller, a creative artist, in which sphere he stands or falls in art. He had, too, a clearer perception of Scott's spiritual mission, the message of comfort and solace which he had for his age. His studies of Scott's life, his imagination, his great faculty of romance, the brilliance and range of his portraiture, the ingredients of his plots, and the classification of his works,

form a noble tribute to the genius of the author and the admiration and humility of the critic.

The nineteenth century to Ruskin was a monstrosity, a thing to be put aside, an age of intellectual, social, and moral narrowness, pervaded by a spirit of smug complacency. Where it is reflected in literature we naturally expect to find Ruskin's strongest antipathies. He does little justice to Dickens, George Eliot, and Thackeray; he cannot separate Wordsworth the poet from Wordsworth the teacher; Byron he admires and despises; on Coleridge, Keats, and Shelley he is unable to arrive at any settled conclusion. Many of the Victorian poets were his personal friends, and there are appreciations, usually with reservations, of Coventry Patmore, the Brownings, Rossetti, Morris, Swinburne, and Tennyson. Most of these are too discursive to be represented here, but they can easily be traced from the Index Volume of the Library Edition of Ruskin.

(xi) SUMMARY

Ruskin sought no place in the history of literary criticism and it is superfluous to give him one. He will always be studied for delight and instruction. His work may not have the same significance for us as it had for his own day, when he was one of the leaders of the great liberal crusade which numbered Carlyle, Ruskin, and Morris on the aesthetic side, and Dickens on the sentimental. Ruskin's literary criticism, like his other themes, was a great broadening influence. Before Arnold was complaining of the insularity of English taste in literature, and reasserting the necessity of accepting only the greatest writers of the world as a standard, Ruskin was explaining to a wide and cosmopolitan audience the merits of Homer, Dante, Shakespeare, and Scott. To criticism more than to the drama Ruskin might have applied the words of Theseus, and his own

likes and dislikes arouse now no more than a passing curiosity. His criticisms are sometimes marred by impatience and petulance, by inconsistencies and peculiarities, by obsessions and lack of restraint, but they are never commonplace. They are always fresh and original, indelibly stamped with the noble character of their author, and consistent with great principles.

Ruskin brought to criticism no new formula with which to test the value of literature; the principles which underlie all his criticism were just those which have been with us since the beginning of art. Like Matthew Arnold, he tended to base his judgments on a moral rather than an aesthetic foundation. "Nobleness" was what he sought in literature. It is significant that he never attempted any detailed criticism of purely didactic writers, men who had some solution to the mystery of life, but who lacked beauty of style and nobility of purpose. Ruskin admired Pope, but his projected exposition of that poet's work was never accomplished. It was moral profundity in its widest sense that Ruskin looked for, that which is found only in whatsoever things are true, honest, just, pure, and lovely. The great writers to him were those who in some way eased the "burthen and the mystery of life", those who had the power to "soothe the cares and lift the thoughts of men". This principle was what made him unjust to many poets, men who had a comfort and solace for humanity which Ruskin was unable to perceive. But it made him the exponent of the greatest minds in the world, and gave him a standard by which to test all literature. He could always rise to a great subject, and, when he is expounding the sublime in works of literature or art, he becomes a great critic.

Ruskin sought moral profundity, but, unlike Matthew Arnold, he added to his equipment a strong aesthetic theory. "*Modern Painters*", says Sir Leslie Stephen, "whatever its

errors, is the only book in the language which treats to any purpose what may be called aesthetics." It is assailable, but it is built on consistent principles, and is a valuable criterion of literature. The identity of truth and beauty is not often complete in this world, and Ruskin's achievement in literary criticism is to point out where the reconciliation is effected. When his aesthetic sense is satisfied, and literary aptitude has a clear relationship with moral qualities, his criticism is sound and deep. Such are the appreciations of Shakespeare, Dante, Homer, and Scott.

When Ruskin recommended beauty it was not as a luxury, but as a weapon to help in the stern conflict of life. He was always something of a Puritan in his attitude to Romantic art, and it is only when this is combined with moral significance, as in Tennyson, that he can appreciate it at its full value. So he had no sympathy with Shelley and his incessant longing to escape from this life to a transcendental world. It is beauty of a very definite kind that he seeks. He never forgets that when God made the world He looked on it and saw that it was good. No one did more than Ruskin to co-ordinate the sense of beauty with the sense of right, and to teach us that the earth is our spiritual nurse. Behind the glory of great art, whether in literature or painting, he always saw the original. And he never saw nature separately; all the landscapes he loved were intertwined in his mind with their heroic history and their reflection in literature and art.

There is nothing epoch-making in Ruskin's criticism. It was intended for all classes of people, and being universal it could not be revolutionary. His best work was achieved when he set down for us

What oft was thought, but ne'er so well expressed.

He endeavoured only to point out what he thought worthy of admiration in literature, as in all other arts, and we can

usually trust to his good taste, and always to the accuracy
of his intuitions for beauty and harmony. "He neither invents, nor creates, nor imagines", says his biographer, "he
links up." And this is the essence of his achievement: he
brings before us noble themes, and expounds them in a
stimulating and suggestive way. Minor details are often
wrong, but the truth in his major premises is precious, and
Ruskin is never in danger of being unread. At times he
missed the path, but he never lost sight of the goal.

CHRONOLOGICAL LIST OF
RUSKIN'S WORKS

Poems. Collected 1850. 1836–1845.
The Poetry of Architecture. 1837–1838.
Modern Painters, volume I. 1843.
Modern Painters, volume II. 1846.
The Seven Lamps of Architecture. 1849.
The Stones of Venice, volume I. 1851.
Pre-Raphaelitism. 1851.
The Stones of Venice, volumes II and III. 1853.
Modern Painters, volumes III and IV. 1856.
The Harbours of England. 1856.
The Elements of Drawing. 1857.
The Two Paths. 1859.
Modern Painters, volume V. 1860.
Unto this Last. 1860.
Munera Pulveris. 1863.
Sesame and Lilies. 1865.
Ethics of the Dust. 1866
Time and Tide. 1867.
Rede Lecture. 1867.
The Queen of the Air. 1869.
Lectures on Art. 1870.
Aratra Pentelici. 1872.
Fors Clavigera. 1871–1884.
The Eagle's Nest. 1872.
Ariadne Florentina. 1873.
Val D'Arno. 1874.
Mornings in Florence. 1875.
St Mark's Rest. 1877–1884.
The Elements of English Prosody. 1880.
Fiction, Fair and Foul. 1880.
The Art of England. 1883–1884.
The Pleasures of England. 1884–1885.
Praeterita. 1885–1889.

SELECTIONS

ON THE STUDY OF
LITERATURE & LANGUAGE

I. BOOKS

A ll books are divisible into two classes, the books of the hour, and the books of all time. Mark this distinction—it is not one of quality only. It is not merely the bad book that does not last, and the good one that does. It is a distinction of species. There are good books for the hour, and good ones for all time; bad books for the hour, and bad ones for all time. I must define the two kinds before I go farther.

The good book of the hour, then,—I do not speak of the bad ones,—is simply the useful or pleasant talk of some person whom you cannot otherwise converse with, printed for you. Very useful often, telling you what you need to know; very pleasant often, as a sensible friend's present talk would be. These bright accounts of travels; good-humoured and witty discussions of question; lively or pathetic story-telling in the form of novel; firm fact-telling, by the real agents concerned in the events of passing history;—all these books of the hour, multiplying among us as education becomes more general, are a peculiar possession of the present age: we ought to be entirely thankful for them, and entirely ashamed of ourselves if we make no good use of them. But we make the worst possible use if we allow them to usurp the place of true books: for, strictly speaking, they are not books at all, but merely letters or newspapers in good print.

Our friend's letter may be delightful, or necessary, to-day: whether worth keeping or not, is to be considered. The newspaper may be entirely proper at breakfast-time, but assuredly it is not reading for all day. So, though bound up in a volume, the long letter which give you so pleasant an account of the inns, and roads, and weather, last year at such a place, or which tells you that amusing story, or gives you the real circumstances of such and such events, however valuable for occasional reference, may not be, in the real sense of the word, a "book" at all, nor, in the real sense, to be "read". A book is essentially not a talking thing, but a written thing; and written, not with a view of mere communication, but of permanence. The book of talk is printed only because its author cannot speak to thousands of people at once; if he could, he would—the volume is mere *multiplication* of his voice. You cannot talk to your friend in India; if you could, you would; you write instead: that is mere *conveyance* of voice. But a book is written, not to multiply the voice merely, not to carry it merely, but to perpetuate it. The author has something to say which he perceives to be true and useful, or helpfully beautiful. So far as he knows, no one has yet said it; so far as he knows, no one else can say it. He is bound to say it, clearly and melodiously if he may; clearly, at all events. In the sum of his life he finds this to be the thing, or group of things, manifest to him;—this, the piece of true knowledge, or sight, which his share of sunshine and earth has permitted him to seize. He would fain set it down for ever; engrave it on rock, if he could; saying, "This is the best of me; for the rest, I ate, and drank, and slept, loved, and hated, like another; my life was as the vapour, and is not; but this I saw and knew: this, if anything of mine, is worth your memory." That is his "writing"; it is, in his small human way, and with whatever degree of true inspiration is in him, his inscription, or scripture. That is a "Book".

Perhaps you think no books were ever so written?

But, again, I ask you, do you at all believe in honesty, or at all in kindness, or do you think there is never any honesty or benevolence in wise people? None of us, I hope, are so unhappy as to think that. Well, whatever bit of a wise man's work is honestly and benevolently done, that bit is his book or his piece of art. It is mixed always with evil fragments—ill-done, redundant, affected work. But if you read rightly, you will easily discover the true bits, and those *are* the book.

Sesame and Lilies, lect. i, pars. 8–10.

II. HOW TO READ

Books of this kind have been written in all ages by their greatest men:—by great readers, great statesmen, and great thinkers. These are all at your choice; and Life is short. You have heard as much before;—yet have you measured and mapped out this short life and its possibilities? Do you know, if you read this, that you cannot read that—that what you lose to-day you cannot gain to-morrow? Will you go and gossip with your housemaid, or your stableboy, when you may talk with queens and kings; or flatter yourself that it is with any worthy consciousness of your own claims to respect, that you jostle with the hungry and common crowd for *entrée* here, and audience there, when all the while this eternal court is open to you, with its society, wide as the world, multitudinous as its days, the chosen, and the mighty, of every place and time? Into that you may enter always; in that you may take fellowship and rank according to your wish; from that, once entered into it, you can never be an outcast but by your own fault; by your aristocracy of companionship there, your own inherent aristocracy will be assuredly tested, and the motives

with which you strive to take high place in the society of the living, measured, as to all the truth and sincerity that are in them, by the place you desire to take in this company of the Dead.

"The place you desire", and the place you *fit yourself for*, I must also say; because, observe, this court of the past differs from all living aristocracy in this:—it is open to labour and to merit, but to nothing else. No wealth will bribe, no name overawe, no artifice deceive, the guardian of those Elysian gates. In the deep sense, no vile or vulgar person ever enters there. At the portières of that silent Faubourg St Germain, there is but brief question:—"Do you deserve to enter? Pass. Do you ask to be the companion of nobles? Make yourself noble, and you shall be. Do you long for the conversation of the wise? Learn to understand it, and you shall hear it. But on other terms? —no. If you will not rise to us, we cannot stoop to you. The living lord may assume courtesy, the living philosopher explain his thought to you with considerate pain; but here we neither feign nor interpret; you must rise to the level of our thoughts if you would be gladdened by them, and share our feelings, if you would recognize our presence."

This, then, is what you have to do, and I admit that it is much. You must, in a word, love these people, if you are to be among them. No ambition is of any use. They scorn your ambition. You must love them, and show your love in these two following ways.

I. First, by a true desire to be taught by them, and to enter into their thoughts. To enter into theirs, observe; not to find your own expressed by them. If the person who wrote the book is not wiser than you, you need not read it; if he be, he will think differently from you in many respects.

II. Very ready we are to say of a book, "How good this is —that's exactly what I think!" But the right feeling is,

"How strange this is! I never thought of that before, and yet I see it is true; or if I do not now, I hope I shall, some day." But whether thus submissively or not, at least be sure that you go to the author to get *his* meaning, not to find yours. Judge it afterwards if you think yourself qualified to do so; but ascertain it first. And be sure also, if the author is worth anything, that you will not get at his meaning all at once;—nay, that at his whole meaning you will not for a long time arrive in any wise. Not that he does not say what he means, and in strong words too; but he cannot say it all; and what is more strange, *will* not, but in a hidden way and in parable, in order that he may be sure you want it. I cannot quite see the reason of this, nor analyse that cruel reticence in the breasts of wise men which makes them always hide their deeper thought. They do not give it you by way of help, but of reward; and will make themselves sure that you deserve it before they allow you to reach it. But it is the same with the physical type of wisdom, gold. There seems, to you and me, no reason why the electric forces of the earth should not carry whatever there is of gold within it at once to the mountain tops, so that kings and people might know that all the gold they could get was there; and without any trouble of digging, or anxiety, or chance, or waste of time, cut it away, and coin as much as they needed. But Nature does not manage it so. She puts it in little fissures in the earth, nobody knows where: you may dig long and find none; you must dig painfully to find any.

And it is just the same with men's best wisdom. When you come to a good book, you must ask yourself, "Am I inclined to work as an Australian miner would? Are my pickaxes and shovels in good order, and am I in good trim myself, my sleeves well up to the elbow, and my breath good, and my temper?" And, keeping the figure a little longer, even at cost of tiresomeness, for it is a thoroughly useful one, the metal you are in search of being the author's

mind or meaning, his words are as the rock which you have to crush and smelt in order to get at it. And your pickaxes are your own care, wit, and learning; your smelting furnace is your own thoughtful soul. Do not hope to get at any good author's meaning without those tools and that fire; often you will need sharpest, finest chiselling, and patientest fusing, before you can gather one grain of the metal.

And, therefore, first of all, I tell you earnestly and authoritatively (I *know* I am right in this), you must get into the habit of looking intensely at words, and assuring yourself of their meaning, syllable by syllable—nay, letter by letter. For though it is only by reason of the opposition of letters in the function of signs, to sounds in the function of signs, that the study of books is called "literature", and that a man versed in it is called, by the consent of nations, a man of letters instead of a man of books, or of words, you may yet connect with that accidental nomenclature this real fact:—that you might read all the books in the British Museum (if you could live long enough), and remain an utterly "illiterate", uneducated person; but that if you read ten pages of a good book, letter by letter,—that is to say, with real accuracy,—you are for evermore in some measure an educated person. The entire difference between education and non-education (as regards the merely intellectual part of it), consists in this accuracy. A well-educated gentlemen may not know many languages,—may not be able to speak any but his own,—may have read very few books. But whatever language he knows, he knows precisely; whatever word he pronounces, he pronounces rightly; above all, he is learned in the *peerage* of words; knows the words of true descent and ancient blood, at a glance, from words of modern canaille; remembers all their ancestry, their intermarriages, distant relationships, and the extent to which they were admitted, and offices they held, among the national noblesse of words at any time, and

in any country. But an uneducated person may know, by memory, many languages, and talk them all, and yet truly know not a word of any,—not a word even of his own. An ordinarily clever and sensible seaman will be able to make his way ashore at most ports; yet he has only to speak a sentence of any language to be known for an illiterate person: so also the accent, or turn of expression of a single sentence, will at once mark a scholar. And this is so strongly felt, so conclusively admitted, by educated persons, that a false accent or a mistaken syllable is enough, in the parliament of any civilized nation, to assign to a man a certain degree of inferior standing for ever.

Sesame and Lilies, lect. I, pars. 11–15.

> Last came, and last did go,
> The pilot of the Galilean lake.
> Two massy keys he bore of metals twain,
> (The golden opes, the iron shuts amain,)
> He shook his mitred locks, and stern bespake,
> "How well could I have spared for thee, young swain,
> Enow of such as for their bellies' sake
> Creep, and intrude, and climb into the fold!
> Of other care they little reckoning make,
> Than how to scramble at the shearers' feast,
> And shove away the worthy bidden guest;
> Blind mouths! that scarce themselves know how to hold
> A sheep-hook, or have learn'd aught else, the least
> That to the faithful herdman's art belongs!
> What recks it them? What need they? They are sped;
> And when they list, their lean and flashy songs
> Grate on their scrannel pipes of wretched straw;
> The hungry sheep look up, and are not fed,
> But, swoln with wind, and the rank mist they draw,
> Rot inwardly, and foul contagion spread;
> Besides what the grim wolf with privy paw
> Daily devours apace, and nothing said."[1]

Let us think over this passage, and examine its words.

[1] *Lycidas*, 108.

First, is it not singular to find Milton assigning to St Peter, not only his full episcopal function, but the very types of it which Protestants usually refuse most passionately? His "mitred" locks! Milton was no Bishop-lover; how comes St Peter to be "mitred"? "Two massy keys he bore." Is this, then, the power of the keys claimed by the Bishops of Rome? and is it acknowledged here by Milton only in a poetical licence, for the sake of its picturesqueness, that he may get the gleam of the golden keys to help his effect? Do not think it. Great men do not play stage tricks with the doctrines of life and death: only little men do that. Milton means what he says; and means it with his might too—is going to put the whole strength of his spirit presently into the saying of it. For though not a lover of false bishops, he *was* a lover of true ones; and the Lake-pilot is here, in his thoughts, the type and head of true episcopal power. For Milton reads that text, "I will give unto thee the keys of the kingdom of Heaven", quite honestly. Puritan though he be, he would not blot it out of the book because there have been bad bishops; nay, in order to understand *him*, we must understand that verse first; it will not do to eye it askance, or whisper it under our breath, as if it were a weapon of an adverse sect. It is a solemn, universal assertion, deeply to be kept in mind by all sects. But perhaps we shall be better able to reason on it if we go on a little farther, and come back to it. For clearly this marked insistence on the power of the true episcopate is to make us feel more weightily what is to be charged against the false claimants of episcopate; or generally, against false claimants of power and rank in the body of the clergy; they who, "for their bellies' sake, creep, and intrude, and climb into the fold".

Never think Milton uses those three words to fill up his verse, as a loose writer would. He needs all the three;— specially those three, and no more than those—"creep",

and "intrude", and "climb"; no other words would or could serve the turn, and no more could be added. For they exhaustively comprehend the three classes, correspondent to the three characters, of men who dishonestly seek ecclesiastical power. First, those who *"creep"* into the fold; who do not care for office, nor name, but for secret influence, and do all things occultly and cunningly, consenting to any servility of office or conduct, so only that they may intimately discern, and unawares direct, the minds of men. Then those who "intrude" (thrust, that is) themselves into the fold, who by natural insolence of heart, and stout eloquence of tongue, and fearlessly perseverant self-assertion, obtain hearing and authority with the common crowd. Lastly, those who "climb", who, by labour and learning, both stout and sound, but selfishly exerted in the cause of their own ambition, gain high dignities and authorities, and become "lords over the heritage", though not "ensamples to the flock".

Now go on:——

> Of other care they little reckoning make,
> Than how to scramble at the shearers' feast.
> *Blind mouths*——

I pause again, for this is a strange expression; a broken metaphor, one might think, careless and unscholarly.

Not so: its very audacity and pithiness are intended to make us look close at the phrase and remember it. Those two monosyllables express the precisely accurate contraries of right character, in the two great offices of the Church—those of bishop and pastor.

A "Bishop" means "a person who sees".

A "Pastor" means "a person who feeds".

The most unbishoply character a man can have is therefore to be Blind.

The most unpastoral is, instead of feeding, to want to be fed,—to be a Mouth.

Take the two reverses together, and you have "blind mouths". We may advisably follow out this idea a little. Nearly all the evils in the Church have arisen from bishops desiring *power* more than *light*. They want authority, not outlook. Whereas their real office is not to rule; though it may be vigorously to exhort and rebuke: it is the king's office to rule; the bishop's office is to *oversee* the flock; to number it, sheep by sheep; to be ready always to give full account of it. Now it is clear he cannot give account of the souls, if he has not so much as numbered the bodies, of his flock. The first thing, therefore, that a bishop has to do is at least to put himself in a position in which, at any moment, he can obtain the history, from childhood, of every living soul in his diocese, and of its present state. Down in that back street, Bill, and Nancy, knocking each other's teeth out!—Does the bishop know all about it? Has he his eye upon them? Has he *had* his eye upon them? Can he circumstantially explain to us how Bill got into the habit of beating Nancy about the head? If he cannot, he is no bishop, though he had a mitre as high as Salisbury steeple; he is no bishop,—he has sought to be at the helm instead of the mast-head; he has no sight of things. "Nay", you say, "it is not his duty to look after Bill in the back street." What! the fat sheep that have full fleeces—you think it is only those he should look after while (go back to your Milton) "the hungry sheep look up, and are not fed, besides what the grim wolf, with privy paw" (bishops knowing nothing about it) "daily devours apace, and nothing said"?

"But that's not our idea of a bishop." Perhaps not; but it was St Paul's; and it was Milton's. They may be right, or we may be; but we must not think we are reading either one or the other by putting our meaning into their words.

I go on.

But swoln with wind, and the rank mist they draw.

This is to meet the vulgar answer that "if the poor are not looked after in their bodies, they are in their souls; they have spiritual food".

And Milton says, "They have no such thing as spiritual food; they are only swollen with wind." At first you may think that is a coarse type, and an obscure one. But again, it is a quite literally accurate one. Take up your Latin and Greek dictionaries, and find out the meaning of "Spirit". It is only a contraction of the Latin word "breath", and an indistinct translation of the Greek word for "wind". The same word is used in writing, "The wind bloweth where it listeth"; and in writing, "So is every one that is born of the Spirit"; born of the *breath*, that is; for it means the breath of God, in soul and body. We have the true sense of it in our words "inspiration" and "expire". Now, there are two kinds of breath with which the flock may be filled,—God's breath, and man's. The breath of God is health, and life, and peace to them, as the air of heaven is to the flocks on the hills; but man's breath—the word which *he* calls spiritual—is disease and contagion to them, as the fog of the fen. They rot inwardly with it; they are puffed up by it, as a dead body by the vapours of its own decomposition. This is literally true of all false religious teaching; the first and last, and fatalest sign of it is that "puffing up". Your converted children, who teach their parents; your converted convicts, who teach honest men; your converted dunces, who, having lived in cretinous stupefaction half their lives, suddenly awaking to the fact of there being a God, fancy themselves therefore His peculiar people and messengers; your sectarians of every species, small and great, Catholic or Protestant, of high church or low, in so far as they think themselves exclusively in the right and others wrong; and pre-eminently, in every sect, those who hold that men can be saved by thinking rightly instead of doing rightly, by word instead of act, and wish instead of

work;—these are the true fog children—clouds, these,
without water; bodies, these, of putrescent vapour and skin,
without blood or flesh: blown bag-pipes for the fiends to
pipe with—corrupt, and corrupting,—"Swoln with wind,
and the rank mist they draw."

Lastly, let us return to the lines respecting the power of
the keys, for now we can understand them. Note the difference between Milton and Dante in their interpretation
of this power: for once, the latter is weaker in thought; he
supposes *both* the keys to be of the gate of heaven; one is of
gold, the other of silver: they are given by St Peter to the
sentinel angel; and it is not easy to determine the meaning
either of the substances of the three steps of the gate, or of
the two keys. But Milton makes one, of gold, the key of
heaven; the other, of iron, the key of the prison in which the
wicked teachers are to be bound who "have taken away
the key of knowledge, yet entered not in themselves".

We have seen that the duties of bishop and pastor are to
see, and feed; and of all who do so it is said, "He that
watereth, shall be watered also himself." But the reverse
is truth also. He that watereth not, shall be *withered* himself; and he that seeth not, shall himself be shut out of sight
—shut into the perpetual prison-house. And that prison
opens here, as well as hereafter: he who is to be bound in
heaven must first be bound on earth. That command to the
strong angels, of which the rock-apostle is the image,
"Take him, and bind him hand and foot, and cast him
out", issues, in its measure, against the teacher, for every
help withheld, and for every truth refused, and for every
falsehood enforced; so that he is more strictly fettered the
more he fetters, and farther outcast as he more and more
misleads, till at last the bars of the iron cage close upon him,
and as "the golden opes, the iron shuts amain".

We have got something out of the lines, I think, and
much more is yet to be found in them; but we have done

enough by way of example of the kind of word-by-word examination of your author which is rightly called "reading"; watching every accent and expression, and putting ourselves always in the author's place, annihilating our own personality, and seeking to enter into his, so as to be able assuredly to say, "Thus Milton thought", not "Thus *I* thought, in mis-reading Milton". And by this process you will gradually come to attach less weight to your own "Thus I thought" at other times. You will begin to perceive that what *you* thought was a matter of no serious importance;—that your thoughts on any subject are not perhaps the clearest and wisest that could be arrived at thereupon:—in fact, that unless you are a very singular person, you cannot be said to have any "thoughts" at all; that you have no materials for them, in any serious matters;—no right to "think", but only to try to learn more of the facts.

Sesame and Lilies, lect. I, pars. 20–25.

III. THE POET

MEN in their several professed employments, looked at broadly, may be properly arranged under five classes:—

1. Persons who see. These, in modern language, are sometimes called sight-seers, that being an occupation coming more and more into vogue every day. Anciently they used to be called, simply, seers.

2. Persons who talk. These, in modern language, are usually called talkers, or speakers, as in the House of Commons, and elsewhere. They used to be called prophets.

3. Persons who make. These, in modern language, are usually called manufacturers. Anciently they were called poets.

4. Persons who think. There seems to be no very distinct modern title for this kind of person, anciently

called philosophers; nevertheless we have a few of them among us.

5. Persons who do: in modern language, called practical persons; anciently, believers.

Modern Painters, vol. V, Pt. VIII, Ch. I, par. 14.

Every kind of knowledge may be sought from ignoble motives, and for ignoble ends; and in those who so possess it, it is ignoble knowledge; while the very same knowledge is in another mind an attainment of the highest dignity, and conveying the greatest blessing. This is the difference between the mere botanist's knowledge of plants, and the great poet's or painter's knowledge of them. The one notes their distinctions for the sake of swelling his herbarium, the other, that he may render them vehicles of expression and emotion. The one counts the stamens, and affixes a name, and is content; the other observes every character of the plant's colour and form; considering each of its attributes as an element of expression, he seizes on its lines of grace or energy, rigidity or repose; notes the feebleness or the vigour, the serenity or tremulousness of its hues; observes its local habits, its love or fear of peculiar places, its nourishment or destruction by particular influences; he associates it in his mind with all the features of the situations it inhabits, and the ministering agencies necessary to its support. Thenceforward the flower is to him a living creature, with histories written on its leaves, and passions breathing in its motion. Its occurrence in his picture is no mere point of colour, no meaningless spark of light. It is a voice rising from the earth, a new chord of the mind's music, a necessary note in the harmony of his picture, contributing alike to its tenderness and its dignity, nor less to its loveliness than its truth.

Modern Painters, vol. I, Preface, par. 30.

A poet, or creator, is therefore a person who puts things together, not as a watchmaker steel, or a shoemaker leather, but who puts life into them.

His work is essentially this: it is the gathering and arranging of material by imagination, so as to have in it at least the harmony or helpfulness of life, and the passion or emotion of life. Mere fitting and adjustment of material is nothing; that is watchmaking. But helpful and passionate harmony, essentially choral harmony, so called from the Greek word "rejoicing",[1] is the harmony of Apollo and the Muses; the word Muse and Mother being derived from the same root, meaning "passionate seeking", or love, of which the issue is passionate finding, or sacred INVENTION.

Modern Painters, vol. v, Pt. VIII, Ch. 1, par. 20.

IV. KINDS OF POETRY

Do you know, in the first place, what a play is? or what a poem is? or what a novel is? That is to say, do you know the perpetual and necessary distinctions in literary aim which have brought these distinctive names into use? You had better first, for clearness' sake, call all the three "poems", for all the three are so, when they are good, whether written in verse or prose. All truly imaginative account of man is poetic; but there are three essential kinds of poetry —one dramatic, one lyric, and one epic.

Dramatic poetry is the expression by the poet of other people's feelings, his own not being told.

Lyric poetry is the expression by the poet of his own feelings.

Epic poetry is account given by the poet of other people's external circumstances, and of events happening to them, with only such expression either of their feelings, or his own, as he thinks may be conveniently added.

[1] χορούς τε ὠνομακέναι παρὰ τῆς χαρᾶς ἔμφυτον ὄνομα (*De Leg.* II, 1).

The business of Dramatic poetry is therefore with the heart essentially; it despises external circumstance.

Lyric poetry may speak of anything that excites emotion in the speaker; while Epic poetry insists on external circumstances, and no more exhibits the heart-feeling than as it may be gathered from these.

For instance, the fight between the Prince of Wales and Hotspur, in *Henry the Fourth*,[1] corresponds closely, in the character of the event itself, to the fight of Fitz-James with Roderick, in *The Lady of the Lake*.[2] But Shakespeare's treatment of his subject is strictly dramatic; Scott's, strictly epic.

Shakespeare gives you no account whatever of any blow or wound: his stage direction is, briefly, "Hotspur is wounded, and falls". Scott gives you accurate account of every external circumstance, and the finishing touch of botanical accuracy—

> Down came the blow; but in the *heath*
> The erring blade found bloodless sheath,—

makes his work perfect, as epic poetry. And Scott's work is always epic, and it is contrary to his very nature to treat any subject dramatically.

That is the technical distinction, then, between the three modes of work. But the gradation of power in all three depends on the degree of imagination with which the writer can enter into the feelings of other people. Whether in expressing theirs or his own, and whether in expressing their feelings only, or also the circumstances surrounding them, his power depends on his being able to feel as they do; in other words, on his being able to conceive character. And the literature which is not poetry at all, which is essentially unsentimental, or anti-poetic, is that which is produced by persons who have no imagination; and whose merit (for of course I am not speaking of bad literature) is in their wit or sense, instead of their imagination.

Fors Clavigera, vol. II, letter XXXIV.

---

[1] 1 *Henry IV*, v, 4.   [2] Canto v, 14–16.

V. DRAMA

"THE BEST, IN THIS KIND, ARE BUT SHADOWS."

THAT is Shakespeare's judgment of his own art. And by
strange coincidence, he has put the words into the mouth
of the hero whose shadow, or semblance in marble, is ad-
mittedly the most ideal and heroic we possess, of man; yet,
I need not ask you, whether of the two, if it were granted
you to see the statue by Phidias, or the hero Theseus himself, you would choose rather to see the carved stone, or the
living King. Do you recollect how Shakespeare's Theseus
concludes his sentence, spoken of the poor tradesmen's
kindly offered art, in the *Midsummer Night's Dream*?

"The best in this kind are but shadows: and the worst
are no worse, if imagination amend them."[1]

It will not burden your memories painfully, I hope,
though it may not advance you materially in the class list,
if you will learn this entire sentence by heart, being, as it is,
a faultless and complete epitome of the laws of mimetic art.

"BUT SHADOWS!" Make them as beautiful as you
can; use them only to enable you to remember and love
what they are cast by. If ever you prefer the skill of them
to the simplicity of the truth, or the pleasure of them to the
power of the truth, you have fallen into that vice of folly,
(whether you call her κακία or μωρία), which concludes
the subtle description of her given by Prodicus, that she
might be seen continually εἰς τὴν ἑαυτῆς σκιὰν ἀπο-
βλέπειν[2]—to look with love, and exclusive wonder, at *her
own* shadow.

There is nothing that I tell you with more eager
desire that you should believe—nothing with wider ground
in my experience for requiring you to believe, than this,
that you never will love art well, till you love what she
mirrors better.   *Eagle's Nest*, pars. 39–41.

[1] Act V, Sc. i, line 213.   [2] Xenophon, *Memorabilia*, II, i, 22.

VI. TRAGEDY AND EPIC

THE ruling purpose of Greek poetry is the assertion of victory, by heroism, over fate, sin, and death. The terror of these great enemies is dwelt upon chiefly by the tragedians. The victory over them, by Homer.

The adversary chiefly contemplated by the tragedians is Fate, or predestinate misfortune. And that under three principal forms.

(A) Blindness or ignorance; not in itself guilty, but inducing acts which otherwise would have been guilty; and leading, no less than guilt, to destruction.*

(B) Visitation upon one person of the sin of another.

(c) Repression by brutal, or tyrannous strength, of a benevolent will.

In all these cases sorrow is much more definitely connected with sin by the Greek tragedians than by Shakespeare. The "fate" of Shakespeare is, indeed, a form of blindness, but it issues in little more than haste or indiscretion. It is, in the literal sense, "fatal", but hardly criminal.

The "I am fortune's fool" of Romeo,[1] expresses Shakespeare's primary idea of tragic circumstance. Often his victims are entirely innocent, swept away by mere current of strong encompassing calamity (Ophelia, Cordelia, Arthur, Queen Katherine). This is rarely so with the Greeks. The victim may indeed be innocent, as Antigone, but is in some way resolutely entangled with crime, and destroyed by it, as if it struck by pollution, no less than participation.

---

* The speech of Achilles to Priam expresses this idea of fatality and submission clearly, there being two vessels—one full of sorrow, the other of great and noble gifts (a sense of disgrace mixing with that of sorrow, and of honour with that of joy), from which Jupiter pours forth the destinies of men; the idea partly corresponding to the scriptural—"In the hand of the Lord there is a cup, and the wine is red; it is full mixed, and He poureth out of the same."[2] But the title of the gods, nevertheless, both with Homer and Hesiod, is given not from the cup of sorrow, but of good: "givers of good" ($\delta\omega\tau\tilde{\eta}\rho\epsilon\varsigma$ $\dot{\epsilon}\dot{\alpha}\omega\nu$). —Hes. *Theog.* 664; *Odyss.* VIII, 325.

[1] *Romeo and Juliet*, III, I.　　[2] *Iliad*, XXIV, 527 seq.; *Psalm* LXXV, 8.

The victory over sin and death is therefore also with the Greek tragedians more complete than with Shakespeare. As the enemy has more direct moral personality,—as it is sinfulness more than mischance, it is met by a higher moral resolve, a greater preparation of heart, a more solemn patience and purposed self-sacrifice. At the close of a Shakespeare tragedy, nothing remains but dead march and clothes of burial. At the close of a Greek tragedy there are far-off sounds of a divine triumph, and a glory as of resurrection.*

The Homeric temper is wholly different. Far more tender, more practical, more cheerful; bent chiefly on present things and giving victory now, and here, rather than in hope, and hereafter. The enemies of mankind, in Homer's conception, are more distinctly conquerable; they are ungoverned passions, especially anger, and unreasonable impulse generally ($\dot{a}\tau\dot{\eta}$). Hence the anger of Achilles, misdirected by pride, but rightly directed by friendship, is the subject of the *Iliad*. The anger of Ulysses ('Οδυσσεὺς, "the angry"), misdirected at first into idle and irregular hostilities, directed at last to execution of sternest justice, is the subject of the *Odyssey*.

Though this is the central idea of the two poems, it is connected with general display of the evil of all unbridled passions, pride, sensuality, indolence, or curiosity. The pride of Atrides, the passion of Paris, the sluggishness of Elpenor, the curiosity of Ulysses himself about the Cyclops, the impatience of his sailors in untying the winds, and all other faults or follies down to that—(evidently no small one in Homer's mind)—of domestic disorderliness, are throughout shown in contrast with conditions of patient affection and household peace.

Also, the wild powers and mysteries of Nature are in the Homeric mind among the enemies of man; so that all the

* The *Alcestis* is perhaps the central example of the *idea* of all Greek drama.

labours of Ulysses are an expression of the contest of manhood, not only with its own passions or with the folly of others, but with the merciless and mysterious powers of the natural world.[1]

This is perhaps the chief signification of the seven years' stay with Calypso, "the concealer". Not, as vulgarly thought, the concealer of Ulysses, but the great concealer— the hidden power of natural things. She is the daughter of Atlas and the Sea, (Atlas, the sustainer of heaven, and the Sea, the disturber of the Earth). She dwells in the island of Ogygia ("the ancient or venerable"). (Whenever Athens, or any other Greek city, is spoken of with any peculiar reverence, it is called "Ogygian".[2]) Escaping from this goddess of secrets, and from other spirits, some of destructive natural force (Scylla), others signifying the enchantment of mere natural beauty (Circe, daughter of the Sun and Sea), he arrives at last at the Phæacian land, whose king is "strength with intellect", and whose queen, "virtue".[3] These restore him to his country.

Now observe that in their dealing with all these subjects the Greeks never shrink from horror; down to its uttermost depth, to its most appalling physical detail, they strive to sound the secrets of sorrow. For them there is no passing by on the other side, no turning away the eyes to vanity from pain. Literally, they have not "lifted up their souls unto vanity". Whether there be consolation for them or not, neither apathy nor blindness shall be their saviour; if, for them, thus knowing the facts of the grief of earth, any hope, relief, or triumph may hereafter seem possible,— well; but if not, still hopeless, reliefless, eternal, the sorrow shall be met face to face. This Hector, so righteous, so merciful, so brave, has, nevertheless, to look upon his dearest brother in miserablest death. His own soul passes

---

[1] Vide *Odyssey*, X, 266; VIII, 166; XIX, 479.
[2] Vide Aeschylus, *Pers.* 37 and 974; and Sophocles, *Œd. Col.* 1770.
[3] *Odyssey*, VII.

away in hopeless sobs through the throat-wound of the Grecian spear. That is one aspect of things in this world, a fair world truly, but having, among its other aspects, this one, highly ambiguous.

Meeting it boldly as they may, gazing right into the skeleton face of it, the ambiguity remains; nay, in some sort gains upon them. We trusted in the gods;—we thought that wisdom and courage would save us. Our wisdom and courage themselves deceive us to our death. Athena had the aspect of Deiphobus—terror of the enemy. She has not terrified him, but left us, in our mortal need.[1]

And beyond that mortality, what hope have we? Nothing is clear to us on that horizon, nor comforting. Funeral honours; perhaps also rest; perhaps a shadowy life—artless, joyless, loveless. No devices in that darkness of the grave, nor daring, nor delight. Neither marrying nor giving in marriage, nor casting of spears, nor rolling of chariots, nor voice of fame. Lapped in pale Elysian mist, chilling the forgetful heart and feeble frame, shall we waste on for ever? Can the dust of earth claim more of immortality than this? Or shall we have even so much as rest? May we, indeed, lie down again in the dust: or have not our sins hidden from us even the things that belong to that peace? May not chance and the whirl of passion govern us there: when there shall be no thought, nor work, nor wisdom, nor breathing of the soul?*

Be it so. With no better reward, no brighter hope, we will be men while we may: men, just, and strong, and fearless, and up to our power, perfect. Athena herself, our wisdom and our strength, may betray us:—Phœbus, our sun, smite us with plague, or hide his face from us helpless; —Jove and all the powers of fate oppress us, or give us up to destruction. While we live, we will hold fast our in-

---

* τῷ καὶ τεθνειῶτι νόον πόρε Περσεφόνεια,
οἴῳ πεπνῦσθαι· τοὶ δὲ σκιαὶ ἀΐσσουσιν.   Od. X, 495.
[1] Vide *Iliad*, XXII, 226 *seq.*

tegrity; no weak tears shall blind us, no untimely tremors abate our strength of arm nor swiftness of limb. The gods have given us at least this glorious body and this righteous conscience; these will we keep bright and pure to the end. So may we fall to misery, but not to baseness; so may we sink to sleep, but not to shame.

And herein was conquest. So defied, the betraying and accusing shadows shrank back; the mysterious horror subdued itself to majestic sorrow. Death was swallowed up in victory. Their blood, which seemed to be poured out upon the ground, rose into hyacinthine flowers. All the beauty of earth opened to them; they had ploughed into its darkness, and they reaped its gold; the gods, in whom they had trusted through all semblance of oppression, came down to love them and be their helpmates. All nature round them became divine,—one harmony of power and peace. The sun hurt them not by day, nor the moon by night; the earth opened no more her jaws into the pit: the sea whitened no more against them the teeth of his devouring waves. Sun, and moon, and earth, and sea,—all melted into grace and love; the fatal arrows rang not now at the shoulders of Apollo, the healer; lord of life, and of the three great spirits of life—Care, Memory, and Melody. Great Artemis guarded their flocks by night; Selene kissed in love the eyes of those who slept. And from all came the help of heaven to body and soul; a strange spirit lifting the lovely limbs; strange light glowing on the golden hair; and strangest comfort filling the trustful heart, so that they could put off their armour, and lie down to sleep,—their work well done, whether at the gates of their temples[1] or of their mountains;[2] accepting the death they once thought terrible, as the gift of Him who knew and granted what was best.

Modern Painters, vol. v, Pt. ix, Ch. ii, pars. 14–20.

---

[1] οὐκέτι ἀνέστησαν, ἀλλ᾽ ἐν τέλει τούτῳ ἔσχοντο. Herod. I, 31.

[2] ὁ δὲ ἀποπεμπόμενος, αὐτὸς μὲν οὐκ ἀπελίπετο· τὸν δὲ παῖδα συστρατευόμενον ἐόντα οἱ μουνογενέα, ἀπέπεμψε. Herod. vii, 221.

VII. THE NOVEL

With respect to the sore temptation of novel reading, it is not the badness of a novel that we should dread, so much as its overwrought interest. The weakest romance is not so stupefying as the lower forms of religious exciting literature, and the worst romance is not so corrupting as false history, false philosophy, or false political essays. But the best romance becomes dangerous, if, by its excitement, it renders the ordinary course of life uninteresting, and increases the morbid thirst for useless acquaintance with scenes in which we shall never be called upon to act.

I speak therefore of good novels only; and our modern literature is particularly rich in types of such. Well read, indeed, these books have serious use, being nothing less than treatises on moral anatomy and chemistry; studies of human nature in the elements of it. But I attach little weight to this function: they are hardly ever read with earnestness enough to permit them to fulfil it. The utmost they usually do is to enlarge somewhat the charity of a kind reader, or the bitterness of a malicious one; for each will gather, from the novel, food for her own disposition. Those who are naturally proud and envious will learn from Thackeray to despise humanity; those who are naturally gentle, to pity it; those who are naturally shallow, to laugh at it. So, also, there might be a serviceable power in novels to bring before us, in vividness, a human truth which we had before dimly conceived; but the temptation to picturesqueness of statement is so great, that often the best writers of fiction cannot resist it; and our views are rendered so violent and one-sided, that their vitality is rather a harm than good.

Sesame and Lilies, lect. II, pars. 76–77.

LITERATURE AND MORALS

I. ART AND NATIONAL MORALS

THE beginning of art *is in getting our country clean, and our people beautiful.* I have been ten years trying to get this very plain certainty—I do not say believed—but even thought of, as anything but a monstrous proposition. To get your country clean, and your people lovely;—I assure you that is a necessary work of art to begin with! There has indeed been art in countries where people lived in dirt to serve God, but never in countries where they lived in dirt to serve the devil. There has indeed been art where the people were not all lovely—where even their lips were thick—and their skins black, because the sun had looked upon them; but never in a country where the people were pale with miserable toil and deadly shade, and where the lips of youth, instead of being full with blood, were pinched by famine, or warped with poison.

Lectures on Art, par. 116.

II. LANGUAGE AND MORALS

ALL right human song is the finished expression, by art, of the joy or grief of noble persons, for right causes. And accurately in proportion to the rightness of the cause, and purity of the emotion, is the possibility of the fine art. A maiden may sing of her lost love, but a miser cannot sing of his lost money. And with absolute precision, from highest to lowest, *the fineness of the possible art is an index of the moral purity and majesty of the emotion it expresses.* You may test it practically at any instant. Question with yourselves respecting any feeling that has

taken strong possession of your mind, "Could this be sung by a master, and sung nobly, with a true melody and art?" Then it is a right feeling. Could it not be sung at all, or only sung ludicrously? It is a base one. And that is so in all the arts; so that with mathematical precision, subject to no error or exception, the art of a nation, so far as it exists, is an exponent of its ethical state.

An exponent, observe, and exalting influence; but not the root or cause. You cannot paint or sing yourselves into being good men; you must be good men before you can either paint or sing, and then the colour and sound will complete in you all that is best.

And this it was that I called upon you to hear, saying, "listen to me at least now", in the first lecture, namely, that no art teaching could be of use to you, but would rather be harmful, unless it was grafted on something deeper than all art. For indeed not only with this, of which it is my function to show you the laws, but much more with the art of all men, which you came here chiefly to learn, that of language, the chief vices of education have arisen from the one great fallacy of supposing that noble language is a communicable trick of grammar and accent, instead of simply the careful expression of right thought. All the virtues of languages are, in their roots, moral; it becomes accurate if the speaker desires to be true; clear, if he speaks with sympathy and a desire to be intelligible; powerful, if he has earnestness; pleasant, if he has sense of rhythm and order. There are no other virtues of language producible by art than these: but let me mark more deeply for an instant the significance of one of them. Language, I said, is only clear when it is sympathetic. You can, in truth, understand a man's word only by understanding his temper. Your own word is also as of an unknown tongue to him unless he understands yours. And it is this which makes the art of language, if any one is to be chosen separately from

the rest, that which is fittest for the instrument of a gentleman's education. To teach the meaning of a word
thoroughly, is to teach the nature of the spirit that coined
it; the secret of language is the secret of sympathy, and its
full charm is possible only to the gentle. And thus the
principles of beautiful speech have all been fixed by sincere
and kindly speech. On the laws which have been determined by sincerity, false speech, apparently beautiful, may
afterwards be constructed; but all such utterance, whether
in oration or poetry, is not only without permanent power,
but it is destructive of the principles it has usurped. So long
as no words are uttered but in faithfulness, so long the art
of language goes on exalting itself; but the moment it is
shaped and chiselled, on external principles, it falls into
frivolity, and perishes. And this truth would have been
long ago manifest, had it not been that in periods of advanced academical science there is always a tendency to deny
the sincerity of the first masters of language. Once learn
to write gracefully in the manner of an ancient author, and
we are apt to think that he also wrote in the manner of
someone else. But no noble nor right style was ever yet
founded but out of a sincere heart.

No man is worth reading to form your style, who does
not mean what he says; nor was any great style ever invented but by some man who meant what he said. Find
out the beginner of a great manner of writing, and you
have also found the declarer of some true facts or sincere
passions: and your whole method of reading will thus be
quickened, for, being sure that your author really meant
what he said, you will be much more careful to ascertain
what it is that he means.

And of yet greater importance is it deeply to know that
every beauty possessed by the language of a nation is
significant of the innermost laws of its being. Keep the
temper of the people stern and manly; make their associa-

tions grave, courteous, and for worthy objects; occupy them in just deeds; and their tongue must needs be a grand one. Nor is it possible, therefore—observe the necessary reflected action—that any tongue should be a noble one, of which the words are not so many trumpet-calls to action. All great languages invariably utter great things, and command them; they cannot be mimicked but by obedience; the breath of them is inspiration because it is not only vocal, but vital; and you can only learn to speak as these men spoke, by becoming what these men were.

Now for direct confirmation of this, I want you to think over the relation of expression to character in two great masters of the absolute art of language, Virgil and Pope. You are perhaps surprised at the last name; and indeed you have in English much higher grasp and melody of language from more passionate minds, but you have nothing else, in its range, so perfect. I name, therefore, these two men, because they are the two most accomplished *Artists*, merely as such, whom I know in literature; and because I think you will be afterwards interested in investigating how the infinite grace in the words of the one, and the severity in those of the other, and the precision in those of both, arise wholly out of the moral elements of their minds:—out of the deep tenderness in Virgil which enabled him to write the stories of Nisus and Lausus; and the serene and just benevolence which placed Pope, in his theology, two centuries in advance of his time, and enabled him to sum the law of noble life in two lines which, so far as I know, are the most complete, the most concise, and the most lofty expression of moral temper existing in English words:—

> Never elated, while one man's oppress'd;
> Never dejected, while another's bless'd.[1]

I wish you also to remember these lines of Pope, and to make yourselves entirely masters of his system of ethics;

[1] *Essay on Man*, Ep. IV, 323.

because, putting Shakespeare aside as rather the world's than ours, I hold Pope to be the most perfect representative we have, since Chaucer, of the true English mind; and I think the *Dunciad* is the most absolutely chiselled and monumental work "exacted" in our country. You will find, as you study Pope, that he has expressed for you, in the strictest language and within the briefest limits, every law of art, of criticism, of economy, of policy, and, finally, of a benevolence, humble, rational, and resigned, contented with its allotted share of life, and trusting the problem of its salvation to Him in whose hands lies that of the universe.

Lectures on Art, pars. 67–70.

III. LITERATURE AND THE MORAL LAW

ONE farther great, and greatest, sign of the Divinity in this enchanted work of the classic masters, I did not then assert—for, indeed, I had not then myself discerned it,— namely, that this power of noble composition is never given but with accompanying instinct of moral law; and that so severe, that the apparently too complete and ideal justice which it proclaims has received universally the name of "poetical" justice—the justice conceived only by the men of consummate imaginative power. So that to say of any man that he has power of design, is at once to say of him that he is using it on God's side; for it can only have been taught him by that Master, and cannot be taught by the use of it against Him. And therefore every great composi- tion in the world, every great piece of painting or literature —without any exception, from the birth of Man to this hour—is an assertion of moral law, as strict, when we examine it, as the Eumenides or the *Divina Commedia*; while the total collapse of all power of artistic design in

Italy at this day has been signalized and sealed by the production of an epic poem in praise of the Devil, and in declaration that God is a malignant "larva".[1]

And this so-called poetical justice, asserted by the great designers, consists not only in the gracing of virtue with her own proper rewards of mental peace and spiritual victory; but in the proportioning also of worldly prosperity to visible virtue; and the manifestation, therefore, of the presence of the Father in this world, no less than in that which is to come. So that, if the life-work of any man of unquestioned genius does not assert this visible justice, but, on the contrary, exhibits good and gentle persons in unredeemed distress or destruction—that work will invariably be found to show no power of design; but to be merely the consecutive collection of interesting circumstances well described, as continually the best work of Balzac, George Sand, and other good novelists of the second order. In some separate pieces, the great masters will indeed exhibit the darkest mystery of human fate, but never without showing, even then, that the catastrophe is owing in the root of it to the violation of some moral law: "*She hath deceived her father,* —and may thee."[2] The root of the entire tragedy is marked by the mighty master in that one line—the double sin, namely, of daughter and father; of the first in too lawlessly forgetting her own people, and her father's house; and of the second, in allowing his pride and selfishness to conquer his paternal love, and harden him, not only in abandonment of his paternal duty, but in calumnious insult to his child. Nor, even thus, is Shakespeare content without marking, in the name of the victim of Evil Fortune, his purpose in the tragedy, of showing that there *is* such a thing as Destiny,

---

[1] A highly laudatory review of this work, in two successive parts, will be found in the columns of the Venetian journal *Il Tempo*, in the winter of 1876–77.

[2] *Othello*, I, iii.

permitted to veil the otherwise clear Providence, and to leave it only to be found by noble Will, and proved by noble Faith.

Although always, in reading Scott, one thinks the story one has last finished, the best, there can be little question that the one which has right of pre-eminence is the *Heart of Midlothian*, being devoted to the portraiture of the purest life, and most vital religion, of his native country.

It is also the most distinct in its assertion of the moral law; the assignment of earthly reward and punishment being, in this story, as accurately proportioned to the degrees of virtue and vice as the lights and shades of a photograph to the force of the rays. The absolute truth and faith of Jeanie make the suffering through which she has to pass the ultimate cause of an entirely prosperous and peaceful life for herself, her father, and her lover: the falsehood and vanity of Effie prepare for her a life of falsehood and vanity: the pride of David Deans is made the chief instrument of his humiliation; and the self-confidence which separated him from true fellowship with his brother-Christians, becomes the cause of his eternal separation from his child.

Also, there is no other analysis of the good and evil of the pure Protestant faith which can be for a moment compared to that in the *Heart of Midlothian*, showing that in an entirely simple, strong, and modest soul, it brings forth fruit of all good works and kindly thoughts; but that, when it meets with innate pride, and the unconquerable selfishness which comes from want of sympathy, it leads into ludicrous and fatal self-worship, mercilessness to the errors, whether in thought or conduct, of others; and blindness to the teaching of God Himself, where it is contrary to the devotee's own habits of thought. There is no other form of the Christian religion which so insolently ignores all Scripture that makes against it, or gathers with so passionate and irrational embrace all Scripture that makes for it.

And the entire course of the tragic story in the *Heart*

of Midlothian comes of the "Museless" hardness of nature, brought upon David Deans by the persecution in his early life, which changed healthy and innocent passion into religious pride,—

"I bless God, (with that singular worthy, Peter Walker, the packman at Bristo port), that ordered my lot in my dancing days, so that fear of my head and throat, dread of bloody rope and swift bullet, cauld and hunger, wetness and weariness, stopped the lightness of my head, and the wantonness of my feet. And now, if I hear ye, quean lassies, sae muckle as name dancing, or think there's such a thing in the world as flinging to fiddlers' sounds and pipers' springs, as sure as my father's spirit is with the just, ye shall be no more either charge or concern of mine."

Over the bronze sculpture of this insolent pride, Scott instantly casts, in the following sentence ("Gang in then, hinnies", etc.) the redeeming glow of paternal love; but he makes it, nevertheless, the cause of all the misery that follows, to the end of the old man's life:—

"'The objurgation of David Deans, however well meant, was unhappily timed. It created a division of feeling in Effie's bosom, and deterred her from her intended confidence in her sister. 'She wad haud me nae better than the dirt below her feet', said Effie to herself, 'were I to confess that I hae danced wi' him four times on the green down by, and ance at Maggie Macqueen's.'"

Such, and no more than such, the little sin that day concealed—sin only *in* concealment. And the fate of her life turns on the Fear and the Silence of a moment.

Fors Clavigera, vol. IV, letter LXXXIII.

IV. EVIL IN LITERATURE

THERE is one strange, but quite essential, character in us—ever since the Conquest, if not earlier—a delight in the forms of burlesque which are connected in some degree with the foulness of evil. I think the most perfect type of a true English mind in its best possible temper, is that of Chaucer; and you will find that, while it is for the most part full of thoughts of beauty, pure and wild like that of an April morning, there are, even in the midst of this, some-times momentarily jesting passages which stoop to play with evil—while the power of listening to and enjoying the jesting of entirely gross persons, whatever the feeling may be which permits it, afterwards degenerates into forms of humour which render some of quite the greatest, wisest, and most moral of English writers now almost useless for our youth. And yet you will find that whenever English-men are wholly without this instinct, their genius is com-paratively weak and restricted.

Lectures on Art, par. 14.

The imaginative power always purifies; the want of it therefore as essentially defiles; and as the wit-power is apt to develop itself through absence of imagination, it seems as if wit itself had a defiling tendency. In Pindar, Homer, Virgil, Dante, and Scott, the colossal powers of imagination result in absolute virginal purity of thought. The defect of imagination and the splendid rational power in Pope and Horace associate themselves—it is difficult to say in what decided measures—with foulness of thought. The *Candide* of Voltaire, in its gratuitous filth, its acute reasoning, and its entire vacuity of imagination, is a standard of what may perhaps be generally and fitly termed "fimetic literature," still capable, by its wit, and partial truth, of a certain service

in its way. But lower forms of modern literature and art—
Gustave Doré's paintings, for instance,—are the corruption, in national decrepitude, of this pessimist method of
thought; and of these, the final condemnation is true—they
are neither fit for the land, nor *yet* for the dunghill.

It is one of the most curious problems respecting mental
government to determine how far this fimetic taint must
necessarily affect intellects in which the reasoning and
imaginative powers are equally balanced, and both of them
at high level,—as in Aristophanes, Shakespeare, Chaucer,
Molière, Cervantes, and Fielding; but it always indicates
the side of character which is unsympathetic, and therefore
unkind; (thus Shakespeare makes Iago the foulest in
thought, as cruelest in design, of all his villains), but which,
in men of noble nature, is their safeguard against weak en-
thusiasms and ideals. It is impossible, however, that the
highest conditions of tenderness in affectionate conception
can be reached except by the absolutely virginal intellect.
Shakespeare and Chaucer throw off, at noble work, the
lower part of their natures as they would a rough dress; and
you may also notice this, that the power of conceiving
personal, as opposed to general, character, depends on this
purity of heart and sentiment. The men who cannot quit
themselves of the impure taint, never invent character,
properly so called; they only invent symbols of common
humanity. Even Fielding's Allworthy is not a character,
but a type of a simple English gentleman; and Squire
Western is not a character, but a type of the rude English
squire. But Sir Roger de Coverley is a character, as well as
a type; there is no one else like him; and the masters of
Tullyveolan, Ellangowan, Monkbarns, and Osbaldistone
Hall, are all, whether slightly or completely drawn, por-
traits, not mere symbols.

Fors Clavigera, vol. II, letter XXXIV.

POETRY AND TEACHING

You may, perhaps, think it a beneficent ordinance for the generality of men that they do not, with earnestness or anxiety, dwell on such questions of the future because the business of the day could not be done if this kind of thought were taken by all of us for the morrow. Be it so: but at least we might anticipate that the greatest and wisest of us, who were evidently the appointed teachers of the rest, would set themselves apart to seek out whatever could be surely known of the future destinies of their race; and to teach this in no rhetorical or ambiguous manner, but in the plainest and most severely earnest words.

Now, the highest representatives of men who had thus endeavoured, during the Christian era, to search out these deep things, and relate them, are Dante and Milton. There are none who for earnestness of thought, for mastery of word, can be classed with these. I am not at present, mind you, speaking of persons set apart in any priestly or pastoral office, to deliver creeds to us, or doctrines; but of men who try to discover and set forth, as far as by human intellect is possible, the facts of the other world. Divines may perhaps teach us how to arrive there, but only these two poets have in any powerful manner striven to discover, or in any definite words professed to tell, what we shall see and become there; or how those upper and nether worlds are, and have been, inhabited.

And what have they told us? Milton's account of the most important event in his whole system of the universe, the fall of the angels, is evidently unbelievable to himself; and the more so, that it is wholly founded on, and in a great part spoiled and degraded from, Hesiod's account of the

decisive war of the younger gods with the Titans. The rest
of his poem is a picturesque drama, in which every artifice
of invention is visibly and consciously employed; not a single
fact being, for an instant, conceived as tenable by any living
faith. Dante's conception is far more intense, and, by himself, for the time, not to be escaped from; it is indeed a
vision, but a vision only, and that one of the wildest that
ever entranced a soul—a dream in which every grotesque
type or phantasy of heathen tradition is renewed, and
adorned; and the destinies of the Christian Church, under
their most sacred symbols, become literally subordinate to
the praise, and are only to be understood by the aid, of one
dear Florentine maiden.

I tell you truly that, as I strive more with this strange
lethargy and trance in myself, and awake to the meaning and
power of life, it seems daily more amazing to me that men
such as these should dare to play with the most precious
truths, (or the most deadly untruths,) by which the whole
human race listening to them could be informed, or deceived;—all the world their audiences for ever, with
pleased ear, and passionate heart;—and yet, to this submissive infinitude of souls, and evermore succeeding and
succeeding multitude, hungry for bread of life, they do but
play upon sweetly modulated pipes; with pompous nomenclature adorn the councils of hell;[1] touch a troubadour's
guitar to the courses of the suns;[2] and fill the openings of
eternity, before which prophets have veiled their faces, and
which angels desire to look into,[3] with idle puppets of their
scholastic imagination, and melancholy lights of frantic faith
in their lost mortal love.

Is not this a mystery of life?

But more. We have to remember that these two great
teachers were both of them warped in their temper, and
thwarted in their search for truth. They were men of

[1] *Par. Lost*, II, X, 10.   [2] *Divina Commedia*.   [3] *Isaiah*, vi, 2.

intellectual war, unable, through darkness of controversy, or stress of personal grief, to discern where their own ambition modified their utterances of the moral law; or their own agony mingled with their anger at its violation. But greater men than these have been—innocent-hearted— too great for contest. Men, like Homer and Shakespeare, of so unrecognized personality, that it disappears in future ages, and becomes ghostly, like the tradition of a lost heathen god. Men, therefore, to whose unoffended, uncondemning sight, the whole of human nature reveals itself in pathetic weakness, with which they will not strive; or in mournful and transitory strength, which they dare not praise. And all Pagan and Christian civilization thus becomes subject to them. It does not matter how little, or how much, any of us have read, either of Homer or Shakespeare; everything round us, in substance, or in thought, has been moulded by them. All Greek gentlemen were educated under Homer. All Roman gentlemen, by Greek literature. All Italian, and French, and English gentlemen, by Roman literature, and by its principles. Of the scope of Shakespeare, I will say only, that the intellectual measure of every man since born, in the domains of creative thought, may be assigned to him, according to the degree in which he has been taught by Shakespeare. Well, what do these two men, centres of mortal intelligence, deliver to us of conviction respecting what it most behoves that intelligence to grasp? What is their hope—their crown of rejoicing? What manner of exhortation have they for us, or of rebuke? what lies next their own hearts, and dictates their undying words? Have they any peace to promise to our unrest—any redemption to our misery?

Take Homer first, and think if there is any sadder image of human fate than the great Homeric story. The main features in the character of Achilles are its intense desire of justice, and its tenderness of affection. And in that bitter

song of the *Iliad*, this man, though aided continually by the wisest of the gods, and burning with the desire of justice in his heart, becomes yet, through ill-governed passion, the most unjust of men: and, full of the deepest tenderness in his heart, becomes yet, through ill-governed passion, the most cruel of men. Intense alike in love and in friendship, he loses, first his mistress, and then his friend; for the sake of the one, he surrenders to death the armies of his own land; for the sake of the other, he surrenders all. Will a man lay down his life for his friend? Yea—even for his *dead* friend, this Achilles, though goddess-born, and goddess-taught, gives up his kingdom, his country, and his life— casts alike the innocent and guilty, with himself, into one gulf of slaughter, and dies at last by the hand of the basest of his adversaries. Is not this a mystery of life?

But what, then, is the message to us of our own poet, and searcher of hearts, after fifteen hundred years of Christian faith have been numbered over the graves of men? Are his words more cheerful than the heathen's— is his hope more near—his trust more sure—his reading of fate more happy? Ah, no! He differs from the Heathen poet chiefly in this—that he recognizes, for deliverance, no gods nigh at hand; and that, by petty chance—by momentary folly—by broken message—by fool's tyranny—or traitor's snare, the strongest and most righteous are brought to their ruin, and perish without word of hope. He indeed, as part of his rendering of character, ascribes the power and modesty of habitual devotion to the gentle and the just. The death-bed of Katharine[1] is bright with visions of angels; and the great soldier-king, standing by his few dead,[2] acknowledges the presence of the hand that can save alike by many or by few. But observe that from those who with deepest spirit, meditate, and with deepest passion, mourn, there are no such words as these; nor in their hearts are any

[1] *Henry VIII*, IV, ii.   [2] *Henry V*, IV, viii.

such consolations. Instead of the perpetual sense of the helpful presence of the Deity, which, through all heathen tradition, is the source of heroic strength, in battle, in exile, and in the valley of the shadow of death, we find only in the great Christian poet, the consciousness of a moral law, through which "the gods are just, and of our pleasant vices make instruments to scourge us";[1] and of the resolved arbitration of the destinies, that conclude into precision of doom what we feebly and blindly began; and force us, when our indiscretion serves us, and our deepest plots do pall, to the confession, that "there's a divinity that shapes our ends, rough hew them how we will".[2]

Is not this a mystery of life?

Sesame and Lilies, lect. III, pars. 110–115.

FAITH IN LITERATURE

NOTICE, for general guidance, the gradations of impression on the feelings of men of strong and well-rounded intellect, by which fancy rises towards faith.

I. The lowest stage is that of wilfully grotesque fancy, which is recognized as false, yet dwelt upon with delight and finished with accuracy, as the symbol or parable of what is true.

Shakespeare's Puck, and the Dwarf Goblin of the "Lay", are precisely alike in this first level of the imagination. Shakespeare does not believe in Bottom's translation; neither does Scott that, when the boy Buccleugh passes the drawbridge with the dwarf, the sentinel only saw a terrier and lurcher passing out. Yet both of them permit the fallacy, because they acknowledge the Elfin power in nature, to make things, sometimes for good, sometimes for harm, seem what they are not. Nearly all the grotesque

[1] *King Lear*, v, iii, 170.   [2] *Hamlet*, v, ii, 7.

sculpture of the great ages, beginning with the Greek Chimæra, has this nascent form of Faith for its impulse.

II. The ghosts and witches of Shakespeare, and the Bodach Glas and White Lady of Scott, are expressions of real belief, more or less hesitating and obscure. Scott's worldliness too early makes him deny his convictions, and in the end effaces them. But Shakespeare remains sincerely honest in his assertion of the uncomprehended spiritual presence; with this further subtle expression of his knowledge of mankind, that he never permits a spirit to show itself but to men of the highest intellectual power. To Hamlet, to Brutus, to Macbeth, to Richard III; but the royal Dane does not haunt his own murderer,—neither does Arthur, King John; neither Norfolk, King Richard II; nor Tybalt, Romeo.

III. The faith of Horace in the spirit of the fountain of Brundusium, in the Faun of his hillside, and in the help of the greater gods, is constant, vital, and practical; yet in some degree still tractable by his imagination, as also that of the great poets and painters of Christian times. In Milton, the tractability is singular; he hews his gods out to his own fancy, and then believes in them; but in Giotto and Dante the art is always subjected to the true vision.

IV. The faith of the saints and prophets, rising into serenity of knowledge, "I know that my Redeemer liveth", is a state of mind of which ordinary men cannot reason; but which in the practical power of it, has always governed the world, and must for ever. No dynamite will ever be invented that can rule;—it can but dissolve and destroy. Only the Word of God and the heart of man can govern.

Fors Clavigera, vol. IV, letter XCII.

THE BEAUTIFUL

I. INTRODUCTION

By the term Beauty, then, properly are signified two things. First, that external quality of bodies already so often spoken of, and which, whether it occur in a stone, flower, beast, or in man, is absolutely identical, which, as I have already asserted, may be shown to be in some sort typical of the Divine attributes, and which therefore I shall, for distinction's sake, call Typical Beauty: and, secondarily, the appearance of felicitous fulfilment of function in living things, more especially of the joyful and right exertion of perfect life in man; and this kind of beauty I shall call Vital Beauty.

Any application of the word Beautiful to other appearances or qualities than these is either false or metaphorical; as, for instance, to the splendour of a discovery, the fitness of a proportion, the coherence of a chain of reasoning, or the power of bestowing pleasure which objects receive from association, a power confessedly great, and interfering, as we shall presently find, in a most embarassing way with the attractiveness of inherent beauty.

Modern Painters, vol. ii, sec. i, ch. iii, par. 16.

II. FALSE IDEAS OF BEAUTY

Those erring or inconsistent positions which I would at once dismiss are: the first, that the Beautiful is the True; the second, that the Beautiful is the Useful; the third, that it is dependent on Custom; and the fourth, that it is dependent on the Association of Ideas.

To assert that the Beautiful is the True, appears, at first, like asserting that propositions are matter, and matter propositions. But giving the best and most rational interpretation we can, and supposing the holders of this strange position to mean only that things are beautiful which appear what they indeed are, and ugly which appear what they are not, we find them instantly contradicted by each and every conclusion of experience. A stone looks as truly a stone as a rose looks a rose, and yet is not so beautiful: a cloud may look more like a castle than a cloud, and be the more beautiful on that account. The mirage of the desert is fairer than its sands; the false image of the under heaven fairer than the sea. I am at a loss to know how any so untenable a position could ever have been advanced; but it may, perhaps, have arisen from some confusion of the beauty of art with the beauty of nature, and from an illogical expansion of the very certain truth, that nothing is beautiful in art, which, professing to be an imitation, or a statement, is not as such in some sort true.

That the Beautiful is the Useful, is an assertion evidently based on that limited and false sense of the latter term which I have already deprecated. As it is the most degrading and dangerous supposition which can be advanced on the subject, so, fortunately, it is the most palpably absurd. It is to confound admiration with hunger, love with lust, and life with sensation; it is to assert that the human creature has no ideas and no feelings except those ultimately referable to its brutal appetites. It has not a single fact nor appearance of fact to support it, and needs no combating; at least until its advocates have obtained the consent of the majority of mankind, that the most beautiful productions of nature are seeds and roots; and of art, spades and millstones.

Somewhat more rational grounds appear for the assertion that the sense of the Beautiful arises from Familiarity with

the object, though even this could not long be maintained by a thinking person. For all that can be alleged in defence of such a supposition is, that familiarity deprives some objects, which at first appeared ugly, of much of their repulsiveness; whence it is as rational to conclude that familiarity is the cause of beauty, as it would be to argue that because it is possible to acquire a taste for olives, therefore custom is the cause of lusciousness in grapes. Nevertheless, there are some phenomena resulting from the tendency of our nature to be influenced by habit, of which it may be well to observe the limits.

Custom has a two-fold operation; the one to deaden the frequency and force of repeated impressions, the other to endear the familiar object to the affections. Commonly, where the mind is vigorous, and the power of sensation very perfect, it has rather the last operation than the first; with meaner minds, the first takes place in the higher degree, so that they are commonly characterized by a desire of excitement, and the want of the loving, fixed, theoretic power. But both take place in some degree with all men; so that as life advances impressions of all kinds become less rapturous, owing to their repetition. It is however beneficently ordained that repulsiveness shall be diminished by custom in a far greater degree than the sensation of beauty; so that the anatomist in a little time loses all sense of horror in the torn flesh and carious bone, while the sculptor ceases not to feel, to the close of his life, the deliciousness of every line of the outward frame. So then, as in that with which we are made familiar the repulsiveness is constantly diminishing, and such claims as it may be able to put forth on the affections are daily becoming stronger, while, in what is submitted to us of new or strange, that which may be repulsive is felt in its full force while no hold is as yet laid on the affections, there is a very strong preference induced in most minds for that to which they are accustomed over

that they know not, and this is strongest in those which are least open to sensations of positive beauty. But however far this operation may be carried, its utmost effect is but the deadening and approximating of the sensations of beauty and ugliness. It never mixes, nor crosses, nor in any way alters them; it has not the slightest connection with, or power over, their nature. By tasting two wines alternately, we may deaden our perception of their flavour; nay, we may even do more than can ever be done in the case of sight, we may confound the two flavours together; but it will hardly be argued, therefore, that custom is the cause of either flavour. And so, though by habit we may deaden the effect of ugliness or beauty, it is not for that reason to be affirmed that habit is the cause of either sensation. We may keep a skull beside us as long as we please, we may overcome its repulsiveness, we may render ourselves capable of perceiving many qualities of beauty about its lines, we may contemplate it for years together if we will,—it and nothing else,—but we shall not get ourselves to think as well of it as of a child's fair face.

It would be easy to pursue the subject farther, but I believe that every thoughtful reader will be perfectly well able to supply farther illustrations, and sweep away the sandy fountains of the opposite theory, unassisted. Let it, however, be observed, that, in spite of all custom, an Englishman instantly acknowledges, and at first sight, the superiority of the turban to the hat, or of the plaid to the coat; that, whatever the dictates of immediate fashion may compel, the superior gracefulness of the Greek or middle-age costumes is invariably felt; and that, respecting what has been asserted of negro nations looking with disgust on the white face, no importance whatever is to be attached to the opinions of races who have never received any ideas of beauty whatsoever (these ideas being only received by minds under some certain degree of cultivation), and whose dis-

gust arises naturally from what they may suppose to be a sign of weakness or ill health. It would be futile to proceed into farther detail.

I pass to the last and most weighty theory, that the agreeableness in objects which we call Beauty, is the result of the Association with them of agreeable or interesting ideas.

Frequent has been the support and wide the acceptance of this supposition, and yet I suppose that no two consecutive sentences were ever written in defence of it, without involving either a contradiction or a confusion of terms. Thus Alison: "There are scenes undoubtedly more beautiful than Runnymede, yet, to those who recollect the great event that passed there, there is no scene perhaps which so strongly seizes on the imagination:"—Where we are wonder-struck at the audacious obtuseness which would prove the power of imagination by its *overcoming that very other power* (of inherent beauty) whose existence the arguer denies. For the only logical conclusion which can possibly be drawn from the above sentence is, that imagination is *not* the source of beauty, for although no scene seizes so strongly on the imagination, yet there are scenes "more beautiful than Runnymede". And though instances of self-contradiction as laconic and complete as this are to be found in few writers except Alison, yet if the arguments on the subject be fairly sifted from the mass of confused language with which they are always encumbered, and placed in logical form, they will be found invariably to involve one of these two syllogisms: either, Association gives pleasure, and Beauty gives pleasure, therefore Association is Beauty; or, the power of Association is stronger than the power of Beauty, therefore the power of Association *is* the power of Beauty.

Nevertheless it is necessary for us to observe the real value and authority of association in the moral system, and

how ideas of actual beauty may be affected by it, otherwise we shall be liable to embarrassment throughout the whole of the succeeding argument.

Association is of two kinds, Rational and Accidental. By Rational Association I understand the interest which any object may bear historically, as having been in some way connected with the affairs or affections of men; an interest shared in the minds of all who are aware of such connection: which to call beauty is mere and gross confusion of terms; it is no theory to be confuted, but a misuse of language to be set aside, a misuse involving the positions that in uninhabited countries the vegetation has no grace, the rock no dignity, the cloud no colour, and that the snowy summits of the Alps receive no loveliness from the sunset light, because they have not been polluted by the wrath, ravage, and misery of men.

By Accidental Association, I understand the accidental connection of ideas and memories with material things, owing to which those material things are regarded as agreeable or otherwise, according to the nature of the feelings or recollections they summon; the association being commonly involuntary and oftentimes so vague as that no distinct image is suggested by the object, but we feel a painfulness in it or pleasure from it, without knowing wherefore. Of this operation of the mind (which is that of which I spoke as causing inextricable embarrassments on the subject of beauty) the experience is constant, so that its more energetic manifestations require no illustration. But I do not think that the minor degrees and shades of this great influence have been sufficiently appreciated. Not only all vivid emotions, and all circumstances of exciting interest, leave their light and shadow on the senseless things and instruments among which, or through whose agency, they have been felt or learned, but I believe that the eye cannot rest on a material form, in a moment of depression or

exultation, without communicating to that form a spirit and
a life,—a life which will make it afterwards in some degree
loved or feared,—a charm or a painfulness for which we shall
be unable to account even to ourselves, which will not indeed be perceptible, except by its delicate influence on our
judgment in cases of complicated beauty. Let the eye but
rest on a rough piece of branch of curious form during a
conversation with a friend, rest however unconsciously,
and though the conversation be forgotten, though every
circumstance connected with it be as utterly lost to the
memory as though it had not been, yet the eye will,
through the whole life after, take a certain pleasure in such
boughs which it had not before, a pleasure so slight, a trace
of feeling so delicate, as to leave us utterly unconscious of
its peculiar power; but undestroyable by any reasoning, a
part, thenceforward, of our constitution, destroyable only
by the same arbitrary process of association by which it was
created. Reason has no effect upon it whatsoever. And
there is probably no one opinion which is formed by any of
us, in matters of taste, which is not in some degree influenced by unconscious association of this kind. In many
who have no definite rules of judgment, preference is
decided by little else, and thus, unfortunately, its opera-
tions are mistaken for, or rather substituted for, those
of inherent beauty, and its real position and value in the
moral system are in a great measure overlooked.

Modern Painters, vol. ii, sec. i, ch. iv, pars. 1–9.

III. QUALITIES OF TYPICAL BEAUTY

(a) INFINITY

ONE, however, of these child instincts, I believe that few forget, the emotion, namely, caused by all open ground, or lines of any spacious kind against the sky, behind which there might be conceived the Sea. It is an emotion more pure than that caused by the sea itself, for I recollect distinctly running down behind the banks of a high beach to get their land line cutting against the sky, and receiving a more strange delight from this than from the sight of the ocean. I am not sure that this feeling is common to all children (or would be common, if they were all in circumstances admitting it,) but I have ascertained it to be frequent among those who possess the most vivid sensibilities for nature; and I am certain that the modification of it which belongs to our after years is common to all, the love, namely, of a light distance appearing over a comparatively dark horizon. This I have tested too frequently to be mistaken, by offering to indifferent spectators forms of equal abstract beauty in half tint, relieved, the one against dark sky, the other against a bright distance. The preference is invariably given to the latter; and it is very certain that this preference arises not from any supposition of there being greater truth in this than the other, for the same preference is unhesitatingly accorded to the same effect in nature herself. Whatever beauty there may result from effects of light on foreground objects,—from the dew of the grass, the flash of the cascade, the glitter of the birch trunk, or the fair daylight hues of darker things (and joyfulness there is in all of them), there is yet a light which the eye invariably seeks with a deeper feeling of the beautiful,—the light of the declining or breaking day, and the flakes of scarlet cloud burning like watch fires in the green sky of the horizon; a deeper feeling, I say,

not perhaps more acute, but having more of spiritual hope
and longing, less of animal and present life, more manifest,
invariably, in those of more serious and determined mind,
(I use the word serious, not as being opposed to cheerful,
but to trivial and volatile,) but I think, marked and unfailing even in those of the least thoughtful dispositions.
I am willing to let it rest on the determination of every
reader, whether the pleasure which he has received from
these effects of calm and luminous distance be not the most
singular and memorable of which he has been conscious;
whether all that is dazzling in colour, perfect in form,
gladdening in expression, be not of evanescent and shallow
appealing, when compared with the still small voice of the
level twilight behind purple hills, or the scarlet arch of
dawn over the dark troublous-edged sea.

Let us try to discover that which effects of this kind
possess or suggest, peculiar to themselves, and which other
effects of light and colour possess not. There *must* be something in them of a peculiar character, and that, whatever it
be, must be one of the primal and most earnest motives of
beauty to human sensation.

Do they show finer characters of form than can be developed by the broader daylight? Not so; for their power
is almost independent of the forms they assume or display;
it matters little whether the bright clouds be simple or
manifold, whether the mountain line be subdued or
majestic; the fairer forms of earthly things are by them
subdued and disguised, the round and muscular growth of
the forest trunks is sunk into skeleton lines of quiet shade,
the purple clefts of the hill-side are labyrinthed in the darkness, the orbed spring and whirling wave of the torrent
have given place to a white, ghastly, interrupted gleaming.
Have they more perfection or fulness of colour? Not so;
for their effect is oftentimes deeper when their hues are
dim, than when they are blazoned with crimson and pale

gold: and assuredly, in the blue of the rainy sky, in the many tints of morning flowers, in the sunlight on summer foliage and field, there are more sources of mere sensual colour-pleasure than in the single streak of wan and dying light. It is not then by nobler form, it is not by positiveness of hue, it is not by intensity of light (for the sun itself at noonday is effectless upon the feelings), that this strange distant space possesses its attractive power. But there is one thing that it has, or suggests, which no other object of sight suggests in equal degree, and that is—Infinity. It is of all visible things the least material, the least finite, the farthest withdrawn from the earth prison-house, the most typical of the nature of God, the most suggestive of the glory of His dwelling-place. For the sky of night, though we may know it boundless, is dark; it is a studded vault, a roof that seems to shut us in and down; but the bright distance has no limit, we feel its infinity, as we rejoice in its purity of light.

Modern Painters, vol. II, sec. I, ch. v, pars. 2–5.

(b) UNITY

There is not any matter, nor any spirit, nor any creature, but it is capable of a unity of some kind with other creatures; and in that unity is its perfection and theirs, and a pleasure also for the beholding of all other creatures that can behold. So the unity of spirits is partly in their sympathy, and partly in their giving and taking, and always in their love; and these are their delight and their strength; for their strength is in their co-working and army fellowship, and their delight is in the giving and receiving of alternate and perpetual good; their inseparable dependency on each other's being, and their essential and perfect depending on their Creator's. And so the unity of earthly creatures is their power and their peace; not like the dead

and cold peace of undisturbed stones and solitary mountains; but the living peace of trust, and the living power of support; of hands that hold each other and are still. And so the unity of matter is, in its noblest form, the organization of it which builds it up into temples for the spirit; and in its lower form, the sweet and strange affinity which gives to it the glory of its orderly elements, and the fair variety of change and assimilation that turns the dust into the crystal, and separates the waters that be above the firmament from the waters that be beneath: and, in its lowest form, it is the working and walking and clinging together that gives their power to the winds, and its syllables and soundings to the air, and their weight to the waves, and their burning to the sunbeams, and their stability to the mountains, and to every creature whatsoever operation is for its glory and for others' good.

Now of that which is thus necessary to the perfection of all things, all appearance, sign, type, or suggestion must be beautiful, in whatever matter it may appear; and the appearance of some species of unity is, in the most determined sense of the word, essential to the perfection of beauty in lines, colours, or forms.

But of the appearances of unity, as of unity itself, there are several kinds, which it will be found hereafter convenient to consider separately. Thus there is the Unity of different and separate things, subjected to one and the same influence, which may be called Subjectional Unity; and this is the unity of the clouds, as they are driven by the parallel winds, or as they are ordered by the electric currents; this the unity of the sea waves, this of the bending and undulation of the forest masses; and in creatures capable of will it is the unity of will or of impulse. And there is Unity of Origin, which we may call Original Unity; which is of things arising from one spring and source, and speaking always of this their brotherhood; and

this in matter is the unity of the branches of the trees, and of the petals and starry rays of flowers, and of the beams of light; and in spiritual creatures it is their filial relation to Him from whom they have their being. And there is Unity of Sequence, which is that of things that form links in chains, and steps in ascents, and stages in journeys; and this, in matter, is the unity of communicable forces in their continuance from one thing to another; and it is the passing upwards and downwards of beneficent effects among all things, the melody of sounds, the continuity of lines, and the orderly succession of motions and times; and in spiritual creatures it is their own constant building up, by true knowledge and continuous reasoning, to higher perfection, and the singleness and straightforwardness of their tendencies to more complete communion with God. And there is the Unity of Membership, which we may call Essential Unity, which is the unity of things separately imperfect into a perfect whole; and this is the great unity of which other unities are but parts and means; it is in matter the harmony of sounds and consistency of bodies, and among spiritual creatures their love and happiness and very life in God.

Modern Painters, vol. ii, sec. i, ch. vi, pars. 1–3.

(c) REPOSE

There is probably no necessity more imperatively felt by the artist, no test more unfailing of the greatness of artistical treatment, than that of the appearance of repose; yet there is no quality whose semblance in matter is more difficult to define or illustrate. Nevertheless, I believe that our instinctive love of it, as well as the cause to which I attribute that love, (although here also, as in the former cases, I contend not for the interpretation, but for the fact,) will be readily allowed by the reader. As opposed to passion, change,

fulness, or laborious exertion, Repose is the especial
and separating characteristic of the eternal mind and
power. It is the "I am" of the Creator opposed to the "I
become" of all creatures; it is the sign alike of the supreme
knowledge which is incapable of surprise, the supreme
power which is incapable of labour, the supreme volition
which is incapable of change; it is the stillness of the beams
of the eternal chambers laid upon the variable waters of
ministering creatures. And as we saw before that the infinity which was a type of the Divine nature on the one
hand, became yet more desirable on the other from its
peculiar address to our prison hopes, and to the expectations
of an unsatisfied and unaccomplished existence; so the
types of this third attribute of the Deity might seem to have
been rendered farther attractive to mortal instinct through
the infliction upon the fallen creature of a curse necessi-
tating a labour once unnatural and still most painful; so that
the desire of rest planted in the heart is no sensual nor unworthy one, but a longing for renovation and for escape
from a state whose every phase is mere preparation for
another equally transitory, to one in which permanence
shall have become possible through perfection. Hence the
great call of Christ to men, that call on which St Augustine
fixed as the essential expression of Christian hope, is accompanied by the promise of rest;[1] and the death bequest
of Christ to men is peace.

Repose, as it is expressed in material things, is either a
simple appearance of permanence and quietness, as in the
massy forms of a mountain or rock, accompanied by the
lulling effect of all mighty sight and sound, which all feel
and none define (it would be less sacred if more explicable)

εὕδουσιν δ᾽ ὀρέων κορυφαί τε καὶ φάραγγες·[2]

or else it is repose proper, the rest of things in which there

[1] *Matt.* xi. 28.   [2] Alcman 44, in Bergk's *Lyrici Gr.*

is vitality or capability of motion actual or imagined: and with respect to these the expression of repose is greater in proportion to the amount and sublimity of the action which is *not* taking place, as well as to the intensity of the negation of it. Thus we do not speak of repose in a pebble, because the motion of a pebble has nothing in it of energy or vitality, neither its repose of stability. But having once seen a great rock come down a mountain side, we have a noble sensation of its rest, now bedded immovably among the fern; because the power and fearfulness of its motion were great, and its stability and negation of motion are now great in proportion. Hence the imagination, which delights in nothing more than in the enhancing of the characters of repose, effects this usually by either attributing to things visibly energetic an ideal stability, or to things visibly stable an ideal activity or vitality. Thus Wordsworth speaks of the Cloud, which in itself has too much of changefulness for his purpose, as one

> That heareth not the loud winds when they call,
> And moveth altogether if it move at all.[1]

And again the children, which, that it may remove from them the child-restlessness, the imagination conceives as rooted flowers,

> Beneath an old grey oak, as violets, lie.[2]

On the other hand, the scattered rocks, which have not, as such, vitality enough for rest, are gifted with it by the living image: they

> Lie crouched around us like a flock of sheep.[3]

Modern Painters, vol. II, sec. I, ch. vii, pars. I–2.

[1] *Resolution and Independence*, XI.
[2] *Descriptive Sketches*.   [3] *Nutting*.

Hence I think that there is no desire more intense or more exalted than that which exists in all rightly disciplined minds for the evidences of repose in external signs: and what I cautiously said respecting infinity, I say fearlessly respecting repose; that no work of art can be great without it, and that all art is great in proportion to the appearance of it. It is the most unfailing test of beauty, whether of matter or of motion; nothing can be ignoble that possesses it, nothing right that has it not; and in strict proportion to its appearance in the work is the majesty of mind to be inferred in the artificer. Without regard to other qualities, we may look to this for our evidence; and by the search for this alone we may be led to the rejection of all that is base, and the accepting of all that is good and great, for the paths of wisdom are all peace. We shall see, by this light, three colossal images standing up side by side, looming in their great rest of spirituality above the whole world-horizon, Phidias, Michael Angelo, and Dante; and then, separated from their great religious thrones only by less fulness and earnestness of faith, Homer and Shakespeare; and from these we may go down step by step among the mighty men of every age, securely and certainly observant of diminished lustre in every appearance of restlessness and effort, until the last trace of true inspiration vanishes in tottering affectation or tortured insanity. There is no art, nor pursuit whatsoever, but its results may be classed by this test alone. Everything of evil is betrayed and winnowed away by it; glitter, confusion, or glare of colour; inconsistency of thought; forced expression; evil choice of subject; redundance of materials, pretence, overcharged decoration, or excessive division of parts; and this in everything. In architecture, in music, in acting, in dancing, in whatsoever art, great or mean, there are yet degrees of greatness or meanness entirely dependent on this single quality of repose. *Modern Painters*, vol. II, sec. I, ch. vii, par. 5.

(*d*) SYMMETRY

We shall not be long detained by the consideration of this, the fourth constituent of beauty, as its nature is universally felt and understood. In all perfectly beautiful objects, there is found the opposition of one part to another, and a reciprocal balance, in animals commonly between opposite sides (note the disagreeableness occasioned by the exception in flat-fish, having the eyes on one side of the head); while in vegetables the opposition is less distinct, as in the boughs on opposite sides of trees, and the leaves and sprays on each side of the boughs; and in dead matter less perfect still, often amounting only to a certain tendency towards a balance, as in the opposite sides of valleys and alternate windings of streams. In things in which perfect symmetry is from their nature impossible or improper, a balance must be at least in some measure expressed before they can be beheld with pleasure. Hence the necessity of what artists require as opposing lines or masses in composition, the propriety of which, as well as their value, depends chiefly on their inartificial and natural invention. Absolute equality is not required, still less absolute similarity. A mass of subdued colour may be balanced by a point of a powerful one, and a long and latent line overpowered by a short and conspicuous one. The only error against which it is necessary to guard the reader, with respect to symmetry, is, the confounding of it with proportion, though it seems strange that the two terms could ever have been used as synonymous. Symmetry is the *opposition* of *equal* quantities to each other; proportion, the *connection* of *unequal* quantities with each other. The property of a tree sending out equal boughs on opposite sides is symmetrical; its sending out shorter and smaller towards the top, proportional. In the human face, its balance of opposite sides is symmetry; its division upwards, proportion.

Modern Painters, vol. II, sec. I, ch. viii, pars. 1–2.

(e) PURITY

In all cases I suppose that pureness is made to us desirable, because expressive of that constant presence and energizing of the Deity by which all things live and move, and have their being; and that foulness is painful as the accompaniment of disorder and decay, and always indicative of the withdrawal of Divine support. And the practical analogies of life, the invariable connection of outward foulness with mental sloth and degradation, as well as with bodily lethargy and disease, together with the contrary indications of freshness and purity belonging to every healthy and active organic frame (singularly seen in the effort of the young leaves when first their inward energy prevails over the earth, pierces its corruption, and shakes its dust away from their own white purity of life), all these circumstances strengthen the instinct by associations countless and irresistible. And then, finally, with the idea of purity comes that of spirituality; for the essential characteristic of matter is its inertia, whence, by adding to it purity or energy, we may in some measure spiritualize even matter itself. Thus in the Apocalyptic descriptions it is the purity of every substance that fits it for its place in heaven; the river of the water of life, that proceeds out of the throne of the Lamb, is clear as crystal, and the pavement of the city is pure gold "like unto clear glass".

Modern Painters, vol. ii, sec. i, ch. ix, pars. 8–9.

(f) MODERATION

If, bringing down our ideas of it from complicated objects to simple lines and colours, we analyze and regard them carefully, I think we shall be able to trace them to an under-current of constantly agreeable feeling, excited by the appearance in material things of a self-restrained liberty; that is to say, by the image of that acting of God

with regard to all His creation, wherein, though free to operate in whatever arbitrary, sudden, violent, or inconstant ways He will, He yet, if we may reverently so speak, restrains in Himself this His omnipotent liberty, and works always in consistent modes, called by us laws. And this restraint or moderation (according to the words of Hooker,[1] "that which doth moderate the force and power, that which doth appoint the form and measure of working, the same we term a Law,") is in the Deity not restraint, such as it is said of creatures, but, as again says Hooker,[2] "the very being of God is a law to His working", so that every appearance of painfulness or want of power and freedom in material things is wrong and ugly; for the right restraint, the image of Divine operation, is, both in them and in men, a willing and not painful stopping short of the utmost degree to which their power might reach, and the appearance of fettering or confinement is the cause of ugliness in the one, as the slightest painfulness or effort in restraint is a sign of sin in the other.

I have put this attribute of beauty last, because I consider it the girdle and safeguard of all the rest, and in this respect the most essential of all; for it is possible that a certain degree of beauty may be attained even in the absence of one of its other constituents, as sometimes in some measure without symmetry or without unity. But the least appearance of violence or extravagance, of the want of moderation and restraint, is, I think, destructive of all beauty whatsoever in everything, colour, form, motion, language, or thought; giving rise to that which in colour we call glaring, in form inelegant, in motion ungraceful, in language coarse, in thought undisciplined, in all unchastened; which qualities are in everything most painful, because the signs of disobedient and irregular operation.

Modern Painters, vol. II, sec. I, ch. x, pars. 5–6.

[1] *Ecclesiastical Polity*, I, ii, 1.　　　　[2] *Ibid.*, 2.

And therefore as that virtue which men last, and with most
difficulty, attain unto, and which many attain not at all,
and yet that which is essential to the conduct and almost
to the being of all other virtues; since neither imagination,
nor invention, nor industry, nor sensibility, nor energy,
nor any other good having, is of full avail without this of
self-command, whereby works truly masculine and mighty
are produced, and by the signs of which they are separated
from that lower host of things brilliant, magnificent, and
redundant, and farther yet from that of the loose, the law-
less, the exaggerated, the insolent, and the profane; I would
have the necessity of it foremost among all our inculcating,
and the name of it largest among all our inscribing, in so
far that, over the doors of every school of Art, I would have
this one word, relieved out in deep letters of pure gold,—
Moderation.   *Modern Painters*, vol. II, sec. I, ch. x, par. 8.

IV. VITAL BEAUTY—(1) RELATIVE

I PROCEED more particularly to examine the nature of
that second kind of Beauty of which I spoke in the third
chapter, as consisting in "the appearance of felicitous fulfilment of function in living things". I have already noticed
the example of very pure and high typical beauty which is
to be found in the lines of gradations of unsullied snow:
if, passing to the edge of a sheet of it, upon the Lower Alps,
early in May, we find, as we are nearly sure to find, two or
three little round openings pierced in it, and through these
emergent, a slender, pensive, fragile flower,[1] whose small,
dark, purple-fringed bell hangs down and shudders over
the icy cleft that it has cloven, as if partly wondering at
its own recent grave, and partly dying of very fatigue after
its hard-won victory; we shall be, or we ought to be, moved

[1] Soldanella alpina.

by a totally different impression of loveliness from that
which we receive among the dead ice and the idle clouds.
There is now uttered to us a call for sympathy, now offered
to us an image of moral purpose and achievement, which,
however unconscious or senseless the creature may indeed
be that so seems to call, cannot be heard without affection,
nor contemplated without worship, by any of us whose
heart is rightly tuned, or whose mind is clearly and surely
sighted.

Throughout the whole of the organic creation every
being in a perfect state exhibits certain appearances or
evidences of happiness; and is in its nature, its desires, its
modes of nourishment, habitation, and death, illustrative or
expressive of certain moral dispositions or principles. Now,
first, in the keenness of the sympathy which we feel in the
happiness, real or apparent, of all organic beings, and which,
as we shall presently see, invariably prompts us, from the
joy we have in it, *to look upon those as most lovely which
are most happy*; and, secondly, in the justness of the moral
sense which rightly reads the lesson they are all intended
to teach, and classes them in orders of worthiness and beauty
according to the rank and nature of that lesson, whether it
be of warning or example, in those that wallow or in those
that soar;—in our right accepting and reading of all this,
consists, I say, the ultimately perfect condition of that noble
Theoretic faculty, whose place in the system of our nature
I have already partly vindicated with respect to typical, but
which can only fully be established with respect to vital
beauty.   *Modern Painters*, vol. II, sec. I, ch. xii, par. I.

(a) CHARITY

Its first perfection, therefore, relating to Vital Beauty, is
the kindness and unselfish fulness of heart, which receives
the utmost amount of pleasure from the happiness of all

things. Of which in high degree the heart of man is incapable; neither what intense enjoyment the angels may have in all that they see of things that move and live, and in the part they take in the shedding of God's kindness upon them, can we know or conceive: only in proportion as we draw near to God, and are made in measure like unto Him, can we increase this our possession of Charity, of which the entire essence is in God only. But even the ordinary exercise of this faculty implies a condition of the whole moral being in some measure right and healthy, and to the entire exercise of it there is necessary the entire perfection of the Christian character; for he who loves not God, nor his brother, cannot love the grass beneath his feet, and the creatures which live not for his uses, filling those spaces in the universe which he needs not; while on the other hand, none can love God, nor his human brother, without loving all things which his Father loves; nor without looking upon them, every one, as in that respect his brethren also, and perhaps worthier than he, if, in the under concords they have to fill, their part is touched more truly. It is good to read of that kindness and humbleness of St Francis of Assisi, who spoke never to bird nor to cicala, nor even to wolf and beast of prey, but as his brother; and so we find are moved the minds of all good and mighty men, as in the lesson that we have from the Mariner of Coleridge, and yet more truly and rightly taught in the *Hartleap Well*,

> Never to blend our pleasure, or our pride,
> With sorrow of the meanest thing that feels;

and again in the *White Doe of Rylstone*, with the added teaching, that anguish of our own—

> Is tempered and allayed by sympathies,
> Aloft ascending and descending deep,
> Even to the inferior kinds.

So that I know not of anything more destructive of the

whole Theoretic faculty, not to say of the Christian character and human intellect, than those accursed sports in which man makes of himself, cat, tiger, serpent, chætodon, and alligator in one; and gathers into one continuance of cruelty, for his amusement, all the devices that brutes sparingly and at intervals use against each other for their necessities.

As we pass from those beings of whose happiness and pain we are certain, to those in which it is doubtful, or only seeming, as possibly in plants (though I would fain hold, if I might, "the faith that every flower enjoys the air it breathes,") yet our feeling for them has in it more of sympathy than of actual love, as receiving from them in delight far more than we can give; for love, I think, chiefly grows in giving; at least its essence is the desire of doing good or giving happiness. Still the sympathy of very sensitive minds usually reaches so far as to the conception of life in the plant, and so to love, as with Shakespeare always, as he has taught us in the sweet voices of Ophelia and Perdita, and Wordsworth always, as of the daffodils and the celandine:

> It doth not love the shower, nor seek the cold.
> This neither is its courage, nor its choice,
> But its necessity in being old:

and so all other great poets[1]; nor do I believe that any mind, however rude, is without some slight perception or acknowledgment of joyfulness in breathless things, as most certainly there are none but feel instinctive delight in the appearances of such enjoyment.

Modern Painters, vol. II, sec. I, ch. xii, pars. 2–3.

---

[1] Compare Milton:
> They at her coming sprung,
> And, touched by her fair tendance, gladlier grew.
> [*Par. Lost*, VIII, 46.]

(b) JUSTICE OF MORAL JUDGMENT

If therefore, as I think appears from all evidence, it is the sense of felicity which we first desire in organic form, those forms will be the most beautiful (always, observe, leaving typical beauty out of the question) which exhibit most of power, and seem capable of most quick and joyous sensation. Hence we find gradations of beauty, from the impenetrable hide and slow movement of the elephant and the rhinoceros, from the foul occupation of the vulture, from the earthy struggling of the worm, to the brilliancy of the moth, the buoyancy of the bird, the swiftness of the fawn and the horse, the fair and kingly sensibility of man.

Thus far then, the Theoretic faculty is concerned with the *happiness* of animals, and its exercise depends on the cultivation of the affections only. Let us next observe how it is concerned with the *moral functions* of animals, and therefore how it is dependent on the cultivation of every moral sense. There is not any organic creature but, in its history and habits, will exemplify or illustrate to us some moral excellence or deficiency, or some point of God's providential government, which it is necessary for us to know. Thus the functions and the fates of animals are distributed to them, with a variety which exhibits to us the dignity and results of almost every passion and kind of conduct: some filthy and slothful, pining and unhappy; some rapacious, restless, and cruel; some ever earnest and laborious, and, I think, unhappy in their endless labour; creatures, like the bee, that heap up riches and cannot tell who shall gather them, and others employed, like angels, in endless offices of love and praise. Of which, when in right condition of mind, we esteem those most beautiful, whose functions are the most noble, whether as some, in mere energy, or as others, in moral honour: so that we look with hate on the foulness of the sloth, and the subtlety of

the adder, and the rage of the hyæna; with the honour due to their earthly wisdom we invest the earnest ant and unwearied bee; but we look with full perception of sacred function to the tribes of burning plumage and choral voice.* And so what lesson we might receive for our earthly conduct from the creeping and laborious things, was taught us by that earthly King who made silver to be in Jerusalem as stones (yet thereafter was less rich toward God).[1] But from the lips of a heavenly King, who had not where to lay His head, we were taught what lesson we have to learn from those higher creatures who sow not, nor reap, nor gather into barns, for their Heavenly Father feedeth them.

Modern Painters, vol. II, sec. I, ch. xii, pars. 7–8.

V. VITAL BEAUTY—(2) GENERIC.

HITHERTO we have observed the conclusions of the Theoretic faculty with respect to the relations of happiness, and of *more or less exalted* function existing between *different orders* of organic being. But we must pursue the inquiry farther yet, and observe what impressions of beauty are connected with more or less perfect fulfilment of the *appointed* function by *different individuals* of the same species. We are now no longer called to pronounce upon worthiness of occupation or dignity of disposition; but both employment and capacity being known, and the animal's position and duty fixed, we have to regard it in that respect alone, comparing it with other individuals of its species, and to determine how far it worthily executes its office; whether, if scorpion, it have poison enough, or if tiger, strength enough, or if dove, innocence enough, to sustain rightly

* True to the kindred points of heaven and home.
                    WORDSWORTH, *To the Skylark*.
[1] I *Kings*, x, 27.

its place in creation, and come up to the perfect idea of dove, tiger, or scorpion.

In the first or sympathetic operation of the Theoretic faculty, it will be remembered, we receive pleasure from the signs of mere happiness in living things. In the second theoretic operation of comparing and judging, we constituted ourselves such judges of the lower creatures as Adam was made by God when they were brought to him to be named; and we allowed of beauty in them as they reached, more or less, to that standard of moral perfection by which we test ourselves. But in the third place we are to come down again from the judgment seat, and, taking it for granted that every creature of God is in some way good, and has a duty and specific operation providentially accessary to the wellbeing of all, we are to look, in this faith, to that employment and nature of each, and to derive pleasure from their entire perfection and fitness for the duty they have to do, and in their entire fulfilment of it; and so we are to take pleasure and find beauty in the magnificent binding together of the jaws of the ichthyosaurus for catching and holding, and in the adaptation of the lion for springing, and of the locust for destroying, and of the lark for singing, and in every creature for the doing of that which God has made it to do. Which faithful pleasure in the perception of the perfect operation of lower creatures I have placed last among the perceptions of the Theoretic faculty concerning them, because it is commonly last acquired, both owing to the humbleness and trustfulness of heart which it demands, and because it implies a knowledge of the habits and structure of every creature, such as we can but imperfectly possess.

Modern Painters, vol. II, sec. I, ch. xiii, par. I.

VI. CONCLUSION

WE have seen that this subject matter is referable to four general heads. It is either the record of conscience, written in things external, or it is a symbolizing of Divine attributes in matter, or it is the felicity of living things, or the perfect fulfilment of their duties and functions. In all cases it is something Divine; either the approving voice of God, the glorious symbol of Him, the evidence of His kind presence, or the obedience to His will by Him induced and supported.

All these subjects of contemplation are such as we may suppose will remain sources of pleasure to the perfected spirit throughout eternity. Divine in their nature, they are addressed to the immortal part of men.

Modern Painters, vol. II, sec. I, ch. xv, par. 4.

THE IMAGINATION

I. INTRODUCTION

We have hitherto been exclusively occupied with those sources of pleasure which exist in the external creation, and which in any faithful copy of it must to a certain extent exist also.

These sources of beauty, however, are not presented by any very great work of art in a form of pure transcript. They invariably receive the reflection of the mind under whose influence they have passed, and are modified or coloured by its image.

This modification is the Work of Imagination.

As, in the course of our succeeding investigation, we shall be called upon constantly to compare sources of beauty existing in nature with the images of them received by the human mind, it is very necessary for us shortly to review the conditions and limits of the Imaginative faculty, and to ascertain by what tests we may distinguish its sane, healthy, and profitable operation, from that which is erratic, diseased, and dangerous.

It is neither desirable nor possible here to examine or illustrate in full the essence of this mighty faculty. Such an examination would require a review of the whole field of literature, and would alone demand a volume. Our present task is not to explain or exhibit full portraiture of this function of the mind in all its relations, but only to obtain some certain tests by which we may determine whether it be very Imagination or not, and unmask all impersonations of it; and this chiefly with respect to art, for in literature the faculty takes a thousand forms, according to the matter it has to treat, and becomes like the

princess of the Arabian tale,[1] sword, eagle, or fire, according to the war it wages; sometimes piercing, sometimes soaring, sometimes illumining, retaining no image of itself, except its supernatural power; so that I shall content myself with tracing that particular form of it, and unveiling those imitations of it only, which are to be found, or feared, in painting, referring to other creations of mind only for illustration.

Modern Painters, vol. ii, sec. ii, ch. i, par. i.

II. FUNCTIONS

UNFORTUNATELY, the works of metaphysicians will afford us in this most interesting inquiry, no aid whatsoever. They who are constantly endeavouring to fathom and explain the essence of the faculties of mind, are sure, in the end, to lose sight of all that cannot be explained (though it may be defined and felt); and because, as I shall presently show, the essence of the Imaginative faculty is utterly mysterious and inexplicable, and to be recognized in its results only, or in the negative results of its absence, the metaphysicians, as far as I am acquainted with their works, miss it altogether, and never reach higher than a definition of Fancy by a false name.

What I understand by Fancy will presently appear; not that I contend for nomenclature, but only for distinction between two mental faculties, by whatever name they be called; one the source of all that is great in the poetic arts, the other merely decorative and entertaining; but which are often confounded together, and which have so much in common as to render strict definition of either difficult.

Dugald Stewart's meagre definition may serve us for a starting point. "Imagination", he says, "includes conception or simple apprehension, which enables us to form a notion of those former objects of perception or of know-

[1] *Arabian Nights*, ch. iii, *Story of Second Royal Mendicant.*

ledge, out of which we are to make a selection; abstraction, which separates the selected materials from the qualities and circumstances which are connected with them in nature; and judgment or taste, which selects the materials and directs their combination. To these powers we may add that particular habit of association to which I formerly gave the name of Fancy, as it is this which presents to our choice all the different materials which are subservient to the efforts of imagination, and which may therefore be considered as forming the ground-work of poetical genius."[1]

(By Fancy in this passage, we find on referring to the chapter treating of it, that nothing more is meant than the rapid occurrence of ideas of sense to the mind.)

Now, in this definition, the very point and purpose of all the inquiry is missed. We are told that judgment or taste "directs the combination". In order that anything may be directed, an end must be previously determined; what is the faculty that determines this end? and of what frame and make, how boned and fleshed, how conceived or seen, is the end itself? Bare judgment or taste, cannot approve of what has no existence; and yet by Dugald Stewart's definition we are left to their catering among a host of conceptions, to produce a combination which, as they work for, they must see and approve before it exists. This power of prophecy is the very essence of the whole matter, and it is just that inexplicable part which the metaphysician misses.

As might be expected from his misunderstanding of the faculty he has given an instance entirely nugatory.[2] It

[1] *Philosophy of Human Mind*, Part I, ch. VIII.

[2] He continues thus: "To illustrate these observations, let us consider the steps by which Milton must have proceeded, in creating his imaginary garden of Eden. When he first proposed to himself that subject of description, it is reasonable to suppose that a variety of the most striking scenes which he had seen, crowded into his mind. The association of ideas suggested them, and the power of conception placed each of them before him with all its beauties and imperfections. In every natural scene, if we destine it for any particular purpose, there

would be difficult to find in Milton a passage in which less power of imagination was shown, than the description of Eden, if, as I suppose, this be the passage meant, at the beginning of the fourth book, where I can find three expressions only in which this power is shown; the "*burnished* with golden rind, hung amiable", of the Hesperian fruit, the "*lays forth* her purple grape" of the vine, and the "*fringed* bank with myrtle crowned" of the lake: and these are not what Stewart meant, but only that accumulation of bowers, groves, lawns, and hillocks, which is not imagination at all, but composition, and that of the commonest kind. Hence, if we take any passage in which there is real imagination, we shall find Stewart's hypothesis not only inefficient and obscure, but utterly inapplicable.

Take one or two at random.

> On the other side,
> Incensed with indignation, Satan stood
> Unterrified, and like a comet burned,
> That fires the length of Ophiuchus huge
> In the arctic sky, and from his horrid hair
> Shakes pestilence and war.[1]

(Note that the word incensed is to be taken in its literal and material sense, set on fire.) What taste or judgment was it that directed this combination? or is there nothing more than taste or judgment here?

> Ten paces huge
> He back recoiled; the tenth on bended knee
> His massy spear upstaid; as if on earth
> Winds under ground, or waters forcing way,
> *Sidelong had pushed a mountain from his seat,*
> *Half-sunk with all his pines.*[2]

are defects and redundancies, which art may sometimes, but cannot always correct. But the power of Imagination is unlimited. She can create and annihilate, and dispose at pleasure, her woods, her rocks, and her rivers. Milton, accordingly, would not copy his Eden from any one scene, but would select from each the features which were most eminently beautiful. The power of abstraction enabled him to make the separation, and taste directed him in the selection."

[1] *Par. Lost*, II, 707.   [2] *Par. Lost*, VI, 193.

Together both, ere the high lawns appeared
Under the opening eyelids of the morn,
We drove afield, and both together heard
What time the grey-fly winds her *sultry* horn.[1]

Missing thee, I walk unseen
On the dry smooth-shaven green,
To behold the wandering moon,
Riding near her highest noon,
Like one that had been led astray
Through the heaven's wide pathless way;
And oft, *as if her head she bowed*,
Stooping through a fleecy cloud.[2]

It is evident that Stewart's explanation utterly fails in all these instances; for there is in them no "combination" whatsoever, but a particular mode of regarding the qualities or appearances of a single thing, illustrated and conveyed to us by the image of another; and the act of imagination, observe, is not the selection of this image, but the mode of regarding the object.

But the metaphysician's definition fails yet more utterly, when we look at the imagination neither as regarding, nor combining, but as penetrating,

My gracious silence, hail!
Wouldst thou have laugh'd, had I come coffin'd home,
That weep'st to see me triumph? Ah, my dear,
Such eyes the widows in Corioli wear,
And mothers that lack sons.[3]

How did Shakespeare *know* that Virgilia could not speak?

This knowledge, this intuitive and penetrative perception, is still one of the forms, the highest, of imagination, but there is no combination of images here.

We find, then, that the Imagination has three totally distinct functions. It combines, and by combination creates new forms; but the secret principle of this combination has

[1] *Lycidas*, 25.   [2] *Il Penseroso*, 65.   [3] *Coriolanus*, II, i.

not been shown by the analysts. Again, it treats, or regards, both the simple images and its own combinations in peculiar ways; and, thirdly, it penetrates, analyzes, and reaches truths by no other faculty discoverable. These its three functions, I shall endeavour to illustrate, but not in this order: the most logical mode of treatment would be to follow the order in which commonly the mind works; that is, penetrating first, combining next, and treating or regarding, finally; but this arrangement would be inconvenient, because the acts of penetration and of regard are so closely connected, and so like in their relations to other mental acts, that I wish to examine them consecutively; and the rather, because they have to do with higher subject matter than the mere act of combination, whose distinctive nature, that property which makes it imagination and not composition, it will, I think, be best to explain at setting out, as we easily may, in subjects familiar and material. I shall therefore examine the Imaginative faculty in these three forms; first, as Combining or Associative; secondly, as Analytic or Penetrative; thirdly, as Regardant or Contemplative.

Modern Painters, vol. II, sect. II, ch. i, pars. 2–6.

III. THE IMAGINATION ASSOCIATIVE

(a) COMPOSITION

WE will suppose a man to retain such clear image of a large number of the material things he has seen, as to be able to set down any of them on paper, with perfect fidelity and absolute memory of their most minute features.

In thus setting them down on paper, he works, I suppose, exactly as he would work from nature, only copying the remembered image in his mind, instead of the

real thing. He is, therefore, still nothing more than a copyist. There is no exercise of imagination in this whatsoever.

But over these images, vivid and distinct as nature herself, he has a command which over nature he has not. He can summon any that he chooses; and if, therefore, any group of them which he received from nature be not altogether to his mind, he is at liberty to remove some of the component images, add others foreign, and re-arrange the whole.

Let us suppose, for instance, that he has perfect knowledge of the forms of the Aiguilles Verte and Argentière, and of the great glacier between them at the upper extremity of the valley of Chamonix. The forms of the mountains please him, but the presence of the glacier suits not his purpose. He removes the glacier, sets the mountains farther apart, and introduces between them part of the valley of the Rhone.

This is composition, and is what Dugald Stewart mistook for imagination, in the kingdom of which noble faculty it has no part nor lot.

The essential acts of Composition, properly so called, are the following. The mind which desires the new feature summons up before it those images which it supposes to be the kind wanted; of these it takes the one which it supposes to be fittest, and tries it; if it will not answer, it tries another, until it has obtained such an association as pleases it.

In this operation, if it be of little sensibility, it regards only the absolute beauty or value of the images brought before it; and takes that or those which it thinks fairest or most interesting, without any regard to their sympathy with those for whose company they are destined. Of this kind is all vulgar composition; the "Mulino" of Claude, being a characteristic example.

If the mind be of higher feeling, it will look to the sympathy or contrast of the features, to their likeness or

dissimilarity: it will take, as it thinks best, features resembling or discordant; and if, when it has put them together, it be not satisfied, it will repeat the process on the features themselves, cutting away one part and putting in another; so working more and more delicately down to the lowest details, until by dint of experiment, of repeated trials and shiftings, and constant reference to principles (as that two lines must not mimic one another, that one mass must not be equal to another), etc., it has mortised together a satisfactory result.

This process will be more and more rapid and effective, in proportion to the artist's powers of conception and association, these in their turn depending on his knowledge and experience. The distinctness of his powers of conception will give value, point, and truth to every fragment that he draws from memory. His powers of association, and his knowledge of nature, will pour out before him, in greater or less number and appositeness, the images from which to choose. His experience guides him to quick discernment in the combination, when made, of the parts that are offensive and require change.

The most elevated power of mind of all these, is that of association, by which images apposite or resemblant, or of whatever kind wanted, are called up quickly and in multitudes. When this power is very brilliant, it is called Fancy; not that this is the only meaning of the word Fancy; but it is the meaning of it in relation to that function of the imagination which we are here considering; for fancy has three functions; one subordinate to each of the three functions of the imagination.

Great differences of power are manifested among artists in this respect; some having hosts of distinct images always at their command, and rapidly discerning resemblance or contrast; others having few images, and obscure, at their disposal, nor readily governing those they have.

Where the powers of fancy are very brilliant, the picture becomes highly interesting; if her images are systematically and rightly combined, and truthfully rendered, it will become even impressive and instructive; if wittily and curiously combined, it will be captivating and entertaining.

But all this time the imagination has not once shown itself. All this (except the gift of fancy) may be taught; all this is easily comprehended and analyzed; but imagination is neither to be taught, nor by any efforts to be attained, nor by any acuteness of discernment dissected or analyzed.

Modern Painters, vol. II, sec. II, ch. ii, pars. 2–6.

(*b*) DEFINITION

It has been said that in composition the mind can only take cognizance of likeness or dissimilarity, or of abstract beauty among the ideas it brings together. But neither likeness nor dissimilarity secures harmony. We saw in the Chapter on Unity that likeness destroyed harmony or unity of membership; and that difference did not necessarily secure it, but only that particular *imperfection* in each of the harmonizing parts which can only be supplied by its fellow part. If, therefore, the combination made is to be harmonious, the artist must induce in each of its component parts (suppose two only, for simplicity's sake), such imperfection as that the other shall put it right. If one of them be perfect by itself, the other will be an excrescence. Both must be faulty when separate, and each corrected by the presence of the other. If he can accomplish this, the result will be beautiful; it will be a whole, an organized body with dependent members;—he is an inventor. If not, let his separate features be as beautiful, as apposite, or as resemblant as they may, they form no whole. They are two members glued together. He is only a carpenter and joiner.

Now, the conceivable imperfections of any single feature are infinite. It is impossible, therefore, to fix upon a form of imperfection in the one, and try with this all the forms of imperfection of the other until one fits; but the two imperfections must be co-relatively and simultaneously conceived.

This is Imagination, properly so called; imagination associative, the grandest mechanical power that the human intelligence possesses, and one which will appear more and more marvellous the longer we consider it. By its operation, two ideas are chosen out of an infinite mass (for it evidently matters not whether the imperfections be conceived out of the infinite number conceivable, or selected out of a number recollected), two ideas which are *separately wrong*, which together shall be right, and of whose unity, therefore, the idea must be formed at the instant they are seized, as it is only in that unity that either is good, and therefore only the *conception of that unity can prompt the preference*.   *Modern Painters*, vol. II, sec. II. ch. ii, pars. 6–7.

(c) DIGNITY

A powerfully imaginative mind seizes and combines at the same instant, not only two, but all the important ideas of its poem or picture; and while it works with any one of them, it is at the same instant working with and modifying all in their relations to it, never losing sight of their bearings on each other; as the motion of a snake's body goes through all parts at once, and its volition acts at the same instant in coils that go contrary ways.

This faculty is indeed something that looks as if man were made after the image of God. It is inconceivable, admirable, altogether divine; and yet, wonderful as it may seem, it is palpably evident that no less an operation is necessary for the production of any great work: for, by the

definition of Unity of Membership (the essential characteristic of greatness), not only certain couples or groups of parts, but *all* the parts of a noble work must be separately imperfect; each must imply, and ask for all the rest, and the glory of every one of them must consist in its relation to the rest; neither while so much as one is wanting can any be right. And it is evidently impossible to conceive, in each separate feature, a certain want or wrongness which can only be corrected by the other features of the picture (not by one or two merely, but by all), unless, together with the want, we conceive also of what is wanted, that is, of all the rest of the work or picture.

Modern Painters, vol. II, sec. II, ch. ii, par. 9.

(*d*) TESTS OF IMAGINATION

The Imaginative artist owns no laws. He defies all restraint, and cuts down all hedges. There is nothing within the limits of natural possibility that he dares not do, or that he allows the necessity of doing. The laws of nature he knows; these are to him no restraint. They are his own nature. All other laws or limits he sets at utter defiance; his journey is over an untrodden and pathless plain. But he sees his end over the waste from the first, and goes straight at it; never losing sight of it, nor throwing away a step. Nothing can stop him, nothing turn him aside; falcons and lynxes are of slow and uncertain sight compared with his. He saw his tree, trunk, boughs, foliage and all, from the first moment; not only the tree, but the sky behind it; not only that tree or sky, but all the other great features of his picture: by what intense power of instantaneous selection and amalgamation cannot be explained, but by this it may be proved and tested; that, if we examine the tree of the unimaginative painter, we shall find that on removing any part or parts of it, though the rest will indeed suffer, as being deprived of the proper

development of a tree, and as involving a blank space that
wants occupation, yet the portions left are not made discordant or disagreeable. They are absolutely and in themselves as valuable as they can be; every stem is a perfect
stem, and every twig a graceful twig, or at least as perfect
and as graceful as they were before the removal of the rest.
But if we try the same experiment on the imaginative
painter's work, and break off the merest stem or twig of
it, it all goes to pieces like a Prince Rupert's drop. There is
not so much as a seed of it but it lies on the tree's life, like
the grain upon the tongue of Chaucer's sainted child.[1] Take
it away, and the boughs will sing to us no longer. All is
dead and cold.

This then is the first sign of the presence of real imagination as opposed to composition. But here is another not less
important.

We have seen that as each part is selected and fitted by
the unimaginative painter, he renders it, in itself, as beautiful as he is able. If it be ugly it remains so; he is incapable
of correcting it by the *addition of another ugliness*, and therefore he chooses all his features as fair as they may be (at
least if his object be beauty). But a small proportion only of
the ideas he has at his disposal will reach his standard of
absolute beauty. The others will be of no use to him: and
among those which he permits himself to use, there will
be so marked a family likeness that he will be more and
more cramped, as his picture advances, for want of material,
and tormented by multiplying resemblances, unless disguised by some artifice of light and shade or other forced
difference; and with all the differences he can imagine,
his tree will yet show a sameness and sickening repetition
in all its parts, and all his trees will be like one another,
except so far as one leans east and another west, one is
broadest at the top and another at the bottom: while

[1] *The Prioresses Tale*, line 1852.

through all this insipid repetition, the means by which he forces contrast, dark boughs opposed to light, rugged to smooth, etc., will be painfully evident, to the utter destruction of all dignity and repose. The imaginative work is necessarily the absolute opposite of all this. As all its parts are imperfect, and as there is an unlimited supply of imperfection (for the ways in which things may be wrong are infinite), the imagination is never at a loss, nor ever likely to repeat itself; nothing comes amiss to it; but whatever rude matter it receives, it instantly so arranges that it comes right; all things fall into their place, and appear in that place perfect, useful, and evidently not to be spared; so that of its combinations there is endless variety, and every intractable and seemingly unavailable fragment that we give to it, is instantly turned to some brilliant use, and made the nucleus of a new group of glory; however poor or common the gift, it will be thankful for it, treasure it up, and pay in gold; and it has that life in it and fire, that wherever it passes, among the dead bones and dust of things, behold! a shaking, and the bones come together bone to his bone.

And now we find what noble sympathy and unity there are between the Imaginative and Theoretic faculties. Both agree in this, that they reject nothing, and are thankful for all; but the Theoretic faculty takes out of everything that which is beautiful, while the Imaginative faculty takes hold of the very imperfections which the Theoretic rejects; and, by means of these angles and roughnesses, it joints and bolts the separate stones into a mighty temple, wherein the Theoretic faculty, in its turn, does deepest homage. Thus sympathetic in their desires, harmoniously diverse in their operation, each working for the other with what the other needs not, all things external to man are by one or other turned to good.

Modern Painters, vol. II, sec. II, ch. ii, pars. 13–16.

(e) TRUTH OF IMAGINATION

There remains but one question to be determined relating to this faculty; what operation, namely, supposing it possessed in high degree, it has or ought to have in the artist's treatment of natural scenery?

I have just said that nature is always imaginative, but it does not follow that her imagination is always of high subject, or that the imagination of all the parts is of a like and sympathetic kind; the boughs of every bramble bush are imaginatively arranged, so are those of every oak and cedar; but it does not follow that there is imaginative sympathy between bramble and cedar. There are few natural scenes whose harmonies are not conceivably improvable either by banishment of some discordant point, or by addition of some sympathetic one; it constantly happens that there is a profuseness too great to be comprehended, or an inequality in the pitch, meaning, and intensity of different parts. The imagination will banish all that is extraneous; it will seize out of the many threads of different feeling which nature has suffered to become entangled, one only; and where that seems thin and likely to break, it will spin it stouter, and in doing this, it never knots, but weaves in the new thread; so that all its work looks as pure and true as nature itself, and cannot be guessed from it but by its exceeding simplicity (*known* from it, it cannot be); so that herein we find another test of the imaginative work, that it looks always as if it had been gathered straight from nature, whereas the unimaginative shows its joints and knots, and is visibly composition.

And here, then, we arrive at an important conclusion (though one somewhat contrary to the positions commonly held on the subject), namely, that if anything looks unnatural, there can be no imagination in it (at least not associative). We frequently hear works that have no truth

in them, justified or elevated on the score of being imaginative. Let it be understood once for all, that imagination
never deigns to touch anything but truth; and though it
does not follow that where there is the appearance of truth,
there has been imaginative operation, of this we may be
assured, that where there is appearance of falsehood, the
imagination has had no hand.

Modern Painters, vol. II, sec. II, ch. ii, pars. 21–22.

(f) CONCLUSION

The final tests, therefore, of the work of Associative
imagination are, its intense simplicity, its perfect harmony,
and its absolute truth. It may be a harmony, majestic or
humble, abrupt or prolonged, but it is always a governed
and perfect whole; evidencing in all its relations the weight,
prevalence, and universal dominion of an awful inexplicable Power; a chastising, animating, and disposing Mind.

Modern Painters, vol. II, sec. II, ch. ii, par. 22.

IV. THE IMAGINATION PENETRATIVE

(a) IMAGINATION AND FANCY

Thus far we have been defining that combining operation
of the Imagination, which appears to be in a sort mechanical,
yet takes place in the same inexplicable modes, whatever
be the order of conception submitted to it, though I choose
to illustrate it by its dealings with mere matter before taking
cognizance of any nobler subjects of imagery. We must
now examine the dealing of the Imagination with its
separate conceptions, and endeavour to understand, not
only its principles of selection, but its modes of apprehension
with respect to what it selects.

When Milton's Satan first "rears from off the pool his
mighty stature", the image of leviathan before suggested

not being yet abandoned, the effect of the fire-wave is described as of the upheaved monster on the ocean stream:

> On each hand the flames
> Driven backward, slope their pointing spires, and, rolled
> In billows, leave i' the midst a horrid vale.[1]

And then follows a fiercely restless piece of volcanic imagery:

> As when the force
> Of subterranean wind transports a hill
> Torn from Pelorus, or the shattered side
> Of thundering Ætna, whose combustible
> And fuelled entrails thence conceiving fire,
> Sublimed with mineral fury, aid the winds,
> And leave a singëd bottom all involved
> With stench and smoke: such resting found the sole
> Of unblest feet.

Yet I think all this is too far detailed, and deals too much with externals: we feel rather the form of the fire-waves than their fury; we walk upon them too securely; and the fuel, sublimation, smoke, and singeing seem to me images only of partial combustion; they vary and extend the conception, but they lower the thermometer. Look back, if you will, and add to the description the glimmering of the livid flames; the sulphurous hail and red lightning; yet all together, however they overwhelm us with horror, fail of making us thoroughly, unendurably *hot*. The essence of intense flame has not been given. Now hear Dante:

> Feriami 'l Sole in su l' omero destro,
>   Che già raggiando tutto l' Occidente
>   *Mutava in bianco aspetto di cilestro.*
> Ed io facea *con l' ombra più rovente*
>   *Parer la fiamma.*[2]

---

[1] *Par. Lost*, I, 222.   [2] *Purg.* XXVI, 4. Cary translates:
                                                The sun
                     Now all the western clime irradiate changed
                     From azure tint to white; and, as I passed,
                     My passing shadow made the umbered flame
                     Burn ruddier.

That is a slight touch; he has not gone to Ætna or Pelorus for fuel; but we shall not soon recover from it, he has taken our breath away, and leaves us gasping. No smoke nor cinders there. Pure white, hurtling, formless flame; very fire crystal, we cannot make spires nor waves of it, nor divide it, nor walk on it; there is no question about singeing soles of feet. It is lambent annihilation.

Such is always the mode in which the highest imaginative faculty seizes its materials. It never stops at crusts or ashes, or outward images of any kind; it ploughs them all aside, and plunges into the very central fiery heart; nothing else will content its spirituality; whatever semblances and various outward shows and phases its subject may possess go for nothing; it gets within all fence, cuts down to the root, and drinks the very vital sap of that it deals with: once therein, it is at liberty to throw up what new shoots it will, so always that the true juice and sap be in them, and to prune and twist them at its pleasure, and bring them to fairer fruit than grew on the old tree; but all this pruning and twisting is work that it likes not, and often does ill; its function and gift are the getting at the root, its nature and dignity depend on its holding things always by the heart. Take its hand from off the beating of that, and it will prophesy no longer; it looks not in the eyes, it judges not by the voice, it describes not by outward features; all that it affirms, judges, or describes, it affirms, from within.

It may seem to the reader that I am incorrect in calling this penetrating possession-taking faculty Imagination. Be it so; the name is of little consequence; the faculty itself, called by what name we will, I insist upon as the highest intellectual power of man. There is no reasoning in it; it works not by algebra, nor by integral calculus; it is a piercing pholas-like mind's tongue, that works and tastes into the very rock heart; no matter what be the subject submitted to it, substance or spirit; all is alike divided

asunder, joint and marrow, whatever utmost truth, life, principle it has, laid bare, and that which has no truth, life, nor principle, dissipated into its original smoke at a touch. The whispers at men's ears it lifts into visible angels. Vials that have lain sealed in the deep sea a thousand years it unseals, and brings out of them Genii.[1]

Every great conception of poet or painter is held and treated by this faculty. Every character that is so much as touched by men like Æschylus, Homer, Dante, or Shakespeare, is by them held by the heart; and every circumstance or sentence of their being, speaking, or seeming, is seized by process from within, and is referred to that inner secret spring of which the hold is never lost for an instant: so that every sentence, as it has been thought out from the heart, opens for us a way down to the heart, leads us to the centre, and then leaves us to gather what more we may. It is the Open Sesame of a huge, obscure, endless cave, with inexhaustible treasure of pure gold scattered in it: the wandering about and gathering the pieces may be left to any of us, all can accomplish that; but the first opening of that invisible door in the rock is of the imagination only.

Hence there is in every word set down by the imaginative mind an awful under-current of meaning, and evidence and shadow upon it of the deep places out of which it has come. It is often obscure, often half-told; for he who wrote it, in his clear seeing of the things beneath, may have been impatient of detailed interpretation: but, if we choose to dwell upon it and trace it, it will lead us always securely back to that metropolis of the soul's dominion from which we may follow out all the ways and tracks to its farthest coasts.

I think the "Quel giorno più non vi leggemmo avante"[2] of Francesca di Rimini, and the "He has no children" of

---

[1] *Arab. Nights,* ch. ii (Lane).
[2] "That day we read no farther": *Inferno,* v, 138.

Macduff,[1] are as fine instances as can be given; but the sign and mark of it are visible on every line of the four great men above instanced.

The unimaginative writer on the other hand, as he has never pierced to the heart, so he can never touch it. If he has to paint a passion, he remembers the external signs of it, he collects expressions of it from other writers, he searches for similes, he composes, exaggerates, heaps term on term, figure on figure, till we groan beneath the cold disjointed heap; but it is all faggot and no fire; the life breath is not in it; his passion has the form of the leviathan, but it never makes the deep boil; he fastens us all at anchor in the scaly rind of it; our sympathies remain as idle as a painted ship upon a painted ocean.

And that virtue of originality that men so strain after is not newness, as they vainly think (there is nothing new), it is only genuineness; it all depends on this single glorious faculty of getting to the spring of things and working out from that; it is the coolness, and clearness, and deliciousness of the water fresh from the fountain head, opposed to the thick, hot, unrefreshing drainage from other men's meadows.

This freshness, however, is not to be taken for an infallible sign of imagination, inasmuch as it results also from a vivid operation of fancy, whose parallel function to this division of the imaginative faculty it is here necessary to distinguish.

I believe it will be found that the entirely unimaginative mind *sees* nothing of the object it has to dwell upon or describe, and is therefore utterly unable, as it is blind itself, to set anything before the eyes of the reader.

The fancy sees the outside, and is able to give a portrait of the outside, clear, brilliant, and full of detail.

The imagination sees the heart and inner nature, and

---

[1] *Macbeth*, IV, iii.

makes them felt, but is often obscure, mysterious, and interrupted, in its giving of outer detail.

Take an instance. A writer with neither imagination nor fancy, describing a fair lip, does not see it, but thinks about it, and about what is said of it, and calls it well turned, or rosy, or delicate, or lovely, or afflicts us with some other quenching and chilling epithet. Now hear Fancy speak:

> Her lips were red, and one was thin,
> Compared with that was next her chin,
> Some bee had stung it newly.[1]

The real, red, bright being of the lip is there in a moment. But it is all outside; no expression yet, no mind. Let us go a step farther with Warner, of Fair Rosamond struck by Eleanor:

> With that she dashed her on the lips
> So dyëd double red;
> Hard was the heart that gave the blow,
> Soft were those lips that bled.[2]

The tenderness of mind begins to mingle with the outside colour, the Imagination is seen in its awakening. Next Shelley:

> Lamp of life, thy lips are burning
> Through the veil that seems to hide them,
> As the radiant lines of morning
> Through thin clouds ere they divide them.[3]

There dawns the entire soul in that morning; yet we may stop if we choose at the image still external, at the crimson clouds. The imagination is contemplative rather than penetrative. Last, hear Hamlet:

Here hung those lips that I have kissed, I know not how oft. Where be your gibes now, your gambols, your songs, your flashes of merriment that were wont to set the table on a roar?[4]

[1] Quoted from Sir J. Suckling in Leigh Hunt's *Imagination and Fancy*.
[2] Quoted from William Warner, in Leigh Hunt.
[3] *Prometheus Unbound*, II, v, 54.   [4] *Hamlet*, v, i, 181.

There is the essence of lip, and the full power of the imagination.

Again, compare Milton's flowers in *Lycidas* with Perdita's. In Milton it happens, I think, generally, and in the case before us most certainly, that the imagination is mixed and broken with fancy, and so the strength of the imagery is part of iron and part of clay:

Bring the rathe primrose, that forsaken dies,	*Imagination.*
The tufted crow-toe and pale jessamine,	*Nugatory.*
The white pink, and the pansy freaked with jet,	*Fancy.*
The glowing violet,	*Imagination.*
The musk rose, and the well-attired woodbine,	*Fancy*, vulgar.
With cowslips wan that hang the pensive head,	*Imagination.*
And every flower that sad embroidery wears.	*Mixed.*

Then hear Perdita:

> O Proserpina,
> For the flowers now, that, frighted, thou let'st fall
> From Dis's waggon! daffodils,
> That come before the swallow dares, and take
> The winds of March with beauty; violets, dim,
> But sweeter than the lids of Juno's eyes,
> Or Cytherea's breath; pale primroses,
> That die unmarried, ere they can behold
> Bright Phœbus in his strength, a malady
> Most incident to maids.[1]

Observe how the imagination in these last lines goes into the very inmost soul of every flower, after having touched them all at first with that heavenly timidness, the shadow of Proserpine's, and gilded them with celestial gathering, and never stops on their spots, or their bodily shape; while Milton sticks in the stains upon them, and puts us off with that unhappy freak of jet in the very flower that, without this bit of paper-staining, would have been the most precious to us of all. "There is pansies, that's for thoughts."[2]

[1] *Winter's Tale*, IV, iii.   [2] *Hamlet*, IV, v.

So, I believe, it will be found throughout the operation of the fancy, that it has to do with the outsides of things, and is content therewith; of this there can be no doubt in such passages as that description of Mab so often given as an illustration of it,[1] and many other instances will be found in Leigh Hunt's work already referred to. Only some embarrassment is caused by passages in which Fancy is seizing the outward signs of emotion, understanding them as such, and yet, in pursuance of her proper function, taking for her share, and for that which she chooses to dwell upon, the outside sign rather than the emotion. Note in *Macbeth* that brilliant instance:

> Where the Norweyan banners flout the sky,
> And fan our people cold.[2]

The outward shiver and coldness of fear is seized on, and irregularly but admirably attributed by the fancy to the drift of the banners. Compare Solomon's Song, where the imagination stays not at the outside, but dwells on the fearful emotion itself:

> Who is she that looketh forth as the morning; fair as the moon, clear as the sun, and terrible as an army with banners?

Now, if these be the prevailing characteristics of the two faculties, it is evident that certain other collateral differences will result from them. Fancy, as she stays at the externals, can never feel. She is one of the hardest-hearted of the intellectual faculties, or rather one of the most purely and simply intellectual. She cannot be made serious, no edge-tools but she will play with. Whereas the Imagination is in all things the reverse. She cannot be but serious; she sees too far, too darkly, too solemnly, too earnestly ever to smile. There is something in the heart of everything, if we can reach it, that we shall not be inclined to laugh at.

---

[1] *Romeo and Juliet*, i, iv.   [2] Act i, Sc. ii, line 51.

And thus there is reciprocal action between the intensity of moral feeling and the power of imagination; for, on the one hand, those who have keenest sympathy are those who look closest and pierce deepest, and hold securest; and on the other, those who have so pierced and seen the melancholy deeps of things are filled with the most intense passion and gentleness of sympathy. Hence, I suppose that the powers of the imagination may always be tested by accompanying tenderness of emotion; and thus, as Byron said,[1] there is no tenderness like Dante's, neither any intensity nor seriousness like his, such seriousness that it is incapable of perceiving that which is commonplace or ridiculous, but fuses all down into its own white-hot fire. And, on the other hand, I suppose the chief bar to the action of imagination, and stop to all greatness in this present age of ours, is its mean and shallow love of jest; so that if there be in any good and lofty work a flaw, failing, or undipped vulnerable part, where sarcasm may stick or stay, it is caught at, and pointed at, and buzzed about, and fixed upon, and stung into, as a recent wound is by flies; and nothing is ever taken seriously or as it was meant, but always, if it may be, turned the wrong way, and misunderstood; and while this is so, there is not, nor cannot be, any hope of achievement of high things; men dare not open their hearts to us, if we are to broil them on a thorn-fire.

This, then, is one essential difference between imagination and fancy; and another is like it and resultant from it, that the imagination being at the heart of things, poises herself there, and is still, quiet, and brooding, comprehending all around her with her fixed look; but the fancy staying at the outside of things, cannot see them all at once; but runs hither and thither, and round and about to see more and more, bounding merrily from point to point, and glittering here and there, but necessarily always settling, if she settle

[1] Byron's *Diary*, Jan. 29, 1821.

at all, on a point only, never embracing the whole. And from these single points she can strike out analogies and catch resemblances, which, so far as the point she looks at is concerned, are true, but would be false, if she could see through to the other side. This, however, she cares not to do; the point of contact is enough for her, and even if there be a gap left between the two things and they do not quite touch, she will spring from one to the other like an electric spark, and be seen brightest in her leaping.

Now these differences between the imagination and the fancy hold, not only in the way they lay hold of separate conceptions, but even in the points they occupy of time; for the fancy loves to run hither and thither in time, and to follow long chains of circumstances from link to link; but the imagination, if it may, gets hold of a moment or link in the middle that implies all the rest, and fastens there. Hence Fuseli's aphorism: "Invention never suffers the action to expire, nor the spectator's fancy to consume itself in preparation, or stagnate into repose. It neither begins from the egg, nor coldly gathers the remains."

Modern Painters, vol. ii, sec. ii, ch. iii, pars. 1–12.

(b) PERCEPTION OF TRUTH

Now, in all these instances, let it be observed—for it is to that end alone that I have been arguing all along—that the virtue of the Imagination is its reaching, by intuition and intensity of gaze (not by reasoning, but by its authoritative opening and revealing power), a more essential truth than is seen at the surface of things. I repeat that it matters not whether the reader is willing to call this faculty Imagination or not; I do not care about the name; but I would be understood when I speak of imagination hereafter, to mean this, the base of whose authority and being is its perpetual thirst for truth and purpose to be true. It has no food, no

delight, no care, no perception, except of truth; it is for ever looking under masks, and burning up mists; no fairness of form, no majesty of seeming will satisfy it; the first condition of its existence is incapability of being deceived; and though it sometimes dwells upon and substantiates the fictions of fancy, yet its own operation is to trace to their farthest limit the true laws and likelihoods even of the fictitious creation.

Modern Painters, vol. ii, sec. ii, ch. iii, par. 29.

V. THE IMAGINATION CONTEMPLATIVE

We have, in the two preceding chapters, arrived at definite conclusions respecting the power and essence of the imaginative faculty. In these two acts of penetration and combination, its separating and characteristic attributes are entirely developed; it remains for us only to observe a certain habit or mode of operation in which it frequently delights, and by which it addresses itself to our perceptions more forcibly, and asserts its presence more distinctly than in those mighty but more secret workings wherein its life consists.

In our examination of the combining imagination, we chose to assume the first or simple conception to be as clear in the absence as in the presence of the object of it. This, I suppose, is, in point of fact, never the case, nor is an approximation to such distinctness of conception always a characteristic of the imaginative mind. Many persons have thorough and felicitous power of drawing from memory, yet never originate a thought, nor excite an emotion.

The form in which conception actually occurs to ordinary minds appears to derive value and preciousness from indefiniteness; for there is an unfailing charm in the memory and anticipation of things beautiful, more sunny and spiritual

than attaches to their presence; for with their presence it is possible to be sated, and even wearied, but with the imagination of them never; in so far that it needs some self-discipline to prevent the mind from falling into a morbid condition of dissatisfaction with all that it immediately possesses, and continual longing for things absent: and yet I think this charm is not justly to be attributed to the mere vagueness and uncertainty of the conception, except thus far, that of objects whose substantial presence was painful, the sublimity and impressiveness, if there were any, are retained in the conception, while the sensual offensiveness is withdrawn; thus circumstances of horror may be safely touched in verbal description, and for a time dwelt upon by the mind as often by Homer and Spenser (by the latter frequently with too much grossness), which could not for a moment be regarded or tolerated in their reality, or on canvas; and besides this mellowing and softening operation on those it retains, the conceptive faculty has the power of letting go many of them altogether out of its groups of ideas, and retaining only those where the "meminisse juvabit"[1] will apply; and in this way the entire group of memories becomes altogether delightful. But of those parts of anything which are in themselves beautiful, I think the indistinctness no benefit, but that the brighter they are the better; and that the peculiar charm we feel in conception results from its grasp and blending of ideas, rather than from their obscurity; for we do not usually recall, as we have seen, one part at a time only of a pleasant scene, one moment only of a happy day; but together with each single object we summon up a kind of crowded and involved shadowing forth of all the other glories with which it was associated, and into every moment we concentrate an epitome of the day; and it will happen frequently that even when the visible objects or actual circumstances are

[1] Vergil, *Aeneid*, I, 203.

not in detail remembered, the feeling and joy of them are obtained we know not how or whence: and so, with a kind of conceptive burning-glass, we bend the sunshine of all the day, and the fulness of all the scene upon every point that we successively seize; and this together with more vivid action of Fancy, for I think that the wilful and playful seizures of the points that suit her purpose, and help her springing, whereby she is distinguished from simple conception, take place more easily and actively with the memory of things than in presence of them. But, however this be, and I confess that there is much that I cannot satisfactorily to myself unravel with respect to the nature of simple conception, it is evident that this agreeableness, whatever it be, is not by art attainable, for all art is, in some sort, realization; it may be the realization of obscurity or indefiniteness, but still it must differ from the mere *conception* of obscurity and indefiniteness; so that whatever emotions depend absolutely on imperfectness of conception, as the horror of Milton's Death, cannot be rendered by art; for art can only lay hold of things which have shape, and destroys by its touch the fearfulness or pleasurableness of those which "shape have none".[1]

But on this indistinctness of conception, itself comparatively valueless and unaffecting, is based the operation of the Imaginative faculty with which we are at present concerned, and in which its glory is consummated; whereby, depriving the subject of material and bodily shape, and regarding such of its qualities only as it chooses for particular purpose, it forges these qualities together in such groups and forms as it desires, and gives to their abstract being consistency and reality, by striking them as it were with the die of an image belonging to other matter, which stroke having once received, they pass current at once in the peculiar conjunction and for the peculiar value desired.

[1] *Par. Lost*, II, 667.

Thus, in the description of Satan, "And like a comet burned," the bodily shape of the angel is destroyed, the inflaming of the formless spirit is alone regarded; and this, and his power of evil, associated in one fearful and abstract conception, are stamped to give them distinctness and permanence with the image of the comet, "That fires the length of Ophiuchus huge." Yet this could not be done, but that the image of the comet itself is in a measure indistinct, capable of awful expansion, and full of threatening and fear. Again, in his fall, the imagination gathers up the thunder, the resistance, the massy prostration, separates them from the external form, and binds them together by the help of that image of the mountain half sunk; which again would be unfit but for its own indistinctness, and for that glorious addition "with all his pines", whereby a vitality and spear-like hostility are communicated to its falling form; and the fall is marked as not utter subversion, but sinking only, the pines remaining in their uprightness and unity, and threatening of darkness upon the descended precipice; and again, in that yet more noble passage at the close of the fourth book, where almost every operation of the contemplative imagination is concentrated; the angelic squadron first gathered into one burning mass by the single expression "sharpening in mooned horns", then told out in their unity and multitude and stooped hostility, by the image of the wind upon the corn; Satan endowed with god-like strength and endurance in that mighty line, "Like Teneriff or Atlas, unremoved", with infinitude of size the next instant, and with all the vagueness and terribleness of spiritual power, by the "Horrour plumed", and the "*what seemed* both spear and shield".[1]

The third function of Fancy, already spoken of as subordinate to this of the Imagination, is the highest of

[1] Vide *Par. Lost*, IV, 979-990.

which she is capable; like the Imagination, she beholds in
the things submitted to her treatment things different from
the actual; but the suggestions she follows are not in their
nature essential in the object contemplated; and the images
resulting, instead of illustrating, may lead the mind away
from it, and change the current of contemplative feeling:
for, as in her operation parallel to Imagination penetrative
we saw her dwelling upon external features, while the
nobler sister faculty entered within; so now, when both,
from what they see and know in their immediate object,
are conjuring up images illustrative or elevatory of it,
the Fancy necessarily summons those of mere external
relationship, and therefore of unaffecting influence; while
the Imagination, by every ghost she raises, tells tales about
the prison house, and therefore never loses her power over
the heart, nor her unity of emotion. On the other hand,
the regardant or contemplative action of Fancy is in this
different from, and in this nobler than, that mere seizing
and likeness-catching operation we saw in her before; that,
when contemplative, she verily believes in the truth of the
vision she has summoned, loses sight of actuality, and beholds the new and spiritual image faithfully and even
seriously; whereas, before, she summoned no spiritual
image, but merely caught the vivid actuality, or the curious
resemblance of the real object; not that these two opera-
tions are separate, for the Fancy passes gradually from mere
vivid sight of reality, and witty suggestion of likeness, to
a ghostly sight of what is unreal; and through this, in proportion as she begins to feel, she rises towards and partakes
of Imagination itself; for Imagination and Fancy are continually united, and it is necessary, when they are so,
carefully to distinguish the feelingless part which is Fancy's,
from the sentient part which is Imagination's. Let us
take a few instances. Here is Fancy, first, very beautiful,
in her simple capacity of likeness-catching:

> To-day we purpose—ay, this hour we mount,
> To spur three leagues towards the Apennine.
> Come down, we pray thee, ere the *hot sun count*
> *His dewy rosary* on the eglantine.[1]

Seizing on the outside resemblances of bead form, and on the slipping from their threading bough one by one, the fancy is content to lose the heart of the thing, the solemnity of prayer: or perhaps I do the glorious poet wrong in saying this, for the sense of a sun worship and orison in beginning its race, may have been in his mind; and so far as it was so, the passage is imaginative and not fanciful. But that which most readers would accept from it, is the mere flash of the external image, in whose truth the Fancy herself does not yet believe, and therefore is not yet contemplative. Here, however, is Fancy believing in the images she creates:

> It feeds the quick growth of the serpent-vine,
> And the dark linked ivy tangling wild,
> And budding, blown, or odour-faded blooms,
> Which *star the winds with points of coloured light*
> As they rain through them; and *bright golden globes*
> *Of fruit suspended in their own green heaven.*[2]

It is not, observe, a mere likeness that is caught here; but the flowers and fruit are entirely deprived by the fancy of their material existence, and contemplated by her seriously and faithfully as stars and worlds; yet it is only external likeness that she catches; she forces the resemblance, and lowers the dignity of the adopted image.

Next take two delicious stanzas of Fancy regardant (believing in her creations), followed by one of heavenly imagination, from Wordsworth's address to the daisy:

> A Nun demure—of lowly port;
> Or sprightly maiden, of Love's court,
> In thy simplicity the sport
> Of all temptations.

[1] Keats, *Isabella*, XXIV.   [2] Shelley, *Prometheus*, III, 3.

A queen in crown of rubies drest,
A starveling in a scanty vest,
Are all, as seems to suit thee best—
Thy appellations.

I see thee glittering from afar—
And then thou art a pretty star;
Not quite so fair as many are
In heaven above thee!
Yet like a star, with glittering crest,
Self-poised in air thou seem'st to rest;—
May peace come never to his nest
Who shall reprove thee!

Bright flower! for by that name at last,
When all my reveries are past,
I call thee, and to that cleave fast,
Sweet silent creature!
That breath'st with me, in sun and air,
Do thou, as thou art wont, repair
My heart with gladness, and a share
Of thy meek nature!

Observe how spiritual, yet how wandering and playful, the fancy is in the first two stanzas, and how far she flies from the matter in hand; never stopping to brood on the character of any one of the images she summons, and yet for a moment truly seeing and believing in them all; while in the last stanza the imagination returns with its deep feeling to the heart of the flower, and "*cleaves fast*" to that. Compare the operation of the Imagination in Coleridge, on one of the most trifling objects that could possibly have been submitted to its action:

The thin blue flame
Lies on my low-burnt fire, and quivers not:
Only that film which fluttered on the grate
Still flutters there, the sole unquiet thing.
Methinks its motion in this hush of nature
Gives it dim sympathies with me, who live,
Making it a companionable form,

> Whose puny flaps and freaks the idling spirit
> By its own moods interprets, everywhere
> Echo or mirror seeking of itself,
> And makes a toy of thought.[1]

Lastly, observe the sweet operation of Fancy regardant, in the following well-known passage from Scott, where both her beholding and transforming powers are seen in their simplicity:

> The rocky summits, split and rent,
> Formed turret, dome or battlement,
> Or seemed fantastically set
> With cupola or minaret.
> Nor were these earth-born castles bare,
> Nor lacked they many a banner fair,
> For, from their shivered brows displayed,
> Far o'er th' unfathomable glade,
> All twinkling with the dew-drop sheen,
> The briar-rose fell, in streamers green,
> And creeping shrubs of thousand dyes
> Waved in the west wind's summer sighs.[2]

Let the reader refer to this passage, with its pretty tremulous conclusion above the pine tree, "where glistening streamers waved and danced", and then compare with it the following, where the Imagination operates on a scene nearly similar:

> Grey rocks did peep from the spare moss, and stemmed
> The struggling brook; tall spires of windle strae
> Threw their thin shadows down the rugged slope,
> And nought but gnarled roots of ancient pines,
> Branchless and blasted, clenched, with grasping roots,
> Th' unwilling soil.   .   .   .
>   .   .   .   A gradual change was here,
> Yet ghastly. For, *as fast years flow away,*
> *The smooth brow gathers, and the hair grows thin*
> *And white; and, where irradiate dewy eyes*
> *Had shone, gleam stony orbs;—so from his steps*

----

[1] *Frost at Midnight.*   [2] *The Lady of the Lake,* I, xi.

Bright flowers departed, and the beautiful shade
Of the green groves, with all their odorous winds
And musical motions.   .   .   .   .   .

.   .   .   .   Where the pass extends
Its stony jaws, the abrupt mountain breaks,
And seems with its accumulated crags
To overhang the world; for wide expand
Beneath the wan stars, and descending moon,
Islanded seas, blue mountains, mighty streams,
Dim tracts and vast, robed in the lustrous gloom
Of leaden-coloured even, and fiery hills
Mingling their flames with twilight, on the verge
Of the remote horizon. The near scene,
In naked and severe simplicity,
Made contrast with the universe. A pine
Rock-rooted, stretch'd athwart the vacancy
Its swinging boughs, to each *inconstant blast*
Yielding one only response at each pause,
In most familiar cadence, with the howl,
The thunder, and the hiss of *homeless* streams,
Mingling its solemn song.[1]

In this last passage, the mind never departs from its
solemn possession of the solitary scene, the Imagination
only giving weight, meaning, and strange human sympathies to all its sights and sounds.

In that from Scott* the Fancy, led away by the outside
resemblance of floating form and hue to the banners, loses

* Let it not be supposed that I mean to compare the sickly dreaming
of Shelley over clouds and waves, with the masculine and magnificent
grasp of men and things which we find in Scott; it only happens that
these two passages are more illustrative, by the likeness of the scenery
they treat, than any others I could have opposed, and that Shelley is
peculiarly distinguished by the faculty of Contemplative imagination.
Scott's healthy and truthful feeling would not allow him to represent
the benighted hunter, provoked by loss of game, horse, and way at
once, as indulging in any more exalted flights of imagination than
those naturally consequent on the contrast between the night's lodging
he expected, and that which befitted him.
[1] Shelley, *Alastor*, 527.

the feeling and possession of the scene, and places herself in circumstances of character completely opposite to the quietness and grandeur of the natural objects; this would have been unjustifiable, but that the resemblance occurs to the mind of the monarch, rather than to that of the poet; and it is that which, of all others, would have been the most likely to occur at the time; from this point of view it has high imaginative propriety. Of the same fanciful character is that transformation of the tree trunks into dragons noticed before in Turner's *Jason*; and in the same way this becomes imaginative, as it exhibits the effect of Fear in disposing to morbid perception. Compare with it the real and high action of the Imagination on the same matter in Wordsworth's *Yew trees* (perhaps the most vigorous and solemn bit of forest landscape ever painted):—

> Each particular trunk a growth
> Of intertwisted fibres serpentine,
> Up-coiling and inveterately convolved,
> *Nor uninformed with Phantasy, and looks*
> *That threaten the profane.*

It is too long to quote, but the reader should refer to it: let him note especially, if painter, that pure touch of colour, "By sheddings from the pining umbrage tinged."

I have been led perhaps into too great detail in illustrating these points; but I think it is of no small importance to prove how in all cases the Imagination is based upon, and appeals to, a deep heart feeling; and how faithful and earnest it is in contemplation of the subject-matter, never losing sight of it, nor disguising it, but depriving it of extraneous and material accidents, and regarding it in its disembodied essence.

Modern Painters, vol. II, sec. II, ch. iv, pars. 1–7.

THE GROTESQUE IN
LITERATURE

A FINE grotesque is the expression, in a moment, by a series of symbols thrown together in bold and fearless connection, of truths which it would have taken a long time to express in any verbal way, and of which the connection is left for the beholder to work out for himself; the gaps, left or over-leaped by the haste of the imagination, forming the grotesque character.

For instance, Spenser desires to tell us, (1) that envy is the most untamable and unappeasable of the passions, not to be soothed by any kindness; (2) that with continual labour it invents evil thoughts out of its own heart; (3) that even in this, its power of doing harm is partly hindered by the de-caying and corrupting nature of the evil it lives in; (4) that it looks every way, and that whatever it sees is altered and discoloured by its own nature; (5) which discolouring, how-ever, is to it a veil, or disgraceful dress, in the sight of others; (6) and that it never is free from the most bitter suffering, (7) which cramps all its acts and movements, enfolding and crushing it while it torments. All this it has required a somewhat long and languid sentence for me to say in unsymbolical terms,—not, by the way, that they *are* unsymbolical altogether, for I have been forced, whether I would or not, to use *some* figurative words; but even with this help the sentence is long and tiresome, and does not with any vigour represent the truth. It would take some prolonged enforcement of each sentence to make it felt, in ordinary ways of talking. But Spenser puts it all into a grotesque, and it is done shortly and at once, so that we feel it fully, and see it, and never forget it. I have numbered

above the statements which had to be made. I now number them with the same numbers, as they occur in the several pieces of the grotesque:—

> And next to him malicious Envy rode
> (1) Upon a ravenous wolfe, and (2, 3) still did chaw
> Between his cankred* teeth a venemous tode,
> That all the poison ran about his jaw.
> (4, 5) All in a kirtle of discolourd say
> He clothed was, y-paynted full of eies;
> (6) And in his bosome secretly there lay
> An hatefull snake, the which his taile uptyes
> (7) In many folds, and mortall sting implyes.[1]

There is the whole thing in nine lines; or, rather in one image, which will hardly occupy any room at all on the mind's shelves, but can be lifted out, whole, whenever we want it. All noble grotesques are concentrations of this kind, and the noblest convey truths which nothing else could convey; and not only so, but convey them, in minor cases with a delightfulness,—in the higher instances with an awfulness,—which no mere utterance of the symbolised truth would have possessed, but which belongs to the effort of the mind to unweave the riddle, or to the sense it has of there being an infinite power and meaning in the thing seen, beyond all that is apparent therein, giving the highest sublimity even to the most trivial object so presented and so contemplated.

"Jeremiah, what seest thou?"
"I see a seething pot; and the face thereof is toward the north.
Out of the north an evil shall break forth upon all the inhabitants
of the land."[2]

And thus in all ages and among all nations, grotesque idealism has been the element through which the most appalling and eventful truth has been wisely conveyed, from

---

* Cankred—because he cannot then bite hard.
[1] *Faërie Queene*, I, iv, 30.   [2] *Jeremiah*, i, 13.

the most sublime words of true Revelation, to the "ἀλλ' ὅτ' ἂν ἡμίονος βασιλεύς", etc., of the oracles,[1] and the more or less doubtful teaching of dreams; and so down to ordinary poetry. No element of imagination has a wider range, a more magnificent use, or so colossal a grasp of sacred truth.   *Modern Painters*, vol. III, ch. viii, pars. 4–5.

The superstitions which represented the devil as assuming various contemptible forms or disguises in order to accomplish his purposes aided this gradual degradation of conception, and directed the study of the workman to the most strange and ugly conditions of animal form, until at last, even in the most serious subjects, the fiends are oftener ludicrous than terrible. Nor, indeed, is this altogether avoidable, for it is not possible to express intense wickedness without some condition of degradation. Malice, subtlety, and pride, in their extreme, cannot be written upon noble forms; and I am aware of no effort to represent the Satanic mind in the angelic form which has succeeded in painting. Milton succeeds only because he separately describes the movements of the mind, and therefore leaves himself at liberty to make the form heroic; but that form is never distinct enough to be painted. Dante, who will not leave even external forms obscure, degrades them before he can feel them to be demoniacal; so also John Bunyan: both of them, I think, having firmer faith than Milton's in their own creations, and deeper insight into the nature of sin. Milton makes his fiends too noble, and misses the foulness, inconstancy, and fury of wickedness. His Satan possesses some virtues, not the less virtues for being applied to evil purpose. Courage, resolution, patience, deliberation in council, this latter being eminently a wise and holy character, as opposed to the "Insania" of excessive

[1] Herodotus, I, 55.

sin: and all this, if not a shallow and false, is a smoothed and artistical, conception. On the other hand, I have always felt that there was a peculiar grandeur in the indescribable ungovernable fury of Dante's fiends, ever shortening its own powers, and disappointing its own purposes; the deaf, blind, speechless, unspeakable rage, fierce as the lightning, but erring from its mark or turning senselessly against itself, and still further debased by foulness of form and action. Something is indeed to be allowed for the rude feelings of the time, but I believe all such men as Dante are sent into the world at the time when they can do their work best; and that, it being appointed for him to give to mankind the most vigorous realisation possible both of Hell and Heaven, he was born both in the country and at the time which furnished the most stern opposition of Horror and Beauty, and permitted it to be written in the clearest terms. And, therefore, though there are passages in the *Inferno* which it would be impossible for any poet now to write, I look upon it as all the more perfect for them. For there can be no question but that one characteristic of excessive vice is indecency, a general baseness in its thoughts and acts concerning the body[1], and that the full portraiture of it cannot be given without marking, and that in the strongest lines, this tendency to corporeal degradation; which, in the time of Dante, could be done frankly, but cannot now. And, therefore, I think the twenty-first and twenty-second books of the *Inferno* the most perfect portraitures of fiendish nature which we possess; and, at the same time, in their mingling of the extreme of horror (for it seems to me that the silent swiftness of the first demon, "con l' ali aperte e sovra i pie leggiero",[2] cannot be surpassed in dread-

---

[1] Let the reader examine, with especial reference to this subject, the general character of the language of Iago.

[2] *Inferno*, XXI, 33: "With wings outstretched, and feet of nimblest tread."

fulness) with ludicrous actions and images, they present the
most perfect instances with which I am acquainted of the
terrible grotesque. But the whole of the *Inferno* is full
of this grotesque, as well as the *Faërie Queene*; and these
two poems, together with the works of Albert Dürer, will
enable the reader to study it in its noblest forms, without
reference to Gothic cathedrals.

Now, just as there are base and noble conditions of the
apathetic grotesque, so also are there of this satirical
grotesque. The condition which might be mistaken for it
is that above described as resulting from the malice of men
given to pleasure, and in which the grossness and foulness
are in the workman as much as in his subject, so that he
chooses to represent vice and disease rather than virtue and
beauty, having his chief delight in contemplating them;
though he still mocks at them with such dull wit as may be
in him, because, as Young has said most truly,

> 'Tis not in folly not to scorn a fool.[1]

Now it is easy to distinguish this grotesque from its noble
counterpart, by merely observing whether any forms of
beauty or dignity are mingled with it or not; for, of course,
the noble grotesque is only employed by its master for good
purposes, and to contrast with beauty: but the base workman cannot conceive anything but what is base; and there
will be no loveliness in any part of his work, or, at the best,
a loveliness measured by line and rule, and dependent on
legal shapes of feature. But, without resorting to this test,
and merely by examining the ugly grotesque itself, it will
be found that, if it belongs to the base school, there will be,
first, no Horror in it; secondly, no Nature in it; and, thirdly,
no Mercy in it.

I say, first, no Horror. For the base soul has no fear of
sin, and no hatred of it: and, however it may strive to make

[1] *Night Thoughts*, i, 416.

its work terrible, there will be no genuineness in the fear; the utmost it can do will be to make its work disgusting.

Secondly, there will be no Nature in it. It appears to be one of the ends proposed by Providence in the appointment of the forms of the brute creation, that the various vices to which mankind are liable should be severally expressed in them so distinctly and clearly as that men could not but understand the lesson; while yet these conditions of vice might, in the inferior animal, be observed without the disgust and hatred which the same vices would excite, if seen in men, and might be associated with features of interest which would otherwise attract and reward contemplation. Thus, ferocity, cunning, sloth, discontent, gluttony, uncleanness, and cruelty are seen, each in its extreme, in various animals; and are so vigorously expressed, that, when men desire to indicate the same vices in connection with human forms, they can do it no better than by borrowing here and there the features of animals. And when the workman is thus led to the contemplation of the animal kingdom, finding therein the expressions of vice which he needs, associated with power, and nobleness, and freedom from disease, if his mind be of right tone he becomes interested in this new study; and all noble grotesque is, therefore, full of the most admirable rendering of animal character. But the ignoble workman is capable of no interest of this kind; and, being too dull to appreciate, and too idle to execute, the subtle and wonderful lines on which the expression of the lower animal depends, he contents himself with vulgar exaggeration, and leaves his work as false as it is monstrous, a mass of blunt malice and obscene ignorance.

Lastly, there will be no Mercy in it. Wherever the satire of the noble grotesque fixes upon human nature, it does so with much sorrow mingled amidst its indignation: in its highest forms there is an infinite tenderness, like that

of the fool in Lear; and even in its more heedless or bitter sarcasm, it never loses sight altogether of the better nature of what it attacks, nor refuses to acknowledge its redeeming or pardonable features. But the ignoble grotesque has no pity: it rejoices in iniquity, and exists only to slander.

I have not space to follow out the various forms of transition which exist between the two extremes of great and base in the satirical grotesque. The reader must always remember, that although there is an infinite distance between the best and worst, in this kind the interval is filled by endless conditions more or less inclining to the evil or the good; impurity and malice stealing gradually into the nobler forms, and invention and wit elevating the lower, according to the countless minglings of the elements of the human soul.

Ungovernableness of the imagination. The reader is always to keep in mind that if the objects of horror in which the terrible grotesque finds its materials, were contemplated in their true light, and with the entire energy of the soul, they would cease to be grotesque, and become altogether sublime; and that therefore it is some shortening of the power, or the will, of contemplation, and some consequent distortion of the terrible image in which the grotesqueness consists. Now this distortion takes place, it was above asserted, in three ways: either through apathy, satire, or ungovernableness of imagination. It is this last cause of the grotesque which we have finally to consider; namely, the error and wildness of the mental impressions, caused by fear operating upon strong powers of imagination, or by the failure of the human faculties in the endeavour to grasp the highest truths.

The grotesque which comes to all men in a disturbed dream is the most intelligible example of this kind, but also the most ignoble; the imagination, in this instance, being entirely deprived of all aid from reason, and incapable of

self-government. I believe, however, that the noblest forms of imaginative power are also in some sort ungovernable, and have in them something of the character of dreams; so that the vision, of whatever kind, comes uncalled, and will not submit itself to the seer, but conquers him, and forces him to speak as a prophet, having no power over his words or thoughts. Only, if the whole man be trained perfectly, and his mind calm, consistent, and powerful, the vision which comes to him is seen as in a perfect mirror, serenely, and in consistence with the rational powers; but if the mind be imperfect and ill trained, the vision is seen as in a broken mirror, with strange distortions and discrepancies, all the passions of the heart breathing upon it in cross ripples, till hardly a trace of it remains unbroken. So that, strictly speaking, the imagination is never governed; it is always the ruling and Divine power: and the rest of the man is to it only as an instrument which it sounds, or a tablet on which it writes; clearly and sublimely if the wax be smooth and the strings true, grotesquely and wildly if they are stained and broken. And thus the *Iliad*, the *Inferno*, the *Pilgrim's Progress*, the *Faërie Queene*, are all of them true dreams; only the sleep of the men to whom they came was the deep, living sleep which God sends, with a sacredness in it, as of death, the revealer of secrets.

Now, observe in this matter, carefully, the difference between a dim mirror and a distorted one; and do not blame me for pressing the analogy too far, for it will enable me to explain my meaning every way more clearly. Most men's minds are dim mirrors, in which all truth is seen, as St Paul tells us, darkly:[1] this is the fault most common and most fatal; dulness of the heart and mistiness of sight, increasing to utter hardness and blindness; Satan breathing upon the glass, so that if we do not sweep the mist laboriously away, it will take no image. But, even so far as we are able to do

[1] 1 *Cor.* xiii, 12.

this, we have still the distortion to fear, yet not to the same extent, for we can in some sort allow for the distortion of an image, if only we can see it clearly. And the fallen human soul, at its best, must be as a diminishing glass, and that a broken one, to the mighty truths of the universe round it; and the wider the scope of its glance, and the vaster the truths into which it obtains an insight, the more fantastic their distortion is likely to be, as the winds and vapours trouble the field of the telescope most when it reaches farthest.

Now, so far as the truth is seen by the imagination in its wholeness and quietness, the vision is sublime; but so far as it is narrowed and broken by the inconsistencies of the human capacity, it becomes grotesque: and it would seem to be rare that any very exalted truth should be impressed on the imagination without some grotesqueness in its aspect, proportioned to the degree of *diminution of breadth* in the grasp which is given of it. Nearly all the dreams recorded in the Bible,—Jacob's, Joseph's, Pharaoh's, Nebuchadnezzar's,—are grotesques; and nearly the whole of the accessory scenery in the books of Ezekiel and the Apocalypse. Thus, Jacob's dream revealed to him the ministry of angels; but because this ministry could not be seen or understood by him in its fulness, it was narrowed to him into a ladder between heaven and earth, which was a grotesque. Joseph's two dreams were evidently intended to be signs of the steadfastness of the Divine purpose towards him, by possessing the clearness of special prophecy; yet were couched in such imagery, as not to inform him prematurely of his destiny, and only to be understood after their fulfilment. The sun, and moon, and stars were at the period, and are indeed throughout the Bible, the symbols of high authority. It was not revealed to Joseph that he should be lord over all Egypt; but the representation of his family by symbols of the most magnificent dominion, and yet as subject to him,

must have been afterwards felt by him as a distinctly prophetic indication of his own supreme power. It was not
revealed to him that the occasion of his brethren's special
humiliation before him should be their coming to buy corn;
but when the event took place, must he not have felt that
there was prophetic purpose in the form of the sheaves of
wheat which first imaged forth their subjection to him?
And these two images of the sun doing obeisance, and the
sheaves bowing down,—narrowed and imperfect intimations of great truth which yet could not be otherwise conveyed,—are both grotesques. The kine of Pharoah eating
each other, the gold and clay of Nebuchadnezzar's image,
the four beasts full of eyes, and other imagery of Ezekiel
and the Apocalypse, are grotesques of the same kind, on
which I need not further insist.

Stones of Venice, vol. III, sec. III, pars. 53–62.

From what we have seen to be its nature, we must, I think,
be led to one most important conclusion; that wherever the
human mind is healthy and vigorous in all its proportions,
great in imagination and emotion no less than in intellect,
and not overborne by an undue or hardened pre-eminence
of the mere reasoning faculties, there the grotesque will
exist in full energy. And, accordingly, I believe that there
is no test of greatness in periods, nations, or men, more
sure than the development, among them or in them, of
a noble grotesque; and no test of comparative smallness
or limitation, of one kind or another, more sure than the
absence of grotesque invention, or incapability of understanding it. I think that the central man of all the world,
as representing in perfect balance the imaginative, moral,
and intellectual faculties, all at their highest, is Dante; and
in him the grotesque reaches at once the most distinct and
the most noble development to which it was ever brought

in the human mind. The two other greatest men whom
Italy has produced, Michael Angelo and Tintoret, show
the same element in no less original strength, but oppressed
in the one by his science, and in both by the spirit of the
age in which they lived; never, however, absent even in
Michael Angelo, but stealing forth continually in a strange
and spectral way, lurking in folds of raiment and knots of
wild hair, and mountainous confusions of craggy limb and
cloudy drapery; and, in Tintoret, ruling the entire conceptions of his greatest works to such a degree that they are
an enigma or an offence, even to this day, to all the petty
disciples of a formal criticism. Of the grotesque in our own
Shakespeare I need hardly speak, nor of its intolerableness
to his French critics; nor of that of Æschylus and Homer,
as opposed to the lower Greek writers; and so I believe it
will be found, at all periods, in all minds of the first order.

Stones of Venice, vol. III, sec. III, par. 67.

THE PATHETIC FALLACY

No w, therefore, putting these tiresome and absurd words quite out of our way, we may go on at our ease to examine the point in question,—namely, the difference between the ordinary, proper, and true appearances of things to us; and the extraordinary, or false appearances, when we are under the influence of emotion, or contemplative fancy; false appearances, I say, as being entirely unconnected with any real power or character in the object, and only imputed to it by us.

For instance—

> The spendthrift crocus, bursting through the mould
> Naked and shivering, with his cup of gold.[1]

This is very beautiful, and yet very untrue. The crocus is not a spendthrift, but a hardy plant; its yellow is not gold, but saffron. How is it that we enjoy so much the having it put into our heads that it is anything else than a plain crocus?

It is an important question. For, throughout our past reasonings about art, we have always found that nothing could be good or useful, or ultimately pleasurable, which was untrue. But here is something pleasurable in written poetry which is nevertheless *un*true. And what is more, if we think over our favourite poetry, we shall find it full of this kind of fallacy, and that we like it all the more for being so.

It will appear also, on consideration of the matter, that this fallacy is of two principal kinds. Either, as in this case of the crocus, it is the fallacy of wilful fancy, which involves no real expectation that it will be believed; or else

[1] O. W. Holmes, *Astraea*.

it is a fallacy caused by an excited state of the feelings, making us, for the time, more or less irrational. Of the cheating of the fancy we shall have to speak presently; but, in this chapter, I want to examine the nature of the other error, that which the mind admits when affected strongly by emotion. Thus, for instance, in *Alton Locke*,—

>They rowed her in across the rolling foam—
>The cruel, crawling foam.

The foam is not cruel, neither does it crawl. The state of mind which attributes to it these characters of a living creature is one in which the reason is unhinged by grief. All violent feelings have the same effect. They produce in us a falseness in all our impressions of external things, which I would generally characterize as the "pathetic fallacy".

Now we are in the habit of considering this fallacy as eminently a character of poetical description, and the temper of mind in which we allow it, as one eminently poetical, because passionate. But I believe, if we look well into the matter, that we shall find the greatest poets do not often admit this kind of falseness,—that it is only the second order of poets who much delight in it.*

Thus, when Dante describes the spirits falling from the bank of Acheron "as dead leaves flutter from a bough",[1] he gives the most perfect image possible of their utter lightness, feebleness, passiveness, and scattering agony of despair, without, however, for an instant losing his own clear perception that *these* are souls, and *those* are leaves; he makes no confusion of one with the other. But when Coleridge speaks of

>The one red leaf, the last of its clan,
>That dances as often as dance it can,[2]

---

* I admit two orders of poets, but no third; and by these two orders I mean the Creative (Shakespeare, Homer, Dante), and Reflective or Perceptive (Wordsworth, Keats, Tennyson). But both of these must be *first*-rate in their range, though their range is different; and with poetry second-rate in *quality* no one ought to be allowed to trouble mankind.   [1] *Inferno*, III, 112.   [2] *Christabel*, pt. I.

he has a morbid, that is to say, a so far false, idea about the
leaf; he fancies a life in it, and will, which there are not;
confuses its powerlessness with choice, its fading death
with merriment, and the wind that shakes it with music.
Here, however, there is some beauty, even in the morbid
passage; but take an instance in Homer and Pope. Without the knowledge of Ulysses, Elpenor, his youngest fol-
lower, has fallen from an upper chamber in the Circean
palace, and has been left dead, unmissed by his leader or
companions, in the haste of their departure. They cross the
sea to the Cimmerian land; and Ulysses summons the shades
from Tartarus. The first which appears is that of the lost
Elpenor. Ulysses, amazed, and in exactly the spirit of
bitter and terrified lightness which is seen in Hamlet[1],
addresses the spirit with the simple, startled words:—

Elpenor? How camest thou under the shadowy darkness?
Hast thou come faster on foot than I in my black ship?[2]

Which Pope renders thus:—

O, say, what angry power Elpenor led
To glide in shades, and wander with the dead?
How could thy soul, by realms and seas disjoined,
Outfly the nimble sail, and leave the lagging wind?

I sincerely hope the reader finds no pleasure here, either
in the nimbleness of the sail, or the laziness of the wind!
And yet how is it that these conceits are so painful now,
when they have been pleasant to us in the other instances?

For a very simple reason. They are not a *pathetic* fallacy
at all, for they are put into the mouth of the wrong passion
—a passion which never could possibly have spoken them—
agonized curiosity. Ulysses wants to know the facts of the
matter; and the very last thing his mind could do at the
moment would be to pause, or suggest in anywise what was

[1] "Well said, old mole! can'st work i' the ground so fast?" (I, v.)
[2] *Odyssey*, XI, 56.

not a fact. The delay in the first three lines, and conceit in the last, jar upon us instantly like the most frightful discord in music. No poet of true imaginative power could possibly have written the passage.*

Therefore we see that the spirit of truth must guide us in some sort, even in our enjoyment of fallacy. Coleridge's fallacy has no discord in it, but Pope's has set our teeth on edge. Without farther questioning, I will endeavour to state the main bearings of this matter.

The temperament which admits the pathetic fallacy, is, as I said above, that of a mind and body in some sort too weak to deal fully with what is before them or upon them; borne away, or over-clouded, or over-dazzled by emotion; and it is a more or less noble state, according to the force of the emotion which has induced it. For it is no credit to a man that he is not morbid or inaccurate in his perceptions, when he has no strength of feeling to warp them; and it is in general a sign of higher capacity and stand in the ranks of being, that the emotions should be strong enough to van-quish, partly, the intellect, and make it believe what they choose. But it is still a grander condition when the in-tellect also rises, till it is strong enough to assert its rule against, or together with, the utmost efforts of the passions; and the whole man stands in an iron glow, white hot, perhaps, but still strong, and in no wise evaporating; even if he melts, losing none of his weight.

* It is worth while comparing the way a similar question is put by the exquisite sincerity of Keats:—
"He wept, and his bright tears
Went trickling down the golden bow he held.
Thus, with half-shut, suffused eyes, he stood;
While from beneath some cumb'rous boughs hard by,
With solemn step, an awful goddess came.
And there was purport in her looks for him,
Which he with eager guess began to read:
Perplexed the while, melodiously he said,
'How cam'st thou over the unfooted sea?'"   (*Hyperion*, III.)

So, then, we have the three ranks: the man who perceives rightly, because he does not feel, and to whom the primrose is very accurately the primrose, because he does not love it. Then, secondly, the man who perceives wrongly, because he feels, and to whom the primrose is anything else than a primrose: a star, or a sun, or a fairy's shield, or a forsaken maiden. And then, lastly, there is the man who perceives rightly in spite of his feelings, and to whom the primrose is for ever nothing else than itself—a little flower apprehended in the very plain and leafy fact of it, whatever and how many soever the associations and passions may be, that crowd around it. And, in general, these three classes may be rated in comparative order, as the men who are not poets at all, and the poets of the second order, and the poets of the first; only however great a man may be, there are always some subjects which *ought* to throw him off his balance; some, by which his poor human capacity of thought should be conquered, and brought into the inaccurate and vague state of perception, so that the language of the highest inspiration becomes broken, obscure, and wild in metaphor, resembling that of the weaker man, overborne by weaker things.

And thus, in full, there are four classes: the men who feel nothing, and therefore see truly; the men who feel strongly, think weakly, and see untruly (second order of poets); the men who feel strongly, think strongly, and see truly (first order of poets); and the men who, strong as human creatures can be, are yet submitted to influences stronger than they, and see in a sort untruly, because what they see is inconceivably above them. This last is the usual condition of prophetic inspiration.

I separate these classes, in order that their character may be clearly understood; but of course they are united each to the other by imperceptible transitions, and the same mind, according to the influences to which it is subjected, passes

at different times into the various states. Still, the difference between the great and less man is, on the whole, chiefly in this point of *alterability*. That is to say, the one knows too much, and perceives and feels too much of the past and future, and of all things beside and around that which immediately affects him, to be in anywise shaken by it. His mind is made up; his thoughts have an accustomed current; his ways are steadfast; it is not this or that new sight which will at once unbalance him. He is tender to impression at the surface, like a rock with deep moss upon it; but there is too much mass of him to be moved. The smaller man, with the same degree of sensibility, is at once carried off his feet; he wants to do something he did not want to do before; he views all the universe in a new light through his tears; he is gay or enthusiastic, melancholy or passionate, as things come and go to him. Therefore the high creative poet might even be thought, to a great extent, impassive (as shallow people think Dante stern), receiving indeed all feelings to the full, but having a great centre of reflection and knowledge in which he stands serene, and watches the feeling, as it were, from far off.

Dante, in his most intense moods, has entire command of himself, and can look around calmly, at all moments, for the image or the word that will best tell what he sees to the upper or lower world. But Keats and Tennyson, and the poets of the second order, are generally themselves subdued by the feelings under which they write, or, at least, write as choosing to be so; and therefore admit certain expressions and modes of thought which are in some sort diseased or false.

Now so long as we see that the *feeling* is true, we pardon, or are even pleased by, the confessed fallacy of sight which it induces: we are pleased, for instance, with those lines of Kingsley's, above quoted, not because they fallaciously describe foam, but because they faithfully describe sorrow. But the moment the mind of the speaker becomes cold,

that moment every such expression becomes untrue, as being for ever untrue in the external facts. And there is no greater baseness in literature than the habit of using these metaphorical expressions in cold blood. An inspired writer, in full impetuosity of passion, may speak wisely and truly of "raging waves of the sea foaming out their own shame";[1] but it is only the basest writer who cannot speak of the sea without talking of "raging waves", "remorseless floods", "ravenous billows", etc.; and it is one of the signs of the highest power in a writer to check all such habits of thought, and to keep his eyes fixed firmly on the *pure fact*, out of which if any feeling comes to him or his reader, he knows it must be a true one.

To keep to the waves, I forget who it is who represents a man in despair, desiring that his body may be cast into the sea,

Whose changing mound, and foam that passed away,
Might mock the eye that questioned where I lay.

Observe, there is not a single false, or even overcharged, expression. "Mound" of the sea wave is perfectly simple and true; "changing" is as familiar as may be; "foam that passed away", strictly literal; and the whole line descriptive of the reality with a degree of accuracy which I know not any other verse, in the range of poetry, that altogether equals. For most people have not a distinct idea of the clumsiness and massiveness of a large wave. The word "wave" is used too generally of ripples and breakers, and bendings in light drapery or grass: it does not by itself convey a perfect image. But the word "mound" is heavy, large, dark, definite; there is no mistaking the kind of wave meant, nor missing the sight of it. Then the term "changing" has a peculiar force also. Most people think of waves as rising and falling. But if they look at the sea carefully, they will perceive that the waves do not rise and fall. They

[1] *Jude*, 13.

change. Change both place and form, but they do not fall; one wave goes on, and on, and still on; now lower, now higher, now tossing its mane like a horse, now building itself together like a wall, now shaking, now steady, but still the same wave, till at last it seems struck by something, and changes, one knows not how,—becomes another wave.

The close of the line insists on this image, and paints it still more perfectly,—"foam that passed away". Not merely melting, disappearing, but passing on, out of sight, on the career of the wave. Then, having put the absolute ocean fact as far as he may before our eyes, the poet leaves us to feel about it as we may, and to trace for ourselves the opposite fact,—the image of the green mounds that do not change, and the white and written stones that do not pass away; and thence to follow out also the associated images of the calm life with the quiet grave, and the despairing life with the fading foam:—

Let no man move his bones.
As for Samaria, her king is cut off like the foam upon the water.[1]

But nothing of this is actually told or pointed out, and the expressions, as they stand, are perfectly severe and accurate, utterly uninfluenced by the firmly governed emotion of the writer. Even the word "mock" is hardly an exception, as it may stand merely for "deceive" or "defeat", without implying any impersonation of the waves.

It may be well, perhaps, to give one or two more instances to show the peculiar dignity possessed by all passages which thus limit their expression to the pure fact, and leave the hearer to gather what he can from it. Here is a notable one from the *Iliad*. Helen, looking from the Scæan gate of Troy over the Grecian host, and telling Priam the names of its captains, says at last:—

[1] 2 *Kings*, xxiii, 18; *Hosea*, x, 7.

I see all the other dark-eyed Greeks; but two I cannot see,—Castor and Pollux,—whom one mother bore with me. Have they not followed from fair Lacedæmon, or have they indeed come in their sea-wandering ships, but now will not enter into the battle of men, fearing the shame and the scorn that is in Me?

Then Homer:

So she spoke. But them, already, the life-giving earth possessed, there in Lacedæmon, in the dear fatherland.[1]

Note, here, the high poetical truth carried to the extreme. The poet has to speak of the earth in sadness, but he will not let that sadness affect or change his thoughts of it. No; though Castor and Pollux be dead, yet the earth is our mother still, fruitful, life-giving. These are the facts of the thing. I see nothing else than these. Make what you will of them.

Take another very notable instance from Casimir de la Vigne's terrible ballad, "La Toilette de Constance." I must quote a few lines out of it here and there, to enable the reader who has not the book by him, to understand its close.

Vite, Anna, vite; au miroir
    Plus vite, Anna. L'heure s'avance,
Et je vais au bal ce soir
    Chez l'ambassadeur de France.

Y pensez-vous, ils sont fanés, ces nœuds,
    Ils sont d'hier, mon Dieu, comme tout passe!
Que du réseau qui retient mes cheveux
    Les glands d'azur retombent avec grâce.
Plus haut! Plus bas! Vous ne comprenez rien!
    Que sur mon front ce saphir étincelle:
Vous me piquez, maladroite. Ah, c'est bien,
    Bien,—chère Anna! Je t'aime, je suis belle.

Celui qu'en vain je voudrais oublier
    (Anna, ma robe) il y sera, j'espère.
(Ah, fi, profane, est-ce là mon collier?
    Quoi! ces grains d'or bénits par le Saint-Père!)

---

[1] *Iliad*, III, 243.

Il y sera; Dieu, s'il pressait ma main,
    En y pensant, à peine je respire;
Père Anselmo doit m'entendre demain,
    Comment ferai-je, Anna, pour tout lui dire?

    Vite, un coup d'œil au miroir,
        Le dernier. ——J'ai l'assurance
    Qu'on va m'adorer ce soir
        Chez l'ambassadeur de France.

Près du foyer, Constance s'admirait.
    Dieu! sur sa robe il vole une étincelle!
Au feu. Courez! Quand l'espoir l'enivrait
    Tout perdre ainsi! Quoi! Mourir,—et si belle!

L'horrible feu ronge avec volupté
    Ses bras, son sein, et l'entoure, et s'élève,
Et sans pitié dévore sa beauté,
    Ses dix-huit ans, hélas, et son doux rêve!

    Adieu, bal, plaisir, amour!
        On disait, Pauvre Constance!
    Et on dansait, jusqu'au jour,
        Chez l'ambassadeur de France.[1]

Yes, that is the fact of it. Right or wrong, the poet does not say. What you may think about it, he does not know. He has nothing to do with that. There lie the ashes of the dead girl in her chamber. There they danced, till the morning, at the Ambassador's of France. Make what you will of it.

If the reader will look through the ballad, of which I have quoted only about the third part, he will find that there is not, from beginning to end of it, a single poetical (so called) expression, except in one stanza. The girl speaks as simple prose as may be; there is not a word she would not have actually used as she was dressing. The poet stands by, impassive as a statue, recording her words just as they come. At last the doom seizes her, and in the very presence

---

[1] *Œuvres Posthumes—Derniers Chants.*

of death, for an instant, his own emotions conquer him. He records no longer the facts only, but the facts as they seem to him. The fire gnaws with *voluptuousness—without pity.* It is soon past. The fate is fixed for ever; and he retires into his pale and crystalline atmosphere of truth. He closes all with the calm veracity,

> They said, "Poor Constance!"

Now in this there is the exact type of the consummate poetical temperament. For, be it clearly and constantly remembered, that the greatness of a poet depends upon the two faculties, acuteness of feeling, and command of it. A poet is great, first in proportion to the strength of his passion, and then, that strength being granted, in proportion to his government of it; there being, however, always a point beyond which it would be inhuman and monstrous if he pushed this government, and, therefore, a point at which all feverish and wild fancy becomes just and true. Thus the destruction of the kingdom of Assyria cannot be contemplated firmly by a prophet of Israel. The fact is too great, too wonderful. It overthrows him, dashes him into a confused element of dreams. All the world is, to his stunned thought, full of strange voices. "Yea, the fir-trees rejoice at thee, and the cedars of Lebanon, saying, 'Since thou art gone down to the grave, no feller is come up against us.'" [1] So, still more, the thought of the presence of Deity cannot be borne without this great astonishment. "The mountains and the hills shall break forth before you into singing, and all the trees of the field shall clap their hands." [2]

But by how much this feeling is noble when it is justified by the strength of its cause, by so much it is ignoble when there is not cause enough for it; and beyond all other ignobleness is the mere affectation of it, in hardness of heart. Simply bad writing may almost always, as above noticed,

---

[1] *Isaiah,* xiv, 8.   [2] *Isaiah,* lv, 12.

be known by its adoption of these fanciful metaphorical expressions as a sort of current coin; yet there is even a worse, at least a more harmful condition of writing than this, in which such expressions are not ignorantly and feelinglessly caught up, but, by some master, skilful in handling, yet insincere, deliberately wrought out with chill and studied fancy; as if we should try to make an old lava stream look red-hot again, by covering it with dead leaves, or white-hot, with hoar-frost.

When Young is lost in veneration, as he dwells on the character of a truly good and holy man, he permits himself for a moment to be overborne by the feeling so far as to exclaim—

> Where shall I find him? angels, tell me where.
> You know him; he is near you; point him out.
> Shall I see glories beaming from his brow,
> Or trace his footsteps by the rising flowers?[1]

This emotion has a worthy cause, and is thus true and right. But now hear the cold-hearted Pope say to a shepherd girl—

> Where'er you walk, cool gales shall fan the glade;
> Trees, where you sit, shall crowd into a shade;
> Your praise the birds shall chant in every grove,
> And winds shall waft it to the powers above.
> But would you sing, and rival Orpheus' strain,
> The wondering forests soon should dance again;
> The moving mountains hear the powerful call,
> And headlong streams hang, listening, in their fall.[2]

This is not, nor could it for a moment be mistaken for, the language of passion. It is simple falsehood, uttered by hypocrisy; definite absurdity, rooted in affectation, and coldly asserted in the teeth of nature and fact. Passion will indeed go far in deceiving itself; but it must be a strong passion, not the simple wish of a lover to tempt his mistress

---

[1] *Night Thoughts*, II, 345.   [2] *Pastorals: Summer, or Alexis.*

to sing. Compare a very closely parallel passage in Wordsworth, in which the lover has lost his mistress:

> Three years had Barbara in her grave been laid,
> When thus his moan he made:—
>
> "Oh, move, thou cottage, from behind yon oak,
>   Or let the ancient tree uprooted lie,
> That in some other way yon smoke
>   May mount into the sky.
> If still behind yon pine-tree's ragged bough,
>   Headlong, the waterfall must come,
>   Oh, let it, then, be dumb—
> Be anything, sweet stream, but that which thou art now."[1]

Here is a cottage to be moved, if not a mountain, and a
water-fall to be silent, if it is not to hang listening: but with
what different relation to the mind that contemplates them!
Here, in the extremity of its agony, the soul cries out wildly
for relief, which at the same moment it partly knows to
be impossible, but partly believes possible, in a vague impression that a miracle *might* be wrought to give relief even
to a less sore distress,—that nature is kind, and God is kind,
and that grief is strong: it knows not well what *is* possible
to such grief. To silence a stream, to move a cottage wall,
—one might think it could do as much as that!

I believe these instances are enough to illustrate the main
point I insist upon respecting the pathetic fallacy,—that so
far as it *is* a fallacy, it is always the sign of a morbid state of
mind, and comparatively of a weak one. Even in the most
inspired prophet it is a sign of the incapacity of his human
sight or thought to bear what has been revealed to it. In
ordinary poetry, if it is found in the thoughts of the poet
himself, it is at once a sign of his belonging to the inferior
school; if in the thoughts of the characters imagined by
him, it is right or wrong according to the genuineness of the

---

[1] "'Tis said, that some have died for love...."

emotion from which it springs; always, however, implying necessarily *some* degree of weakness in the character.

Take two most exquisite instances from master hands. The Jessy of Shenstone, and the Ellen of Wordsworth, have both been betrayed and deserted. Jessy, in the course of her most touching complaint, says:

> If through the garden's flowery tribes I stray,
>   Where bloom the jasmines that could once allure,
> "Hope not to find delight in us", they say,
>   "For we are spotless, Jessy; we are pure."

Compare with this some of the words of Ellen:

> "Ah, why", said Ellen, sighing to herself,
> "Why do not words, and kiss, and solemn pledge,
> And nature, that is kind in woman's breast,
> And reason, that in man is wise and good,
> And fear of Him who is a righteous Judge,—
> Why do not these prevail for human life,
> To keep two hearts together, that began
> Their springtime with one love, and that have need
> Of mutual pity and forgiveness sweet
> To grant, or be received; while that poor bird—
> O, come and hear him! Thou who hast to me
> Been faithless, hear him;—though a lowly creature,
> One of God's simple children that yet know not
> The Universal Parent, *how* he sings!
> As if he wished the firmament of heaven
> Should listen, and give back to him the voice
> Of his triumphant constancy and love;
> The proclamation that he makes, how far
> His darkness doth transcend our fickle light."[1]

The perfection of both these passages, as far as regards truth and tenderness of imagination in the two poets, is quite insuperable. But of the two characters imagined, Jessy is weaker than Ellen, exactly in so far as something appears to her to be in nature which is not. The flowers do not

---

[1] *Excursion*, VI.

really reproach her. God meant them to comfort her, not to taunt her; they would do so if she saw them rightly.

Ellen, on the other hand, is quite above the slightest erring emotion. There is not the barest film of fallacy in all her thoughts. She reasons as calmly as if she did not feel. And, although the singing of the bird suggests to her the idea of its desiring to be heard in heaven, she does not for an instant admit any veracity in the thought. "As if", she says,—"I know he means nothing of the kind; but it does verily seem as if." The reader will find, by examining the rest of the poem, that Ellen's character is throughout consistent in this clear though passionate strength.*

It then being, I hope, now made clear to the reader in all respects that the pathetic fallacy is powerful only so far as it is pathetic, feeble so far as it is fallacious, and, therefore, that the dominion of Truth is entire, over this, as over every other natural and just state of the human mind, we may go on to the subject for the dealing with which this prefatory inquiry became necessary; and why necessary, we shall see forthwith.

Modern Painters, vol. III, ch. xii, pars. 4–15.

---

* I cannot quit this subject without giving two more instances, both exquisite, of the pathetic fallacy, which I have just come upon, in *Maud:*
                  "For a great speculation had fail'd;
And ever he mutter'd and madden'd, and ever wann'd with despair;
And out he walk'd, when the wind like a broken worldling wail'd,
And the *flying gold of the ruin'd woodlands drove thro' the air.*"

        "There has fallen a splendid tear
          From the passion-flower at the gate.
        The red rose cries, 'She is near, she is near!'
          And the white rose weeps, 'She is late.'
        The larkspur listens, 'I hear, I hear!'
          And the lily whispers, 'I wait.'"

LANDSCAPE IN LITERATURE

I. CLASSICAL LANDSCAPE

(a) PATHETIC FALLACY

My reason for asking the reader to give so much of his time to the examination of the pathetic fallacy was, that, whether in literature or in art, he will find it eminently characteristic of the modern mind; and in the landscape, whether of literature or art, he will also find the modern painter endeavouring to express something which he, as a living creature, imagines in the lifeless object, while the classical and mediæval painters were content with expressing the unimaginary and actual qualities of the object itself. It will be observed that, according to the principle stated long ago, I use the words painter and poet quite indifferently, including in our inquiry the landscape of literature, as well as that of painting; and this the more because the spirit of classical landscape has hardly been expressed in any other way than by words.

Taking, therefore, this wide field, it is surely a very notable circumstance, to begin with, that this pathetic fallacy is eminently characteristic of modern painting. For instance, Keats, describing a wave breaking out at sea, says of it—

> Down whose green back the short-lived foam, all hoar,
> Bursts gradual, with a wayward indolence.[1]

That is quite perfect, as an example of the modern manner. The idea of the peculiar action with which foam rolls down a long, large wave could not have been given by any other words so well as by this "wayward indolence".

[1] *Endymion*, II, 350.

But Homer would never have written, never thought of, such words. He could not by any possibility have lost sight of the great fact that the wave, from the beginning to the end of it, do what it might, was still nothing else than salt water; and that salt water could not be either wayward or indolent. He will call the waves "over-roofed", "full-charged", "monstrous", "compact-black", "dark-clear", "violet-coloured", "wine-coloured", and so on. But every one of these epithets is descriptive of pure physical nature. "Over-roofed" is the term he invariably uses of anything—rock, house, or wave—that nods over at the brow; the other terms need no explanation; they are as accurate and intense in truth as words can be, but they never show the slightest feeling of anything animated in the ocean. Black or clear, monstrous or violet-coloured, cold salt water it is always, and nothing but that.

"Well, but the modern writer, by his admission of the tinge of fallacy, has given an idea of something in the action of the wave which Homer could not, and surely, therefore, has made a step in advance? Also there appears to be a degree of sympathy and feeling in the one writer, which there is not in the other; and as it has been received for a first principle that writers are great in proportion to the intensity of their feelings, and Homer seems to have no feelings about the sea but that it is black and deep, surely in this respect also the modern writer is the greater?"

Stay a moment. Homer *had* some feeling about the sea; a faith in the animation of it much stronger than Keats's. But all this sense of something living in it, he separates in his mind into a great abstract image of a Sea Power. He never says the waves rage, or the waves are idle. But he says there is somewhat in, and greater than, the waves, which rages, and is idle, and *that* he calls a god.

Modern Painters, vol. III, ch. xiii, pars. 1–3.

(b) CLASSICAL LANDSCAPE

Such being their general idea of the gods, we can now easily understand the habitual tone of their feelings towards what was beautiful in nature. With us, observe, the idea of the Divinity is apt to get separated from the life of nature; and imagining our God upon a cloudy throne, far above the earth, and not in the flowers or waters, we approach those visible things with a theory that they are dead, governed by physical laws, and so forth. But coming to them, we find the theory fail; that they are not dead; that, say what we choose about them, the instinctive sense of their being alive is too strong for us; and in scorn of all physical law, the wilful fountain sings, and the kindly flowers rejoice. And then, puzzled, and yet happy; pleased, and yet ashamed of being so; accepting sympathy from nature, which we do not believe it gives, and giving sympathy to nature, which we do not believe it receives,—mixing, besides, all manner of purposeful play and conceit with these involuntary fellowships,—we fall necessarily into the curious web of hesitating sentiment, pathetic fallacy, and wandering fancy, which form a great part of our modern view of nature. But the Greek never removed his god out of nature at all; never attempted for a moment to contradict his instinctive sense that God was everywhere. "The tree *is* glad", said he, "I know it is; I can cut it down: no matter, there was a nymph in it". "The water *does* sing", said he; "I can dry it up; but no matter, there was a naiad in it." But in thus clearly defining his belief, observe, he threw it entirely into a human form, and gave his faith to nothing but the image of his own humanity. What sympathy and fellowship he had, were always for the spirit *in* the stream, not for the stream; always for the dryad *in* the wood, not for the wood. Content with this human sympathy, he approached the actual waves and woody fibres with no sympathy at all.

The spirit that ruled them, he received as a plain fact. Them, also, ruled and material, he received as plain facts; they, without their spirit, were dead enough. A rose was good for scent, and a stream for sound and coolness; for the rest, one was no more than leaves, the other no more than water; he could not make anything else of them; and the divine power, which was involved in their existence, having been all distilled away by him into an independent Flora or Thetis, the poor leaves or waves were left, in mere cold corporealness, to make the most of their being discernibly red and soft, clear and wet, and unacknowledged in any other power whatsoever.

Then, observe farther, the Greeks lived in the midst of the most beautiful nature, and were as familiar with blue sea, clear air, and sweet outlines of mountain, as we are with brick walls, black smoke, and level fields. This perfect familiarity rendered all such scenes of natural beauty unexciting, if not indifferent to them, by lulling and overwearying the imagination as far as it was concerned with such things; but there was another kind of beauty which they found it required effort to obtain, and which, when thoroughly obtained, seemed more glorious than any of this wild loveliness—the beauty of the human countenance and form. This, they perceived, could only be reached by continual exercise of virtue; and it was in Heaven's sight, and theirs, all the more beautiful because it needed this self-denial to obtain it. So they set themselves to reach this, and having gained it, gave it their principal thoughts, and set it off with beautiful dress as best they might. But making this their object, they were obliged to pass their lives in simple exercise and disciplined employments. Living wholesomely, giving themselves no fever fits, either by fasting or over-eating, constantly in the open air, and full of animal spirit and physical power, they became incapable of every morbid condition of mental emotion. Unhappy

love, disappointed ambition, spiritual despondency, or any other disturbing sensation, had little power over the well-braced nerves, and healthy flow of the blood; and what bitterness might yet fasten on them was soon boxed or raced out of a boy, and spun or woven out of a girl, or danced out of both. They had indeed their sorrows, true and deep, but still, more like children's sorrows than ours, whether bursting into open cry of pain, or hid with shuddering under the veil, still passing over the soul as clouds do over heaven, not sullying it, not mingling with it;—darkening it perhaps long or utterly, but still not becoming one with it, and for the most part passing away in dashing rain of tears, and leaving the man unchanged: in nowise affecting, as our sorrow does, the whole tone of his thought and imagination thenceforward.

How far our melancholy may be deeper and wider than theirs in its roots and view, and therefore nobler, we shall consider presently; but at all events, they had the advantage of us in being entirely free from all those dim and feverish sensations which result from unhealthy state of the body. I believe that a large amount of the dreamy and sentimental sadness, tendency to reverie, and general patheticalness of modern life results merely from derangement of stomach; holding to the Greek life the same relation that the feverish night of an adult does to a child's sleep.

Farther. The human beauty, which, whether in its bodily being or in imagined divinity, had become, for the reasons we have seen, the principal object of culture and sympathy to these Greeks, was, in its perfection, eminently orderly, symmetrical, and tender. Hence, contemplating it constantly in this state, they could not but feel a proportionate fear of all that was disorderly, unbalanced, and rugged. Having trained their stoutest soldiers into a strength so delicate and lovely, that their white flesh, with their blood upon it, should look like ivory stained with

purple[1]; and having always around them, in the motion and majesty of this beauty, enough for the full employment of their imagination, they shrank with dread or hatred from all the ruggedness of lower nature,—from the wrinkled forest bark, the jagged hill-crest, and irregular, inorganic storm of sky; looking to these for the most part as adverse powers, and taking pleasure only in such portions of the lower world as were at once conducive to the rest and health of the human frame, and in harmony with the laws of its gentler beauty.

Modern Painters, vol. III, ch. xiii, pars. 13–15.

(c) RELATION TO HUMAN COMFORT

Thus, as far as I recollect, without a single exception, every Homeric landscape, intended to be beautiful, is composed of a fountain, a meadow, and a shady grove. This ideal is very interestingly marked, as intended for a perfect one, in the fifth book of the *Odyssey*; when Mercury himself stops for a moment, though on a message, to look at a landscape "which even an immortal might be gladdened to behold."[2] This landscape consists of a cave covered with a running vine, all blooming into grapes, and surrounded by a grove of alder, poplar, and sweet-smelling cypress. Four fountains of white (foaming) water, springing *in succession* (mark the orderliness), and close to one another, flow away in different directions, through a meadow full of violets and parsley (parsley, to mark its moisture, being elsewhere called "marsh-nourished", and associated with the lotus[3]); the air is perfumed not only by these violets and by the sweet cypress, but by Calypso's fire of finely chopped cedar wood, which sends a smoke, as of incense, through the island; Calypso herself is singing; and finally, upon the trees are resting, or roosting, owls, hawks, and "long-tongued sea-

[1] *Iliad*, IV, 141.   [2] *Odyssey*, V, 58.   [3] *Iliad*, II, 776.

crows". Whether these last are considered as a part of the ideal landscape, as marine singing-birds, I know not; but the approval of Mercury appears to be elicited chiefly by the fountains and violet meadow.

Now the notable things in this description are, first, the evident subservience of the whole landscape to human comfort, to the foot, the taste, or the smell; and, secondly, that throughout the passage there is not a single figurative word expressive of the things being in any wise other than plain grass, fruit, or flower. I have used the term "spring" of the fountains, because, without doubt, Homer means that they sprang forth brightly, having their source at the foot of the rocks (as copious fountains nearly always have); but Homer does not say "spring", he says simply flow, and uses only one word for "growing softly", or "richly", of the tall trees, the vine, and the violets. There is, however, some expression of sympathy with the sea-birds; he speaks of them in precisely the same terms, as in other places of naval nations, saying they "have care of the works of the sea".[1]

If we glance through the references to pleasant land-scape which occur in other parts of the *Odyssey*, we shall always be struck by this quiet subjection of their every feature to human service, and by the excessive similarity in the scenes. Perhaps the spot intended, after this, to be most perfect, may be the garden of Alcinous,[2] where the principal ideas are, still more definitely, order, symmetry, and fruitfulness; the beds being duly ranged between rows of vines, which, as well as the pear, apple, and fig-trees, bear fruit continually, some grapes being yet sour, while others are getting black; there are plenty of "*orderly* square beds of herbs", chiefly leeks, and two fountains, one running through the garden, and one under the pavement of the palace, to a reservoir for the citizens. Ulysses,

---

[1] *Odyssey*, V, 67.   [2] *Odyssey*, VII, 112.

pausing to contemplate this scene, is described nearly in the same terms as Mercury pausing to contemplate the wilder meadow; and it is interesting to observe, that, in spite of all Homer's love of symmetry, the god's admiration is excited by the free fountains, wild violets, and wandering vine; but the mortal's, by the vines in rows, the leeks in beds, and the fountains in pipes. *Modern Painters*, vol. III, ch. xiii, pars. 16–18.

(d) TREES

But to return more definitely to our Homeric landscape. When it is perfect, we have, as in the above instances, the foliage and meadows together; when imperfect, it is always either the foliage or the meadow; pre-eminently the meadow, or arable field. Thus, meadows of asphodel are prepared for the happier dead; and even Orion, a hunter among the mountains in his lifetime, pursues the ghosts of beasts in these asphodel meadows after death.[1] So the sirens sing in a meadow;[2] and throughout the *Odyssey* there is a general tendency to the depreciation of poor Ithaca, because it is rocky, and only fit for goats, and has "no meadows";[3] for which reason Telemachus refuses Atrides's present of horses, congratulating the Spartan king at the same time on ruling over a plain which has "plenty of lotus in it, and rushes", with corn and barley. Note this constant dwelling on the marsh plants, or, at least, those which grow in flat and well-irrigated land, or beside streams: when Scamander, for instance, is restrained by Vulcan, Homer says, very sorrowfully, that "all his lotus, and reeds, and rushes were burnt";[4] and thus Ulysses, after being shipwrecked and nearly drowned, and beaten about the sea for many days and nights, on raft and mast, at last getting ashore at

---

[1] *Odyssey* XI, 571; XXIV, 13. The couch of Ceres, with Homer's usual faithfulness, is made of a *ploughed* field, v, 127.

[2] *Odyssey*, XII, 45.   [3] *Odyssey*, IV, 601.   [4] *Iliad*, XXI, 351.

the mouth of a large river, casts himself down first upon its
rushes, and then, in thankfulness, kisses the "corn-giving
land", as most opposed, in his heart, to the fruitless and
devouring sea.[1]

In this same passage, also, we find some peculiar expressions of the delight which the Greeks had in trees;
for, when Ulysses first comes in sight of land, which gladdens him, "as the reviving of a father from his sickness
gladdens his children", it is not merely the sight of the land
itself which gives him such pleasure, but of the "land and
wood".[2] Homer never throws away any words, at least in
such a place as this; and what in another poet would have
been merely the filling up of the deficient line with an
otherwise useless word, is in him the expression of the
general Greek sense, that land of any kind was in nowise
grateful or acceptable till there was *wood* upon it (or corn;
but the corn, in the flats, could not be seen so far as the
black masses of forest on the hillsides), and that, as in being
rushy and corn-giving, the low land, so in being woody, the
high land was most grateful to the mind of the man who
for days and nights had been wearied on the engulphing sea.
And this general idea of wood and corn, as the types of the
fatness of the whole earth, is beautifully marked in another
place of the *Odyssey*,[3] where the sailors in a desert island,
having no flour of corn to offer as a meat offering with their
sacrifices, take the leaves of the trees, and scatter them over
the burnt offering instead.

But still, every expression of the pleasure which Ulysses
has in this landing and resting, contains uninterruptedly
the reference to the utility and sensible pleasantness of all
things, not to their beauty. After his first grateful kiss
given to the corn-growing land, he considers immediately
how he is to pass the night; for some minutes hesitating
whether it will be best to expose himself to the misty chill

[1] *Odyssey*, V, 398.   [2] *Odyssey*, V, 395.   [3] *Odyssey*, XII, 357.

from the river, or run the risk of wild beasts in the wood. He decides for the wood, and finds in it a bower formed by a sweet and a wild olive-tree, interlacing their branches, or—perhaps more accurately translating Homer's intensely graphic expression—"changing their branches with each other" (it is very curious how often, in an entanglement of wood, one supposes the branches to belong to the wrong trees) and forming a roof penetrated by neither rain, sun, nor wind. Under this bower Ulysses collects the "*vain* (or *frustrate*) outpouring of the dead leaves"—another exquisite expression, used elsewhere of useless grief or shedding of tears;—and, having got enough together, makes his bed of them, and goes to sleep, having covered himself up with them, "as embers are covered up with ashes".[1]

Nothing can possibly be more intensely possessive of the *facts* than this whole passage; the sense of utter deadness and emptiness, and frustrate fall in the leaves; of dormant life in the human body,—the fire, and heroism, and strength of it, lulled under the dead brown heap, as embers under ashes, and the knitting of interchanged and close strength of living boughs above. But there is not the smallest apparent sense of there being *beauty* elsewhere than in the human being. The wreathed wood is admired simply as being a perfect roof for it; the fallen leaves only as being a perfect bed for it; and there is literally no more excitement of emotion in Homer, as he describes them, nor does he expect us to be more excited or touched by hearing about them, than if he had been telling us how the chambermaid at the Bull aired the four-poster, and put on two extra blankets. *Modern Painters*, vol. III, ch. xiii, pars. 21–23.

[1] *Odyssey*, V, 481.

(e) ROCKS

Now, exactly this same contemplation of subservience to human use makes the Greek take some pleasure in *rocks*, when they assume one particular form, but one only—that of a *cave*. They are evidently quite frightful things to him under any other condition, and most of all if they are rough and jagged; but if smooth, looking "sculptured",[1] like the sides of a ship, and forming a cave or shelter for him, he begins to think them endurable. Hence, associating the ideas of rich and sheltering wood, sea, becalmed and made useful as a port by projecting promontories of rock, and smoothed caves or grottoes in the rocks themselves, we get the pleasantest idea which the Greek could form of a landscape, next to a marsh with poplars in it; not, indeed, if possible, ever to be without these last; thus, in commending the Cyclops' country as one possessed of every perfection, Homer first says: "They have soft *marshy* meadows near the sea, and good, rich, crumbling, ploughing-land, giving fine deep crops, and vines always giving fruit"; then, "a port so quiet, that they have no need of cables in it; and at the head of the port, a beautiful clear spring just *under a cave* and *aspen poplars all round it*."[2]

This, it will be seen, is very nearly Homer's usual "ideal"; but, going into the middle of the island, Ulysses comes on a rougher and less agreeable bit, though still fulfilling certain required conditions of endurableness; a "cave shaded with laurels", which, having no poplars about it, is, however, meant to be somewhat frightful, and only fit to be inhabited by a Cyclops.[3] So in the country of the Læstrygons, Homer, preparing his reader gradually for something very disagreeable, represents the rocks as bare and "exposed to the sun"; only with some smooth and

[1] *Iliad*, II, 88.   [2] *Odyssey*, IX, 132, etc.   [3] *Odyssey*, IX, 183.

slippery roads over them, by which the trucks bring down wood from the higher hills. Any one familiar with Swiss slopes of hills must remember how often he has descended, sometimes faster than was altogether intentional, by these same slippery woodman's truck roads.

And thus, in general, whenever the landscape is intended to be lovely, it verges towards the ploughed lands and poplars; or, at worst, to *woody* rocks; but, if intended to be painful, the rocks are bare and "sharp". This last epithet, constantly used by Homer for mountains, does not altogether correspond, in Greek, to the English term, nor is it intended merely to characterize the sharp mountain summits; for it never would be applied simply to the edge or point of a sword, but signifies rather "harsh", "bitter", or "painful", being applied habitually to fate, death, and in *Od.* II, 333, to a halter; and, as expressive of general objectionableness and unpleasantness, to all high, dangerous, or peaked mountains, as the Maleian promontory (a much-dreaded one), the crest of Parnassus, the Tereian mountain, and a grim or untoward, though, by keeping off the force of the sea, protective, rock at the mouth of the Jardanus; as well as habitually to inaccessible or impregnable fortresses built on heights.

In all this I cannot too strongly mark the utter absence of any trace of the feeling for what we call the picturesque, and the constant dwelling of the writer's mind on what was available, pleasant, or useful; his ideas respecting all landscape being not uncharacteristically summed, finally, by Pallas herself; when, meeting Ulysses, who after his long wandering does not recognize his own country, and meaning to describe it as politely and soothingly as possible, she says[1]:—"This Ithaca of ours is, indeed, a rough country enough, and not good for driving in; but, still, things might be worse: it has plenty of corn, and good wine, and *always*

[1] *Odyssey*, XIII, 236, etc.

rain, and soft nourishing dew, and it has good feeding for goats and oxen, and all manner of wood, and springs fit to drink at all the year round."

It may indeed be thought that I am assuming too hastily that this was the general view of the Greeks respecting landscape, because it was Homer's. But I believe the true mind of a nation, at any period, is always best ascertainable by examining that of its greatest men; and that simpler and truer results will be attainable for us by simply comparing Homer, Dante, and Walter Scott, than by attempting (what my limits must have rendered absurdly inadequate, and in which, also, both my time and knowledge must have failed me) an analysis of the landscape in the range of contemporary literature. All that I can do is to state the general impression which has been made upon me by my desultory reading, and to mark accurately the grounds for this impression, in the works of the greatest men. Now it is quite true that in others of the Greeks, especially in Æschylus and Aristophanes, there is infinitely more of modern feeling, of pathetic fallacy, love of picturesque or beautiful form, and other such elements, than there is in Homer; but then these appear to me just the parts of them which were not Greek, the elements of their minds by which (as one division of the human race always must be with subsequent ones) they are connected with the mediævals and moderns. And without doubt, in his influence over future mankind, Homer is eminently the Greek of Greeks: if I were to associate any one with him it would be Herodotus, and I believe all I have said of the Homeric landscape will be found equally true of the Herodotean, as assuredly it will be of the Platonic;—the contempt, which Plato sometimes expresses by the mouth of Socrates, for the country in general, except so far as it is shady, and has cicadas and running streams to make pleasant noises in it, being almost ludicrous. But Homer is the great type, and the more

notable one because of his influence on Virgil, and, through him, on Dante, and all the after ages: and, in like manner, if we can get the abstract of mediæval landscape out of Dante, it will serve us as well as if we had read all the songs of the troubadours, and help us to the farther changes in derivative temper, down to all modern time.

Modern Painters, vol. III, ch. xiii, pars. 24–27.

II. MEDIEVAL LANDSCAPE

(a) GENERAL CHARACTERISTICS

IN our examination of the spirit of classical landscape, we were obliged to confine ourselves to what is left to us in written description. Some interesting results might indeed have been obtained by examining the Egyptian and Nine-vite landscape sculpture, but in nowise conclusive enough to be worth the pains of the inquiry; for the landscape of sculpture is necessarily confined in range, and usually inexpressive of the complete feelings of the workman, being introduced rather to explain the place and circumstances of events, than for its own sake. In the Middle Ages, how-ever, the case is widely different. We have written land-scape, sculptured landscape, and painted landscape, all bearing united testimony to the tone of the national mind in almost every remarkable locality of Europe.

That testimony, taken in its breadth, is very curiously conclusive. It marks the mediæval mind as agreeing alto-gether with the ancients, in holding that flat land, brooks, and groves of aspens, compose the pleasant places of the earth, and that rocks and mountains are, for inhabitation, altogether to be reprobated and detested; but as disagreeing with the classical mind totally in this other most important respect, that the pleasant flat land is never a ploughed field, nor a rich lotus meadow good for pasture, but *garden* ground

covered with flowers, and divided by fragrant hedges, with a castle in the middle of it. The aspens are delighted in, not because they are good for "coach-making men"[1] to make cart-wheels of, but because they are shady and graceful; and the fruit-trees, covered with delicious fruit, especially apple and orange, occupy still more important positions in the scenery. Singing-birds—not "sea-crows",[2] but nightingales—perch on every bough: and the ideal occupation of mankind is not to cultivate either the garden or the meadow, but to gather roses and eat oranges in the one, and ride out hawking over the other.

Finally, mountain scenery, though considered as disagreeable for general inhabitation, is always introduced as being proper to meditate in, or to encourage communion with higher beings; and in the ideal landscape of daily life, mountains are considered agreeable things enough, so that they be far enough away.

In this great change there are three vital points to be noticed.

The first, the disdain of agricultural pursuits by the nobility; a fatal change, and one gradually bringing about the ruin of that nobility. It is expressed in the mediæval landscape by the eminently pleasurable and horticultural character of everything; by the fences, hedges, castle walls, and masses of useless, but lovely flowers, especially roses. The knights and ladies are represented always as singing, or making love, in these pleasant places. The idea of setting an old knight, like Laertes (whatever his state of fallen fortune), "with thick gloves on to keep his hands from the thorns",[3] to prune a row of vines, would have been regarded as the most monstrous violation of the decencies of life; and a senator, once detected in the home employments of Cincinnatus, could, I suppose, thenceforward hardly have appeared in society.

[1] *Iliad*, IV, 485.　　[2] *Odyssey*, V, 66.　　[3] *Odyssey*, XXIV, 340.

The second vital point is the evidence of a more sentimental enjoyment of external nature. A Greek, wishing really to enjoy himself, shut himself into a beautiful atrium, with an excellent dinner, and a society of philosophical or musical friends. But a mediæval knight went into his pleasance, to gather roses and hear the birds sing; or rode out hunting or hawking. His evening feast, though riotous enough sometimes, was not the height of his day's enjoyment; and if the attractions of the world are to be shown typically to him, as opposed to the horrors of death, they are never represented by a full feast in a chamber, but by a delicate dessert in an orange grove, with musicians under the trees; or a ride on a May morning, hawk on fist.

This change is evidently a healthy, and a very interesting one.

The third vital point is the marked sense that this hawking and apple-eating are not altogether right; that there is something else to be done in the world than that; and that the mountains, as opposed to the pleasant garden-ground, are places where that other something may best be learned;—which is evidently a piece of infinite and new respect for the mountains, and another healthy change in the tone of the human heart.

Modern Painters, vol. III, ch. xiv, pars. 1–5.

Now, assembling all these different sources of the peculiar mediæval feeling towards nature in one view, we have:

1st. Love of the garden instead of love of the farm, leading to a sentimental contemplation of nature, instead of a practical and agricultural one.

2nd. Loss of sense of actual Divine presence, leading to fancies of fallacious animation, in herbs, flowers, clouds, etc.

3rd. Perpetual, and more or less undisturbed, companionship with wild nature.

4th. Apprehension of demoniacal and angelic presence among mountains, leading to a reverent dread of them.
5th. Principalness of delight in human beauty, leading to comparative contempt of natural objects.
6th. Consequent love of order, light, intelligibility, and symmetry, leading to dislike of the wildness, darkness, and mystery of nature.
7th. Inaccuracy of observance of nature, induced by the habitual practice of change on its forms.

From these mingled elements, we should necessarily expect to find resulting, as the characteristic of mediæval landscape art, compared with Greek, a far higher sentiment about it, and affection for it, more or less subdued by still greater respect for the loveliness of man, and therefore subordinated entirely to human interests; mingled with curious traces of terror, piety, or superstition, and cramped by various formalisms,—some wise and necessary, some feeble, and some exhibiting needless ignorance and inaccuracy. *Modern Painters*, vol. III, ch. xiv, par. 15.

(*b*) LANDSCAPE OF DANTE

The thing that must first strike us in this respect, as we turn our thoughts to the poem,[1] is, unquestionably, the *formality* of its landscape.

Milton's effort, in all that he tells us of his Inferno, is to make it indefinite; Dante, to make it *definite*. Both, indeed, describe it as entered through gates; but, within the gate, all is wild and fenceless with Milton, having indeed its four rivers,—the last vestige of the mediæval tradition,—but rivers which flow through a waste of mountain and moorland, and by "many a frozen, many a fiery Alp".[2] But Dante's Inferno is accurately separated

[1] *Divina Commedia.*   [2] *Par. Lost*, II, 620; *Inferno*, III, 1–11.

into circles drawn with well-pointed compasses; mapped and properly surveyed in every direction, trenched in a thoroughly good style of engineering from depth to depth, and divided in the "*accurate* middle" (dritto mezzo)[1] of its deepest abyss, into a concentric series of ten moats and embankments, like those about a castle, with bridges from each embankment to the next; precisely in the manner of those bridges over Hiddekel and Euphrates, which Mr Macaulay thinks so innocently designed, apparently not aware that he is also laughing at Dante. These larger fosses are of rock, and the bridges also; but as he goes farther into detail, Dante tells us of various minor fosses and embankments, in which he anxiously points out to us not only the formality, but the neatness and perfectness, of the stonework. For instance, in describing the river Phlegethon, he tells us that it was "paved with stone at the bottom, and at the sides, and *over the edges of the sides*",[2] just as the water is at the baths of Bulicame; and for fear we should think this embankment at all *larger* than it really was, Dante adds, carefully, that it was made just like the embankments of Ghent or Bruges against the sea, or those in Lombardy which bank the Brenta, only "not so high, nor so wide", as any of these. And besides the trenches, we have two well-built castles; one, like Ecbatana, with seven circuits of wall (and surrounded by a fair stream), wherein the great poets and sages of antiquity live; and another, a great fortified city with walls of iron, red-hot, and a deep fosse round it, and full of "grave citizens",—the city of Dis.

Now, whether this be in what we moderns call "good taste", or not, I do not mean just now to inquire—Dante having nothing to do with taste, but with the facts of what he had seen; only, so far as the imaginative faculty of the two poets is concerned, note that Milton's vagueness is not the sign of imagination, but of its absence, so far as it is

[1] *Inferno*, XI, 16 *seq.*; XVIII, I *seq.*   [2] *Inferno*, XIV, 79.

significative in the matter. For it does not follow, because Milton did not map out his Inferno as Dante did, that he *could* not have done so if he had chosen; only, it was the easier and less imaginative process to leave it vague than to define it. Imagination is always the seeing and asserting faculty; that which obscures or conceals may be judgment, or feeling, but not invention. The invention, whether good or bad, is in the accurate engineering, not in the fog and uncertainty.

When we pass with Dante from the Inferno to Purgatory, we have indeed more light and air, but no more liberty; being now confined on various ledges cut into a mountain side, with a precipice on one hand and a vertical wall on the other; and, lest here also we should make any mistake about magnitudes, we are told that the ledges were eighteen feet wide,[1] and that the ascent from one to the other was by steps, made like those which go up from Florence to the church of San Miniato.[2]

Lastly, though in the Paradise there is perfect freedom and infinity of space, though for trenches we have planets, and for cornices constellations, yet there is more cadence, procession, and order among the redeemed souls than any others; they fly, so as to describe letters and sentences in the air, and rest in circles, like rainbows, or determinate figures, as of a cross and an eagle; in which certain of the more glorified natures are so arranged as to form the eye of the bird, while those most highly blessed are arranged with their white crowds in leaflets, so as to form the image of a white rose in the midst of heaven.

Thus, throughout the poem, I conceive that the first striking character of its scenery is intense definition; precisely the reflection of that definiteness which we have already traced in pictorial art. But the second point which

[1] "Three times the length of the human body."—*Purg.* X, 24.
[2] *Purg.* XII, 93.

seems noteworthy is, that the flat ground and embanked
trenches are reserved for the Inferno: and that the entire
territory of the Purgatory is a mountain, thus marking the
sense of that purifying and perfecting influence in mountains which we saw the mediæval mind was so ready to
suggest. The same general idea is indicated at the very com-
mencement of the poem, in which Dante is overwhelmed
by fear and sorrow in passing through a dark forest, but
revives on seeing the sun touch the top of a hill, afterwards
called by Virgil "the pleasant mount—the cause and source
of all delight."[1]

While, however, we find this greater honour paid to
mountains, I think we may perceive a much greater dread
and dislike of woods. We saw that Homer seemed to attach
a pleasant idea, for the most part, to forests; regarding them
as sources of wealth and places of shelter; and we find
constantly an idea of sacredness attached to them, as being
haunted especially by the gods; so that even the wood
which surrounds the house of Circe is spoken of as a sacred
thicket,[2] or rather, as a sacred glade, or labyrinth of glades
(of the particular word used I shall have more to say
presently); and so the wood is sought as a kindly shelter by
Ulysses, in spite of its wild beasts; and evidently regarded
with great affection by Sophocles, for, in a passage[3] which is
always regarded by readers of Greek tragedy with peculiar
pleasure, the aged and blind Œdipus, brought to rest in
"the sweetest resting-place" in all the neighbourhood of
Athens, has the spot described to him as haunted perpetually by nightingales, which sing "in the green glades
and in the dark ivy, and in the thousand-fruited, sunless,
and windless thickets of the god" (Bacchus); the idea of the
complete shelter from wind and sun being here, as with
Ulysses, the uppermost one. After this come the usual
staples of landscape,—narcissus, crocus, plenty of rain,

[1] *Inferno*, I, 73.   [2] *Odyssey*, X, 275.   [3] *Œd. Col.*, 668–711.

olive trees; and last, and the greatest boast of all,—"it is a good country for horses, and conveniently by the sea"; but the prominence and pleasantness of the thick wood in the thoughts of the writer are very notable; whereas to Dante the idea of a forest is exceedingly repulsive, so that, as just noticed, in the opening of his poem, he cannot express a general despair about life more strongly than by saying he was lost in a wood so savage and terrible, that "even to think or speak of it is distress,—it was so bitter,—it was something next door to death";[1] and one of the saddest scenes in all the Inferno is in a forest, of which the trees are haunted by lost souls: while (with only one exception[2]), whenever the country is to be beautiful, we find ourselves coming out into open air and open meadows.[3]

It is quite true that this is partly a characteristic, not merely of Dante, or of mediæval writers, but of *southern* writers; for the simple reason that the forest, being with them higher upon the hills, and more out of the way than in the north, was generally a type of lonely and savage places; while in England, the "greenwood", coming up to the very walls of the towns, it was possible to be "merry in the good greenwood",[4] in a sense which an Italian could not have understood. Hence Chaucer, Spenser, and Shakespeare send their favourites perpetually to the woods for pleasure or meditation; and trust their tender Canace, or Rosalind, or Helena, or Silvia, or Belphœbe, where Dante would have sent no one but a condemned spirit. Nevertheless, there is always traceable in the mediæval mind a dread of thick foliage, which was not present to that of a Greek; so that, even in the north, we have our sorrowful "children in the wood", and black huntsmen of the Hartz forests, and such other wood terrors; the principal reason for the difference being that a Greek, being by no means

[1] *Inferno*, I, 1–7.   [2] *Purg.* XXVIII.
[3] Vide *Inferno*, IV, 111.   [4] *The Lady of the Lake*, IV, 12.

given to travelling, regarded his woods as so much valuable property; and if he ever went into them for pleasure, expected to meet one or two gods in the course of his walk, but no banditti; while a mediæval, much more of a solitary traveller, and expecting to meet with no gods in the thickets, but only with thieves, or a hostile ambush, or a bear, besides a great deal of troublesome ground for his horse, and a very serious chance, next to a certainty, of losing his way, naturally kept in the open ground as long as he could, and regarded the forests, in general, with anything but an eye of favour.

Modern Painters, vol. III, ch. xiv, pars. 29–33

(c) COLOUR

The Greek sense of colour seems to have been so comparatively dim and uncertain, that it is almost impossible to ascertain what the real idea was which they attached to any word alluding to hue: and above all, colour, though pleasant to their eyes, as to those of all human beings, seems never to have been impressive to their feelings. They liked purple, on the whole, the best; but there was no sense of cheerfulness or pleasantness in one colour, and gloom in another, such as the mediævals had.

For instance, when Achilles goes, in great anger and sorrow, to complain to Thetis of the scorn done him by Agamemnon, the sea appears to him "wine-coloured".[1] One might think this meant that the sea looked dark and reddish-purple to him, in a kind of sympathy with his anger. But we turn to the passage of Sophocles, which has been above quoted,—a passage peculiarly intended to express peace and rest,—and we find that the birds sing among "wine-coloured" ivy.[2] The uncertainty of conception of

[1] *Iliad*, I, 350. [2] *Œd. Col.*, 674.

the hue itself, and entire absence of expressive character in the word, could hardly be more clearly manifested.

Again: I said the Greek liked purple, as a general source of enjoyment, better than any other colour. So he did; and so all healthy persons who have eye for colour, and are unprejudiced about it, do; and will to the end of time, for a reason presently to be noted. But so far was this instinctive preference for purple from giving, in the Greek mind, any consistently cheerful or sacred association to the colour, that Homer constantly calls death "purple death".[1]

Again: in the passage of Sophocles, so often spoken of, I said there was some difficulty respecting a word often translated "thickets". I believe, myself, it means glades; literally, "going places" in the woods,—that is to say, places where, either naturally or by force, the trees separate, so as to give some accessible avenue. Now, Sophocles tells us the birds sang in these "*green* going places"[2]; and we take up the expression gratefully, thinking the old Greek perceived and enjoyed, as we do, the sweet fall of the eminently *green* light through the leaves when they are a little thinner than in the heart of the wood. But we turn to the tragedy of Ajax, and are much shaken in our conclusion about the meaning of the word, when we are told that the body of Ajax is to lie unburied, and be eaten by sea-birds on the "*green* sand".[3] The formation, geologically distinguished by that title, was certainly not known to Sophocles; and the only conclusion which, it seems to me, we can come to under the circumstances,—assuming Ariel's[4] authority as to the colour of pretty sand, and the ancient mariner's (or, rather, his hearer's[5]) as to the colour

[1] Vide *Iliad*, v, 83.   [2] *Œd. Col.*, 673.
[3] *Ajax*, 1064.
[4] "Come unto these *yellow* sands."
[5] "And thou art long, and lank, and *brown*,
    As is the ribbed sea sand."

of ugly sand, to be conclusive,—is that Sophocles really did not know green from yellow or brown.

Now, without going out of the terrestrial paradise, in which Dante last left us, we shall be able at once to compare with this Greek incertitude the precision of the mediæval eye for colour. Some three arrow flights farther up into the wood we come to a tall tree, which is at first barren, but, after some little time, visibly opens into flowers, of a colour "less than that of roses, but more than that of violets".[1]

It certainly would not be possible, in words, to come nearer to the *definition* of the exact hue which Dante meant —that of the apple-blossom. Had he employed any simple colour-phrase, as a "pale pink", or "violet-pink", or any other such combined expression, he still could not have completely got at the delicacy of the hue; he might perhaps have indicated its kind, but not its tenderness; but by taking the rose-leaf as the type of the delicate red, and then enfeebling this with the violet grey, he gets, as closely as language can carry him, to the complete rendering of the vision, though it is evidently felt by him to be in its perfect beauty ineffable; and rightly so felt, for of all lovely things which grace the spring time in our fair temperate zone, I am not sure but this blossoming of the apple-tree is the fairest. At all events, I find it associated in my mind with four other kinds of colour, certainly principal among the gifts of the northern earth, namely:

1st. Bell gentians growing close together, mixed with lilies of the valley, on the Jura pastures.

2nd. Alpine roses with dew upon them, under low rays of morning sunshine, touching the tops of the flowers.

3rd. Bell heather in mass, in full light, at sunset.

4th. White narcissus (red-centred) in mass, on the Vevay pastures, in sunshine after rain.

[1] *Purg.* XXXII, 58.

And I know not where in the group to place the wreaths of apple-blossoms in the Vevay orchards, with the far-off blue of the lake of Geneva seen between the flowers.

A Greek, however, would have regarded this blossom simply with the eyes of a Devonshire farmer, as bearing on the probable price of cider, and would have called it red, cerulean, purple, white, hyacinthine, or generally "aglaos", agreeable, as happened to suit his verse.

Modern Painters, vol. III, ch. xiv, pars. 43–46.

(*d*) GRASS

There are, it seems to me, several important deductions to be made from these facts. The Greeks, we have seen, delighted in the grass for its usefulness; the mediæval, as also we moderns, for its colour and beauty. But both dwell on it as the *first* element of the lovely landscape; we saw its use in Homer, we see also that Dante thinks the righteous spirits of the heathen enough comforted in Hades by having even the *image* of green grass put beneath their feet;[1] the happy resting-place in Purgatory has no other delight than its grass and flowers; and, finally, in the terrestrial paradise, the feet of Matilda pause where the Lethe stream first bends the blades of grass.[2] Consider a little what a depth there is in this great instinct of the human race. Gather a single blade of grass, and examine for a minute, quietly, its narrow sword-shaped strip of fluted green. Nothing, as it seems there, of notable goodness or beauty. A very little strength, and a very little tallness, and a few delicate long lines meeting in a point,—not a perfect point neither, but blunt and unfinished, by no means a creditable or apparently much cared for example of Nature's workmanship; made, as it seems, only to be trodden on to-day, and to-morrow to be cast into the oven; and a little pale and hollow stalk,

[1] Vide *Inferno*, IV, 118.   [2] *Purg.* XVIII, 27.

feeble and flaccid, leading down to the dull brown fibres of roots. And yet, think of it well, and judge whether of all the gorgeous flowers that beam in summer air, and of all strong and goodly trees, pleasant to the eyes or good for food,—stately palm and pine, strong ash and oak, scented citron, burdened vine,—there be any by man so deeply loved, by God so highly graced, as that narrow point of feeble green.

Modern Painters, vol. III, ch. xiv, par. 51.

(e) MOUNTAINS

To Dante, mountains are inconceivable except as great broken stones or crags; all their broad contours and undulations seem to have escaped his eye. It is, indeed, with his usual undertone of symbolic meaning that he describes the great broken stones, and the fall of the shattered mountain, as the entrance to the circle appointed for the punishment of the violent; meaning that the violent and cruel, notwithstanding all their iron hardness of heart, have no true strength, but, either by earthquake, or want of support, fall at last into desolate ruin, naked, loose, and shaking under the tread. But in no part of the poem do we find allusion to mountains in any other than a stern light; nor the slightest evidence that Dante cared to look at them. From that hill of San Miniato, whose steps he knew so well, the eye commands, at the farther extremity of the Val d'Arno, the whole purple range of the mountains of Carrara, peaked and mighty, seen always against the sunset light in silent outline, the chief forms that rule the scene as twilight fades away. By this vision Dante seems to have been wholly unmoved, and, but for Lucan's mention of Aruns at Luna,[1] would seemingly not have spoken of the Carrara hills in the whole course of his poem: when he does allude to them,[2]

---

[1] *Pharsalia*, I, 575.   [2] *Inferno*, xx, 46.

he speaks of their white marble, and their command of stars and sea, but has evidently no regard for the hills themselves. There is not a single phrase or syllable throughout the poem which indicates such a regard. Ugolino, in his dream, seemed to himself to be in the mountains, "by cause of which the Pisan cannot see Lucca";[1] and it is impossible to look up from Pisa to that hoary slope without remembering the awe that there is in the passage; nevertheless, it was as a hunting-ground only that he remembered those hills. Adam of Brescia, tormented with eternal thirst, remembers the hills of Romena, but only for the sake of their sweet waters:

> The rills that glitter down the grassy slopes
> Of Casentino, making fresh and soft
> The banks whereby they glide to Arno's stream,
> Stand ever in my view.[2]

And, whenever hills are spoken of as having any influence on character, the repugnance to them is still manifest; they are always causes of rudeness or cruelty:

> But that ungrateful and malignant race,
> Who in old times came down from Fesole,
> *Ay, and still smack of their rough mountain flint,*
> Will, for thy good deeds, show thee enmity.
> Take heed thou cleanse thee of their ways.[3]

So again—

> As one *mountain-bred,*
> Rugged, and clownish, if some city's walls
> He chance to enter, round him stares agape.[4]

Finally, although the Carrara mountains are named as having command of the stars and sea, the *Alps* are never specially mentioned but in bad weather, or snow. On the sand of the circle of the blasphemers—

---

[1] *Inferno,* XXXIII, 30.   [2] *Inferno,* XXX, 63.
[3] *Inferno,* XV, 61.   [4] *Purg.* XXVI, 60.

> Fell slowly wafting down
> Dilated flakes of fire, as flakes of snow
> On Alpine summit, when the wind is hushed.[1]

So the Paduans have to defend their town and castles against inundations,

> Ere the genial warmth be felt,
> On Chiarentana's top.[2]

The clouds of anger, in Purgatory, can only be figured to the reader who has

> On an Alpine height been ta'en by cloud,
> Through which thou sawest no better than the mole
> Doth through opacous membrane.[3]

And in approaching the second branch of Lethe, the seven ladies pause,—

> Arriving at the verge
> Of a dim umbrage hoar, such as is seen
> Beneath green leaves and gloomy branches oft
> To overbrow a bleak and Alpine cliff.[4]

Modern Painters, vol. III, ch. XV, pars. 17–18.

(f) SKY

There is only one more point to be noticed in the Dantesque landscape; namely, the feeling entertained by the poet towards the sky. And the love of mountains is so closely connected with the love of clouds, the sublimity of both depending much on their association, that, having found Dante regardless of the Carrara mountains as seen from San Miniato, we may well expect to find him equally regardless of the clouds in which the sun sank behind them. Accordingly, we find that his only pleasure in the sky depends on its "white clearness",—that turning into "bianca aspetto di cilestro" which is so peculiarly characteristic of fine days in Italy. His pieces of pure pale light are always exquisite. In the dawn on the purgatorial mountain, first,

[1] *Inferno*, XIV, 25. [2] *Inferno*, XV, 9.
[3] *Purg.* XVII, 2. [4] *Purg.* XXXIII, 107.

in its pale white, he sees the "tremola della marina"—
trembling of the sea; then it becomes vermilion; and at
last, near sunrise, orange.[1] These are precisely the changes
of a calm and perfect dawn. The scenery of Paradise begins
with "Day added to day", the light of the sun so flooding
the heavens, that "never rain nor river made lake so wide";[2]
and throughout the Paradise all the beauty depends on
spheres of light, or stars, never on clouds. But the pit of the
Inferno is at first sight obscure, deep, and so *cloudy* that
at its bottom nothing could be seen.[3] When Dante and
Virgil reach the marsh in which the souls of those who
have been angry and sad in their lives are for ever plunged,
they find it covered with thick fog; and the condemned
souls say to them,—   We once were sad,
In the *sweet air made gladsome by the sun*.
Now in these murky settlings are we sad.[4]

Even the angel crossing the marsh to help them is annoyed
by this bitter marsh smoke, "fummo acerbo", and continually sweeps it with his hand from before his face.[5]

Anger, on the purgatorial mountain, is in like manner
imaged, because of its blindness and wildness, by the Alpine
clouds. As they emerge from its mist they see the white
light radiated through the fading folds of it; and, except this
appointed cloud, no other can touch the mountain of
purification.

Tempest none, shower, hail, or snow,
Hoar-frost, or dewy moistness, higher falls,
Than that brief scale of threefold steps. Thick clouds,
Nor scudding rack, are ever seen, swift glance
Ne'er lightens, nor Thaumantian iris gleams.[6]

Dwell for a little while on this intense love of Dante for
light,—taught, as he is at last by Beatrice, to gaze on the

---

[1] *Purg.* I, 117; II, 7–9.   [2] *Par.* I, 61.
[3] *Inferno*, IV, 10.   [4] *Inferno*, VII, 121.
[5] *Inferno*, IX, 82.   [6] *Purg.* XXI, 46.

sun itself like an eagle[1],—and endeavour to enter into his equally intense detestation of all mist, rack of cloud, or dimness of rain; and then consider with what kind of temper he would have regarded a landscape of Copley Fielding's or passed a day in the Highlands. He has, in fact, assigned to the souls of the gluttonous no other punishment in the Inferno than perpetuity of Highland weather:

> Showers
> Ceaseless, accursed, heavy and cold, unchanged
> For ever, both in kind and in degree,—
> Large hail, discoloured water, sleety flaw,
> Through the dim midnight air streamed down amain.[2]

Modern Painters, vol. III, ch. xv, par. 20.

III. MODERN LANDSCAPE

CHARACTERISTICS

WE turn our eyes, therefore, as boldly and as quickly as may be, from these serene fields and skies of mediæval art, to the most characteristic examples of modern landscape. And, I believe, the first thing that will strike us, or that ought to strike us, is their *cloudiness*.

Out of perfect light and motionless air, we find ourselves on a sudden brought under sombre skies, and into drifting wind; and, with fickle sunbeams flashing in our face, or utterly drenched with sweep of rain, we are reduced to track the changes of the shadows on the grass, or watch the rents of twilight through angry cloud. And we find that whereas all the pleasure of the mediæval was in *stability*, *definiteness*, and *luminousness*, we are expected to rejoice in darkness, and triumph in mutability; to lay the foundation of happiness in things which momentarily change or fade; and to expect the utmost satisfaction and instruction from what it is impossible to arrest, and difficult to comprehend.

[1] *Par.* I, 47.   [2] *Inferno,* VI, 7.

We find, however, together with this general delight in breeze and darkness, much attention to the real form of clouds, and careful drawing of effects of mist; so that the appearance of objects, as seen through it, becomes a subject of science with us; and the faithful representation of that appearance is made of primal importance, under the name of aërial perspective. The aspects of sunset and sunrise, with all their attendant phenomena of cloud and mist, are watchfully delineated; and in ordinary daylight landscape, the sky is considered of so much importance, that a principal mass of foliage, or a whole foreground, is unhesitatingly thrown into shade merely to bring out the form of a white cloud. So that, if a general and characteristic name were needed for modern landscape art, none better could be invented than "the service of clouds".

The next thing that will strike us, after this love of clouds, is the love of liberty. Whereas the mediæval was always shutting himself into castles, and behind fosses, and drawing brickwork neatly, and beds of flowers primly, our painters delight in getting to the open fields and moors; abhor all hedges and moats; never paint anything but free-growing trees, and rivers gliding "at their own sweet will"; eschew formality down to the smallest detail; break and displace the brickwork which the mediæval would have carefully cemented; leave unpruned the thickets he would have delicately trimmed; and, carrying the love of liberty even to license, and the love of wildness even to ruin, take pleasure at last in every aspect of age and desolation which emancipates the objects of nature from the government of men;—on the castle wall displacing its tapestry with ivy, and spreading, through the garden, the bramble for the rose.

Connected with this love of liberty we find a singular manifestation of love of mountains, and see our painters traversing the wildest places of the globe in order to obtain subjects with craggy foregrounds and purple distances.

Some few of them remain content with pollards and flat land; but these are always men of third-rate order; and the leading masters, while they do not reject the beauty of the low grounds, reserve their highest powers to paint Alpine peaks or Italian promontories. And it is eminently noticeable, also, that this pleasure in the mountains is never mingled with fear, or tempered by a spirit of meditation, as with the mediæval; but it is always free and fearless, brightly exhilarating, and wholly unreflective; so that the painter feels that his mountain foreground may be more consistently animated by a sportsman than a hermit; and our modern society in general goes to the mountains, not to fast, but to feast, and leaves their glaciers covered with chicken-bones and egg-shells.

Connected with this want of any sense of solemnity in mountain scenery, is a general profanity of temper in regarding all the rest of nature; that is to say, a total absence of faith in the presence of any deity therein. Whereas the mediæval never painted a cloud, but with the purpose of placing an angel in it; and a Greek never entered a wood without expecting to meet a god in it; *we* should think the appearance of an angel in the cloud wholly unnatural, and should be seriously surprised by meeting a god anywhere. Our chief ideas about the wood are connected with poaching. We have no belief that the clouds contain more than so many inches of rain or hail, and from our ponds and ditches expect nothing more divine than ducks and watercresses.

Finally: connected with this profanity of temper is a strong tendency to deny the sacred element of colour, and make our boast in blackness. For though occasionally glaring or violent, modern colour is on the whole eminently sombre, tending continually to grey or brown, and by many of our best painters consistently falsified, with a confessed pride in what they call chaste or subdued tints; so that,

whereas a mediæval paints his sky bright blue and his foreground bright green, gilds the towers of his castles, and
clothes his figures with purple and white, we paint our sky
grey, our foreground black, and our foliage brown, and
think that enough is sacrificed to the sun in admitting the
dangerous brightness of a scarlet cloak or a blue jacket.

It is evident that the title "Dark Ages", given to the
mediæval centuries, is, respecting art, wholly inapplicable.
They were, on the contrary, the bright ages; ours are the
dark ones. I do not mean metaphysically, but literally. They
were the ages of gold; ours are the ages of umber.

This is partly mere mistake in us; we build brown brick
walls, and wear brown coats, because we have been blun-
deringly taught to do so, and go on doing so mechanically.
There is, however, also some cause for the change in our
own tempers. On the whole, these are much *sadder* ages than
the early ones; not sadder in a noble and deep way, but in a
dim wearied way,—the way of ennui, and jaded intellect,
and uncomfortableness of soul and body. The Middle Ages
had their wars and agonies, but also intense delights. Their
gold was dashed with blood; but ours is sprinkled with dust.
Their life was inwoven with white and purple: ours is one
seamless stuff of brown. Not that we are without apparent
festivity, but festivity more or less forced, mistaken, em-
bittered, incomplete—not of the heart. How wonderfully,
since Shakespeare's time, have we lost the power of laughing
at bad jests! The very finish of our wit belies our gaiety.

The profoundest reason of this darkness of heart is,
I believe, our want of faith. There never yet was a generation of men (savage or civilized) who, taken as a body, so
wofully fulfilled the words "having no hope, and without
God in the world", as the present civilized European race.
A Red Indian or Otaheitan savage has more sense of a
divine existence round him, or government over him, than
the plurality of refined Londoners and Parisians: and those

among us who may in some sense be said to believe, are divided almost without exception into two broad classes, Romanist and Puritan; who, but for the interference of the unbelieving portions of society, would, either of them, reduce the other sect as speedily as possible to ashes; the Romanist having always done so whenever he could, from the beginning of their separation, and the Puritan at this time holding himself in complacent expectation of the destruction of Rome by volcanic fire. Such division as this between persons nominally of one religion, that is to say, believing in the same God, and the same Revelation, cannot but become a stumbling-block of the gravest kind to all thoughtful and far-sighted men,—a stumbling-block which they can only surmount under the most favourable circumstances of early education. Hence, nearly all our powerful men in this age of the world are unbelievers; the best of them in doubt and misery; the worst in reckless defiance; the plurality, in plodding hesitation, doing, as well as they can, what practical work lies ready to their hands. Most of our scientific men are in this last class: our popular authors either set themselves definitely against all religious form, pleading for simple truth and benevolence, (Thackeray, Dickens,) or give themselves up to bitter and fruitless statement of facts, (De Balzac,) or surface-painting, (Scott,) or careless blasphemy, sad or smiling, (Byron, Beranger). Our earnest poets and deepest thinkers are doubtful and indignant, (Tennyson, Carlyle); one or two, anchored, indeed, but anxious or weeping, (Wordsworth, Mrs Browning); and of these two, the first is not so sure of his anchor, but that now and then it drags with him, even to make him cry out,—

Great God, I had rather be
A Pagan suckled in some creed outworn;
So might I, standing on this pleasant lea,
Have glimpses that would make me less forlorn.[1]

[1] *Miscellaneous Sonnets*, pt. 1, no. 33.

In politics, religion is now a name; in art, a hypocrisy or affectation. Over German religious pictures the inscription, "See how Pious I am", can be read at a glance by any clear-sighted person. Over French and English religious pictures, the inscription, "See how Impious I am", is equally legible. All sincere and modest art is, among us, profane.

Modern Painters, vol. III, ch. xvi, pars. 1–2; 5–10.

IV. THE INFLUENCE OF MOUNTAINS

WE seem to have involved the supposition that mountain influence is either unfavourable or inessential to literary power; but for this also the mountain influence is still necessary, only in a subordinate degree. It is true, indeed, that the Avon is no mountain torrent, and that the hills round the vale of Stratford are not sublime; true, moreover, that the cantons Berne and Uri have never yet, so far as I know, produced a great poet; but neither, on the other hand, has Antwerp or Amsterdam. And, I believe, the natural scenery which will be found, on the whole, productive of most literary intellect is that mingled of hill and plain, as all available light is of flame and darkness; the flame being the active element, and the darkness the tempering one.

In noting such evidence as bears upon this subject, the reader must always remember that the mountains are at an unfair disadvantage, in being much *out of the way* of the masses of men employed in intellectual pursuits. The position of a city is dictated by military necessity or commercial convenience: it rises, flourishes, and absorbs into its activity whatever leading intellect is in the surrounding population. The persons who are able and desirous to give

their children education naturally resort to it; the best schools, the best society, and the strongest motives assist and excite those born within its walls; and youth after youth rises to distinction out of its streets, while among the blue mountains, twenty miles away, the goatherds live and die in unregarded lowliness. And yet this is no proof that the mountains have little effect upon the mind, or that the streets have a helpful one. The men who are formed by the schools and polished by the society of the capital, may yet in many ways have their powers shortened by the absence of natural scenery; and the mountaineer, neglected, ignorant, and unambitious, may have been taught things by the clouds and streams which he could not have learned in a college, or a coterie.

And in reasoning about the effect of mountains we are therefore under a difficulty like that which would occur to us if we had to determine the good or bad effect of light on the human constitution, in some place where all corporal exercise was necessarily in partial darkness, and only idle people lived in the light. The exercise might give an advantage to the occupants of the gloom, but we should neither be justified in therefore denying the preciousness of light in general, nor the necessity to the workers of the few rays they possessed; and thus I suppose the hills around Stratford, and such glimpses as Shakespeare had of sandstone and pines in Warwickshire, or of chalk cliffs in Kent, to have been essential to the development of his genius. This supposition can only be proved false by the rising of a Shakespeare at Rotterdam or Bergen-op-Zoom, which I think not probable; whereas, on the other hand, it is confirmed by myriads of collateral evidences. The matter could only be *tested* by placing for half a century the British universities at Keswick and Beddgelert, and making Grenoble the capital of France; but if, throughout the history of Britain and France, we contrast the general invention

and pathetic power, in ballads or legends, of the inhabitants of the Scottish Border with those manifested in Suffolk or Essex; and similarly the inventive power of Normandy, Provence, and the Bearnois with that of Champagne or Picardy, we shall obtain some convincing evidence respecting the operation of hills on the masses of mankind, and be disposed to admit, with less hesitation, that the apparent inconsistencies in the effect of scenery on greater minds proceed in each case from specialties of education, accident, and original temper, which it would be impossible to follow out in detail. Sometimes only, when the original resemblance in character of intellect is very marked in two individuals, and they are submitted to definitely contrary circumstances of education, an approximation to evidence may be obtained. Thus Bacon and Pascal appear to be men naturally very similar in their temper and powers of minds. One, born in York House, Strand, of courtly parents, educated in court atmosphere, and replying, almost as soon as he could speak, to the queen asking how old he was—"Two years younger than Your Majesty's happy reign!"—has the world's meanness and cunning engrafted into his intellect, and remains smooth, serene, unenthusiastic, and in some degree base, even with all his sincere devotion and universal wisdom; bearing, to the end of life, the likeness of a marble palace in the street of a great city, fairly furnished within, and bright in wall and battlement, yet noisome in places about the foundations. The other, born at Clermont, in Auvergne, under the shadow of the Puy de Dôme, though taken to Paris at eight years old, retains for ever the impress of his birthplace; pursuing natural philosophy with the same zeal as Bacon, he returns to his own mountains to put himself under their tutelage, and by their help first discovers the great relations of the earth and the air: struck at last with mortal disease; gloomy, enthusiastic, and superstitious, with a conscience burning like lava, and in-

flexible like iron, the clouds gather about the majesty of him, fold after fold; and, with his spirit buried in ashes, and rent by earthquake, yet fruitful of true thought and faithful affection, he stands like that mound of desolate scoria that crowns the hill ranges of his native land, with its sable summit far in heaven, and its foundations green with the ordered garden and the trellised vine.

When, however, our inquiry thus branches into the successive analysis of individual characters, it is time for us to leave it; noting only one or two points respecting Shakespeare. He seems to have been sent essentially to take universal and equal grasp of the *human* nature; and to have been removed, therefore, from all influences which could in the least warp or bias his thoughts. It was necessary that he should lean *no* way; that he should contemplate, with absolute equality of judgment, the life of the court, cloister, and tavern, and be able to sympathize so completely with all creatures as to deprive himself, together with his personal identity, even of his conscience, as he casts himself into their hearts. He must be able to enter into the soul of Falstaff or Shylock with no more sense of contempt or horror than Falstaff or Shylock themselves feel for or in themselves; otherwise his own conscience and indignation would make him unjust to them; he would turn aside from something, miss some good, or overlook some essential palliation. He must be utterly without anger, utterly without purpose; for if a man has any serious purpose in life, that which runs counter to it, or is foreign to it, will be looked at frowningly or carelessly by him. Shakespeare was forbidden of Heaven to have any *plans*. To *do* any good or *get* any good, in the common sense of good, was not to be within his permitted range of work. Not, for him, the founding of institutions, the preaching of doctrines, or the repression of abuses. Neither he, nor the sun, did on any morning that they rose together, receive charge from their Maker concerning such

things. They were both of them to shine on the evil and good; both to behold unoffendedly all that was upon the earth, to burn unappalled upon the spears of kings, and undisdaining, upon the reeds of the river.

Therefore, so far as nature had influence over the early training of this man, it was essential to his perfectness that the nature should be quiet. No mountain passions were to be allowed in him. Inflict upon him but one pang of the monastic conscience; cast upon him but one cloud of the mountain gloom; and his serenity had been gone for ever—his equity—his infinity. You would have made another Dante of him; and all that he would have ever uttered about poor, soiled, and frail humanity would have been the quarrel between Simon and Adam of Brescia,—speedily retired from, as not worthy a man's hearing, nay, not to be heard without heavy fault. All your Falstaffs, Slenders, Quicklys, Sir Tobys, Lances, Touchstones, and Quinces, would have been lost in that. Shakespeare could be allowed no mountains; nay, not even any supreme natural beauty. He had to be left with his kingcups and clover;—pansies—the passing clouds—the Avon's flow—and the undulating hills and woods of Warwick; nay, he was not to love even these in any exceeding measure, lest it might make him in the least overrate their power upon the strong, full-fledged minds of men. He makes the quarrelling fairies concerned about them; poor lost Ophelia find some comfort in them; fearful, fair, wise-hearted Perdita trust the speaking of her good will and good hostess-ship to them; and one of the brothers of Imogen confide his sorrow to them,—rebuked instantly by his brother for "wench-like words";* but any

*   "With fairest flowers
While summer lasts, and I live here, Fidele,
I'll sweeten thy sad grave. Thou shalt not lack
The flower that's like thy face—pale primrose, nor
The azured harebell—like thy veins; no, nor
The leaf of eglantine, whom not to slander,

thought of them in his mighty men I do not find: it is not usually in the nature of such men; and if he had loved the flowers the *least* better himself, he would assuredly have been offended at this, and given a botanical turn of mind to Cæsar, or Othello.

And it is even among the most curious proofs of the necessity to all high imagination that it should paint straight from the life, that he has *not* given such a turn of mind to some of his great men;—Henry the Fifth, for instance. Doubtless some of my readers, having been accustomed to hear it repeated thoughtlessly from mouth to mouth that Shakespeare conceived the spirit of all ages, were as much offended as surprised at my saying that he only painted human nature as he saw it in his own time. They will find, if they look into his work closely, as much antiquarianism as they do geography, and no more. The commonly received notions about the things that had been, Shakespeare took as he found them, animating them with pure human nature, of any time and all time; but inquiries into the minor detail of temporary feeling, he despised as utterly as he did maps; and wheresoever the temporary feeling was in anywise contrary to that of his own day, he errs frankly, and paints from his own time. For instance in this matter of

> Outsweetened not thy breath. The ruddock would
> With charitable bill bring thee all this;
> Yea, and furr'd moss besides, when flowers are none,
> To winter-ground thy corse.

Gui.   Prithee, have done,
> And do not play in wench-like words with that
> Which is so serious."

Imogen herself, afterwards, in deeper passion, will give weeds—not flowers,—and something more:

>   "And when
> With wildwood leaves and weeds, I have strewed his grave,
> And on it said a century of prayers,
> Such as I can, twice o'er, I'll weep, and sigh,
> And, leaving so his service, follow you."

>   (*Cymbeline*, IV, 2.)

love of flowers; we have traced already, far enough for our general purposes, the mediæval interest in them, whether to be enjoyed in the fields, or to be used for types of ornamentation in dress. If Shakespeare had cared to enter into the spirit even of the early fifteenth century, he would assuredly have marked this affection in some of his knights, and indicated even then, in heroic tempers, the peculiar respect for loveliness of *dress* which we find constantly in Dante. But he could not do this; he had not seen it in real life. In his time dress had become an affectation and absurdity. Only fools, or wise men in their weak moments, showed much concern about it; and the facts of human nature which appeared to him general in the matter were the soldier's disdain, and the coxcomb's care of it. Hence Shakespeare's good soldier is almost always in plain or battered armour; even the speech of Vernon in Henry the Fourth,[1] which, as far as I remember, is the only one that bears fully upon the beauty of armour, leans more upon the spirit and hearts of men—"bated, like eagles having lately bathed"; and has an under-current of slight contempt running through the following line, "Glittering in golden coats, *like images*"; while the beauty of the young Harry is essentially the beauty of fiery and perfect youth, answering as much to the Greek, or Roman, or Elizabethan knight as to the mediæval one; whereas the definite interest in armour and dress is opposed by Shakespere in the French (meaning to depreciate them), to the English rude soldierliness:

Con. Tut, I have the best armour in the world. Would it were day!

Orl. You have an excellent armour, but let my horse have his due.

And again:

My lord constable, the armour that I saw in your tent to-night, are those stars, or suns, upon it?

[1] 1 *Henry IV*, IV, I.

while Henry, half proud of his poorness of array, speaks of armorial splendour scornfully; the main idea being still of its being a gilded show and vanity—

> Our gayness and our *gilt* are all besmirched.[1]

This is essentially Elizabethan. The quarterings on a knight's shield, or the inlaying of his armour, would never have been thought of by him as mere "gayness or gilt" in earlier days.* In like manner, throughout every scale of rank or feeling, from that of the French knights down to Falstaff's "I looked he should have sent me two-and-twenty yards of satin, as I am true knight, and he sends me security!"[2] care for dress is always considered by Shakespeare as contemptible; and Mrs Quickly distinguishes herself from a true fairy by her solicitude to scour the *chairs of order* —and "each fair instalment, coat, and several crest";[3] and the association in her mind of the flowers in the fairy rings with the

> Sapphire, pearl, and rich embroidery,
> Buckled below fair knighthood's bending knee;

while the true fairies, in field simplicity, are only anxious to "sweep the dust behind the door"; and

> With this field dew consecrate,
> Every several chamber bless
> Through this palace with sweet peace.[4]

Note the expression "Field dew consecrate". Shakespeare loved courts and camps; but he felt that sacredness and peace were in the dew of the Fields only.

---

* If the reader thinks that in Henry the Fifth's time the Elizabethan temper might already have been manifesting itself, let him compare the English herald's speech, act 2 scene 2 of King John; and by way of specimen of Shakespeare's historical care, or regard of mediæval character, the large use of *artillery* in the previous scene.

[1] *Henry V*, III, 7; IV, 3.   [2] *2 Henry IV*, I, 2.
[3] *Merry Wives of Windsor*, V, 5.
[4] *Midsummer Night's Dream*, V, 2.

There is another respect in which he was wholly incapable of entering into the spirit of the Middle Ages. He had no great art of any kind around him in his own country, and was, consequently, just as powerless to conceive the general influence of former art, as a man of the most inferior calibre. Shakespeare's evidence in matters of art is as narrow as the range of Elizabethan art in England, and resolves itself wholly into admiration of two things,—mockery of life, as in the instance of Hermione as a statue, or absolute splendour, as in the close of *Romeo and Juliet,* where the notion of *gold* as the chief source of dignity of aspect, coming down to Shakespeare from the times of the Field of the Cloth of Gold, and, as I said before, strictly Elizabethan, would interfere seriously with the pathos of the whole passage, but for the sense of sacrifice implied in it:

> As *rich* shall Romeo by his lady lie
> Poor sacrifices of our enmity.[1]

And observe, I am not giving these examples as proof of any smallness in Shakespeare, but of his greatness; that is to say, of his contentment, like every other great man who ever breathed, to paint nothing but *what he saw*; and therefore giving perpetual evidence that his sight was of the sixteenth, and not of the thirteenth century, beneath all the broad and eternal humanity of his imagination. How far in these modern days, emptied of splendour, it may be necessary for great men having certain sympathies for those earlier ages, to act in this differently from all their predecessors; and how far they may succeed in the resuscitation of the past by habitually dwelling in all their thoughts among vanished generations, are questions, of all practical and present ones concerning art, the most difficult to decide; for already in poetry several of our truest men have set themselves to this task, and have indeed put more vitality

---

[1] *Romeo and Juliet,* v, 3.

into the shadows of the dead than most others can give the presences of the living. Thus Longfellow, in the *Golden Legend*, has entered more closely into the temper of the Monk, for good and for evil, than ever yet theological writer or historian, though they may have given their life's labour to the analysis: and, again, Robert Browning is unerring in every sentence he writes of the Middle Ages; always vital, right, and profound; so that in the matter of art, with which we have been specially concerned, there is hardly a principle connected with the mediæval temper, that he has not struck upon in those seemingly careless and too rugged rhymes of his. There is a curious instance, by the way, in a short poem referring to this very subject of tomb and image sculpture; and illustrating just one of those phases of local human character which, though belonging to Shakespeare's own age, he never noticed, because it was specially Italian and un-English; connected also closely with the influence of mountains on the heart, and therefore with our immediate inquiries. I mean the kind of admiration with which a southern artist regarded the *stone* he worked in; and the pride which populace or priest took in the possession of precious mountain substance, worked into the pavements of their cathedrals, and the shafts of their tombs.

Observe, Shakespeare, in the midst of architecture and tombs of wood, or freestone, or brass, naturally thinks of *gold* as the best enriching and ennobling substance for them;[1] —in the midst also of the fever of the Renaissance he writes, as every one else did, in praise of precisely the most vicious master of that school—Giulio Romano;[2] but the modern poet, living much in Italy, and quit of the Renaissance influence, is able fully to enter into the Italian feeling, and to see the evil of the Renaissance tendency, not because he

[1] Vide *Romeo and Juliet*, v, 3, line 299.
[2] Vide *Winter's Tale*, v, 2.

is greater than Shakespeare, but because he is in another element, and has *seen* other things. I miss fragments here and there not needed for my purpose in the passage quoted, without putting asterisks, for I weaken the poem enough by the omissions, without spoiling it also by breaks.

"*The Bishop orders his tomb in St Praxed's Church*

As here I lie
In this state chamber, dying by degrees,
Hours, and long hours, in the dead night, I ask
Do I live—am I dead? Peace, peace seems all:
St Praxed's ever was the church for peace.
And so, about this tomb of mine. I fought
With tooth and nail to save my niche, ye know;
Old Gandolf[1] cozened me, despite my care.
Shrewd was that snatch from out the corner south
He graced his carrion with.
Yet still my niche is not so cramped but thence
One sees the pulpit o' the epistle side,
And somewhat of the choir, those silent seats;
And up into the aery dome where live
The angels, and a sunbeam's sure to lurk.
And I shall fill my slab of basalt there,
And 'neath my tabernacle take my rest,
With those nine columns round me, two and two,
The odd one at my feet, where Anselm[2] stands;
Peach-blossom marble all.
Swift as a weaver's shuttle fleet our years:
Man goeth to the grave, and where is he?
Did I say basalt for my slab, sons? Black—
'Twas ever antique-black I meant! How else
Shall ye contrast my frieze to come beneath?
The bas-relief in bronze ye promised me,
Those Pans and Nymphs ye wot of, and perchance
Some tripod, thyrsus, with a vase or so,

---

[1] The last bishop.
[2] His favourite son; nominally his nephew.

The Saviour at his sermon on the mount,
St Praxed in a glory, and one Pan,
And Moses with the tables . . . but I know
Ye mark me not! What do they whisper thee,
Child of my bowels, Anselm? Ah, ye hope
To revel down my villas while I gasp,
Bricked o'er with beggar's mouldy travertine,
Which Gandolf from his tomb-top chuckles at!
Nay, boys, ye love me—all of jasper, then!
There's plenty jasper somewhere in the world—
And have I not St Praxed's ear to pray
Horses for ye, and brown Greek manuscripts?
That's if ye carve my epitaph aright,
Choice Latin, picked phrase, Tully's every word,
No gaudy ware like Gandolf's second line—
Tully, my masters? Ulpian serves *his* need."

I know no other piece of modern English, prose or poetry, in which there is so much told, as in these lines, of the Renaissance spirit,—its worldliness, inconsistency, pride, hypocrisy, ignorance of itself, love of art, of luxury, and of good Latin. It is nearly all that I said of the central Renaissance in thirty pages of the *Stones of Venice* put into as many lines, Browning's being also the antecedent work. The worst of it is that this kind of concentrated writing needs so much *solution* before the reader can fairly get the good of it, that people's patience fails them, and they give the thing up as insoluble; though, truly, it ought to be to the current of common thought like Saladin's talisman, dipped in clear water, not soluble altogether, but making the element medicinal.[1]

It is interesting, by the way, with respect to this love of stones in the Italian mind, to consider the difference necessitated in the English temper merely by the general domestic use of wood instead of marble. In that old Shakespearian England, men must have rendered a grateful

[1] Vide Scott: *Talisman*, I, 8–9.

homage to their oak forests, in the sense of all that they owed to their goodly timbers in the wainscot and furniture of the rooms they loved best, when the blue of the frosty midnight was contrasted, in the dark diamonds of the lattice, with the glowing brown of the warm, fire-lighted, crimson-tapestried walls. Not less would an Italian look with a grateful regard on the hill summits, to which he owed, in the scorching of his summer noonday, escape into the marble corridor or crypt palpitating only with cold and smooth variegation of the unfevered mountain veins. In some sort, as, both in our stubbornness and our comfort, we not unfitly describe ourselves typically as Hearts of Oak, the Italians might in their strange and variegated mingling of passion, like purple colour, with a cruel sternness, like white rock, truly describe themselves as Hearts of Stone.

Into this feeling about marble in domestic use, Shakespeare, having seen it even in northern luxury, could partly enter, and marks it in several passages of his Italian plays. But if the reader still doubts his limitation to his own experience in all subjects of imagination, let him consider how the removal from mountain influence in his youth, so necessary for the perfection of his lower human sympathy, prevented him from ever rendering with any force the feelings of the mountain anchorite, or indicating in any of his monks the deep spirit of monasticism. Worldly cardinals or nuncios he can fathom to the uttermost; but where, in all his thoughts, do we find St Francis, or Abbot Samson? The "Friar" of Shakespeare's plays is almost the only stage conventionalism which he admitted; generally nothing more than a weak old man, who lives in a cell, and has a rope about his waist.

While, finally, in such slight allusions as he makes to mountain scenery itself, it is very curious to observe the accurate limitation of his sympathies to such things as he had known in his youth; and his entire preference of

human interest, and of courtly and kingly dignities, to the nobleness of the hills. This is most marked in *Cymbeline*, where the term "mountaineer" is, as with Dante, always one of reproach, and the noble birth of Arviragus and Guiderius is shown by their holding their mountain cave as

> A cell of ignorance; travelling abed;
> A prison for a debtor;

and themselves, educated among hills, as in all things contemptible:

> We are beastly; subtle as the fox, for prey;
> Like warlike as the wolf, for what we eat;
> Our valour is to chase what flies; our cage
> We make our choir, as doth the prisoned bird.[1]

A few phrases occur here and there which might justify the supposition that he had seen high mountains, but never implying awe or admiration. Thus Demetrius:

> These things seem *small* and *indistinguishable*,
> *Like far off mountains, turned into clouds.*[2]

"Taurus snow", and the "frosty Caucasus", are used merely as types of purity or cold; and though the avalanche is once spoken of as an image of power, it is with instantly following depreciation:

> Rush on his host, as doth the melted snow
> Upon the valleys whose low vassal seat
> The Alps doth spit, and void his rheum upon.[3]

There was only one thing belonging to hills that Shakespeare seemed to feel as noble—the pine tree, and that was because he had seen it in Warwickshire, clumps of pine occasionally rising on little sandstone mounds, as at the

[1] *Cymbeline*, III, 3. [2] *Midsummer Night's Dream*, IV, 1.
[3] *Henry V*, III, 5.

place of execution of Piers Gaveston, above the lowland woods. He touches on this tree fondly again and again:

> As rough,
> Their royal blood enchafed, as the rud'st wind,
> That by his top doth take the mountain pine,
> And make him stoop to the vale.[1]

> The strong-based promontory
> Have I made shake, and by the spurs plucked up
> The pine and cedar.[2]

Where note his observance of the peculiar horizontal roots of the pine, spurred as it is by them like the claw of a bird, and partly propped, as the aiguilles by those rock promontories at their bases which I have always called their spurs, this observance of the pine's strength and animal-like grasp being the chief reason for his choosing it, above other trees, for Ariel's prison. Again:

> You may as well forbid the mountain pines
> To wag their high tops, and to make no noise
> When they are fretted with the gusts of heaven.[3]

And yet again:

> But when, from under this terrestrial ball,
> He fires the proud tops of the eastern pines.[4]

We may judge, by the impression which this single feature of hill scenery seems to have made on Shakespeare's mind, because he had seen it in his youth, how his whole temper would have been changed if he had lived in a more sublime country, and how essential it was to his power of contemplation of mankind that he should be removed from the sterner influences of nature. For the rest, so far as Shakespeare's work has imperfections of any kind,—the trivialness of many of his adopted plots, for instance, and

---

[1] *Cymbeline*, IV, 2.   [2] *Tempest*, V, I.
[3] *Merchant of Venice*, IV, I.   [4] *Richard II*, III, 2.

the comparative rarity with which he admits the ideal of an enthusiastic virtue arising out of principle; virtue being with him, for the most part, founded simply on the affections joined with inherent purity in his women, or on mere manly pride and honour in his men;*—in a word, whatever difference, involving inferiority, there exists between him and Dante, in his conceptions of the relation between this world and the next, we may partly trace, as we did the difference between Bacon and Pascal, to the less noble character of the scenes around him in his youth; and admit that, though it was necessary for his special work that he should be put, as it were, on a level with his race, on those

* I mean that Shakespeare almost always implies a total difference in *nature* between one human being and another; one being from the birth pure and affectionate, another base and cruel; and he displays each, in its sphere, as having the nature of dove, wolf, or lion, never much implying the government or change of nature by any external principle. There can be no question that in the main he is right in this view of human nature: still, the other form of virtue does exist occasionally, and was never, as far as I recollect, taken much note of by him. And with this stern view of humanity, Shakespeare joined a sorrowful view of Fate, closely resembling that of the ancients. He is distinguished from Dante eminently by his always dwelling on last causes instead of first causes. Dante invariably points to the moment of the soul's choice which fixed its fate, to the instant of the day when it read no farther, or determined to give bad advice about Penestrino.[1] But Shakespeare always leans on the force of Fate, as it urges the final evil; and dwells with infinite bitterness on the power of the wicked, and the infinitude of result dependent seemingly on little things. A fool brings the last piece of news from Verona, and the dearest lives of its noble houses are lost; they might have been saved if the sacristan had not stumbled as he walked. Othello mislays his handkerchief, and there remains nothing for him but death. Hamlet gets hold of the wrong foil, and the rest is silence. Edmund's runner is a moment too late at the prison, and the feather will not move at Cordelia's lips. Salisbury a moment too late at the tower, and Arthur lies on the stones dead. Goneril and Iago have on the whole, in this world, Shakespeare sees, much their own way, though they come to a bad end. It is a pin that Death pierces the king's fortress wall with; and Carelessness and Folly sit sceptred and dreadful, side by side with the pin-armed skeleton.

[1] *Inferno,* IV, 135; XXVII, 102.

plains of Stratford, we should see in this a proof, instead of a negation, of the mountain power over human intellect. For breadth and perfectness of condescending sight, the Shakespearian mind stands alone; but in *ascending* sight it is limited. The breadth of grasp is innate; the stoop and slightness of it were given by the circumstances of scene: and the difference between those careless masques of heathen gods, or unbelieved, though mightily conceived visions of fairy, witch, or risen spirit, and the earnest faith of Dante's vision of Paradise, is the true measure of the difference in influence between the willowy banks of Avon, and the purple hills of Arno.

Modern Painters, vol. IV, ch. xx, pars. 25–38.

V. THE SEA IN LITERATURE

THE glory of a boat is, first its steadiness of poise—its assured standing on the clear softness of the abyss; and, after that, so much capacity of progress by oar or sail as shall be consistent with this defiance of the treachery of the sea. And, this being understood, it is very notable how commonly the poets, creating for themselves an ideal of motion, fasten upon the charm of a boat. They do not usually express any desire for wings, or, if they do, it is only in some vague and half-unintended phrase, such as "flit or soar", involving wingedness. Seriously, they are evidently content to let the wings belong to Horse, or Muse, or Angel, rather than to themselves; but they all, somehow or other, express an honest wish for a Spiritual Boat. I will not dwell on poor Shelley's paper navies, and seas of quicksilver, lest we should begin to think evil of boats in general because of this traitorous one in Spezzia Bay; but it is a triumph to find the pastorally minded Wordsworth imagine no other way of visiting the stars than in a boat "no bigger than the crescent moon";[1] and to find Tennyson—although his

[1] Prologue to *Peter Bell*.

boating, in an ordinary way, has a very marshy and punt-like character—at last, in his highest inspiration, enter in where the wind began "to sweep a music out of sheet and shroud".[1] But the chief triumph of all is in Dante. He had known all manner of travelling; had been borne through vacancy on the shoulders of chimeras, and lifted through upper heaven in the grasp of its spirits; but yet I do not remember that he ever expresses any positive *wish* on such matters, except for a boat.

> Guido, I wish that Lapo, thou, and I,
>   Led by some strong enchantment, might ascend
>   A magic ship, whose charmëd sails should fly
>   With winds at will where'er our thoughts might wend,
> So that no change nor any evil chance
>   Should mar our joyous voyage; but it might be
>   That even satiety should still enhance
>   Between our souls their strict community:
> And that the bounteous wizard then would place
>   Vanna and Bice, and our Lapo's love,
>   Companions of our wandering, and would grace
> With passionate talk, wherever we might rove,
> Our time, and each were as content and free
> As I believe that thou and I should be.[2]

And of all the descriptions of motion in the *Divina Commedia*, I do not think there is another quite so fine as that in which Dante has glorified the old fable of Charon by giving a boat also to the bright sea which surrounds the mountain of Purgatory, bearing the redeemed souls to their place of trial; only an angel is now the pilot, and there is no stroke of labouring oar, for his wings are the sails.

>   My preceptor silent yet
> Stood, while the brightness that we first discerned
> Opened the form of wings: then, when he knew
> The pilot, cried aloud, "Down, down; bend low

[1] *In Memoriam*, ci.
[2] Dante: *Sonnet to Guido Cavalcanti.*

Thy knees; behold God's angel: fold thy hands:
Now shalt thou see true ministers indeed.
Lo! how all human means he sets at nought;
So that nor oar he needs, nor other sail
Except his wings, between such distant shores.
Lo! how straight up to heaven he holds them reared,
Winnowing the air with those eternal plumes,
That not like mortal hairs fall off or change."
   As more and more toward us came, more bright
Appeared the bird of God, nor could the eye
Endure his splendour near: I mine bent down.
He drove ashore in a small bark so swift
And light, that in its course no wave it drank.
The heavenly steersman at the prow was seen,
Visibly written blessed in his looks.
Within, a hundred spirits and more there sat.[1]

I have given this passage at length, because it seems to
me that Dante's most inventive adaptation of the fable of
Charon to Heaven has not been regarded with the interest
that it really deserves; and because, also, it is a description
that should be remembered by every traveller when first he
sees the white fork of the felucca sail shining on the
Southern Sea. Not that Dante had ever seen such sails;
his thought was utterly irrespective of the form of canvas
in any ship of the period; but it is well to be able to attach
this happy image to those felucca sails, as they now float
white and soft above the blue glowing of the bays of Adria.
Nor are other images wanting in them. Seen far away on
the horizon, the Neapolitan felucca has all the aspect of
some strange bird stooping out of the air and just striking
the water with its claws; while the Venetian, when its
painted sails are at full swell in sunshine, is as beautiful as a
butterfly with its wings half-closed. There is something
also in them that might remind us of the variegated and
spotted angel wings of Orcagna, only the Venetian sail

<hr>

[1] *Purgatorio*, II, 25–45.

never looks majestic; it is too quaint and strange, yet with no peacock's pride or vulgar gaiety,—nothing of Milton's Dalilah:

> So bedecked, ornate and gay
> Like a stately ship
> Of Tarsus, bound for the Isles
> Of Javan or Gadire
> With all her bravery on and tackle trim,
> Sails filled and streamers waving.[1]

That description could only have been written in a time of vulgar women and vulgar vessels. The utmost vanity of dress in a woman of the fourteenth century would have given no image of "sails filled or streamers waving"; nor does the look or action of a really "stately" ship ever suggest any image of the motion of a weak or vain woman. The beauties of the Court of Charles II, and the gilded galleys of the Thames, might fitly be compared; but the pomp of the Venetian fisher-boat is like neither. The sail seems dyed in its fulness by the sunshine, as the rainbow dyes a cloud; the rich stains upon it fade and reappear, as its folds swell or fall; worn with the Adrian storms, its rough woof has a kind of noble dimness upon it, and its colours seem as grave, inherent, and free from vanity as the spots of the leopard, or veins of the seashell.

Yet, in speaking of poets' love of boats, I ought to have limited the love to *modern* poets; Dante, in this respect, as in nearly every other, being far in advance of his age. It is not often that I congratulate myself upon the days in which I happen to live; but I do so in this respect, that, compared with every other period of the world, this nineteenth century (or rather, the period between 1750 and 1850) may not improperly be called the Age of Boats; while the classic and chivalric times, in which boats were partly dreaded, partly despised, may respectively be characterised, with

---

[1] *Samson Agonistes,* 712.

regard to their means of locomotion, as the Age of Chariots, and the Age of Horses.

It is very interesting to note how repugnant every oceanic idea appears to be to the whole nature of our principal English mediæval poet, Chaucer. Read first the *Man of Lawe's Tale*, in which the Lady Constance is continually floated up and down the Mediterranean, and the German Ocean, in a ship by herself; carried from Syria all the way to Northumberland, and there wrecked upon the coast; thence yet again driven up and down among the waves for five years, she and her child; and yet, all this while, Chaucer does not let fall a single word descriptive of the sea, or express any emotion whatever about it, or about the ship. He simply tells us the lady sailed here and was wrecked there; but neither he nor his audience appear to be capable of receiving any sensation, but one of simple aversion, from waves, ships, or sands. Compare with his absolutely apathetic recital, the description by a modern poet of the sailing of a vessel, charged with the fate of another Constance:

> It curled not Tweed alone, that breeze—
> For far upon Northumbrian seas
>   It freshly blew, and strong;
> Where from high Whitby's cloistered pile,
> Bound to St Cuthbert's holy isle,
>   It bore a bark along.
> Upon the gale she stooped her side,
> And bounded o'er the swelling tide
>   As she were dancing home.
> The merry seamen laughed to see
> Their gallant ship so lustily
>   Furrow the green sea foam.[1]

Now just as Scott enjoys this sea breeze, so does Chaucer the soft air of the woods, the moment the older poet lands, he is himself again, his poverty of language in speaking of

[1] *Marmion*, II, 1.

the ship is not because he despises description, but because he has nothing to describe. Hear him upon the ground in Spring:

> These woodes else recoveren greene,
> That drie in winter ben to sene,
> And the erth waxeth proud withall,
> For sweet dewes that on it fall,
> And the poore estate forget,
> In which that winter had it set:
> And than becomes the ground so proude,
> That it wol have a newe shroude,
> And maketh so queint his robe and faire,
> That it had hewes an hundred paire,
> Of grasse and floures, of Inde and Pers,
> And many hewes full divers:
> That is the robe I mean ywis,
> Through which the ground to praisen is.[1]

In like manner, wherever throughout his poems we find Chaucer enthusiastic, it is on a sunny day in the "good greenwood", but the slightest approach to the sea-shore makes him shiver; and his antipathy finds at last positive expression, and becomes the principal foundation of the Frankeleine's Tale, in which a lady, waiting for her husband's return in a castle by the sea, behaves and expresses herself as follows:—

> Another time ther wold she sit and thinke,
> And cast her eyen dounward fro the brinke;
> But whan she saw the grisly rockes blake,
> For veray fere so wold hire herte quake
> That on hire feet she might hire not sustene
> Than wold she sit adoun upon the grene,
> And pitously into the see behold,
> And say right thus, with sorweful sighes cold.
> "Eterne God, that thurgh thy purveance
> Ledest this world by certain governance,
> In idel, as men sain, ye nothing make.
> *But, lord, thise grisly fendly rockes blake,*

[1] *Romaunt of the Rose,* 57–70.

> *That semen rather a foule confusion*
> *Of werk, than any faire creation*
> Of swiche a parfit wise God and stable,
> Why han ye wrought this werk unresonable?"[1]

The desire to have the rocks out of her way is indeed severely punished in the sequel of the tale; but it is not the less characteristic of the age, and well worth meditating upon, in comparison with the feelings of an unsophisticated modern French or English girl among the black rocks of Dieppe or Ramsgate.

On the other hand, much might be said about that peculiar love of *green fields and birds* in the Middle Ages; and of all with which it is connected, purity and health in manners and heart, as opposed to the too frequent condition of the modern mind—

> As for the birds in the thicket,
> Thrush or ousel in leafy niche,
> Linnet or finch—she was far too rich
> To care for a morning concert to which
> She was welcome, without a ticket.[2]

But this would lead us far afield, and the main fact I have to point out to the reader is the transition of human grace and strength from the exercises of the land to those of the sea in the course of the last three centuries.

Harbours of England, Introduction.

---

[1] *Frankeleines Tale*, 129–144.
[2] Thomas Hood: *Miss Kilmansegg and her Precious Leg.*

STYLE

I. POETRY AND FACT

I AM writing at a window which commands a view of the head of the Lake of Geneva; and as I look up from my paper, to consider this point, I see, beyond it, a blue breadth of softly moving water, and the outline of the mountains above Chillon, bathed in morning mist. The first verses which naturally come into my mind are—

> A thousand feet in depth below
> The massy waters meet and flow;
> So far the fathom line was sent
> From Chillon's snow-white battlement.[1]

Let us see in what manner this poetical statement is distinguished from a historical one.

It is distinguished from a truly historical statement, first, in being simply false. The water under the castle of Chillon is not a thousand feet deep, nor anything like it. Herein, certainly, these lines fulfil Reynolds's first requirement in poetry, "that it should be inattentive to literal truth and minute exactness in detail". In order, however, to make our comparison more closely in other points, let us assume that what is stated is indeed a fact, and that it was to be recorded, first historically, and then poetically.

Historically stating it, then, we should say: "The lake was sounded from the walls of the castle of Chillon, and found to be a thousand feet deep."

Now, if Reynolds be right in his idea of the difference between history and poetry, we shall find that Byron leaves out of this statement certain *un*necessary details, and retains

[1] Byron: *Prisoner of Chillon*, VI.

only the invariable,—that is to say, the points which the Lake of Geneva and Castle of Chillon have in common with all other lakes and castles.

Let us hear, therefore.

A thousand feet in depth below.

"Below?" Here is, at all events, a word added (instead of anything being taken away); invariable, certainly in the case of lakes, but not absolutely necessary.

The massy waters meet and flow.

"Massy!" why massy? Because deep water is heavy. The word is a good word, but it is assuredly an added detail, and expresses a character, not which the Lake of Geneva has in common with all other lakes, but which it has in distinction from those which are narrow, or shallow.

"Meet and flow." Why meet and flow? Partly to make up a rhyme; partly to tell us that the waters are forceful as well as massy, and changeful as well as deep. Observe, a farther addition of details, and of details more or less peculiar to the spot, or, according to Reynolds's definition, of "heavy matter, retarding the progress of the imagination".

So far the fathom line was sent.

Why fathom line? All lines for sounding are not fathom lines. If the lake was ever sounded from Chillon, it was probably sounded in metres, not fathoms. This is an addition of another particular detail, in which the only compliance with Reynolds's requirement is, that there is some chance of its being an inaccurate one.

From Chillon's snow-white battlement.

Why snow-white? Because castle battlements are not usually snow-white. This is another added detail, and a detail quite peculiar to Chillon, and therefore exactly the most striking word in the whole passage.

"Battlement!" why battlement? Because all walls have not battlements, and the addition of the term marks the castle to be not merely a prison, but a fortress.

This is a curious result. Instead of finding, as we expected, the poetry distinguished from the history by the omission of details, we find it consist entirely in the *addition* of details; and instead of being characterised by regard only of the invariable, we find its whole power to consist in the clear expression of what is singular and particular!

Modern Painters, vol. III, ch. i, pars. 8–9.

It is evident, therefore, that our author has entangled himself in some grave fallacy, by introducing this idea of invariableness as forming a distinction between poetical and historical art. What the fallacy is, we shall discover as we proceed; but as an invading army should not leave an untaken fortress in its rear, we must not go on with our inquiry into the views of Reynolds until we have settled satisfactorily the question already suggested to us, in what the essence of poetical treatment really consists. For though, as we have seen, it certainly involves the addition of specific details, it cannot be simply that addition which turns the history into poetry. For it is perfectly possible to add any number of details to a historical statement, and to make it more prosaic with every added word. As, for instance, "The lake was sounded out of a flat-bottomed boat, near the crab-tree at the corner of the kitchen-garden, and was found to be a thousand feet nine inches deep, with a muddy bottom." It thus appears that it is not the multiplication of details which constitutes poetry; nor their subtraction which constitutes history, but that there must be something either in the nature of the details themselves, or the method of using them, which invests them with poetical power or historical propriety.

It seems to me, and may seem to the reader, strange that we should need to ask the question, "What is poetry?" Here is a word we have been using all our lives, and, I suppose, with a very distinct idea attached to it; and when I am now called upon to give a definition of this idea, I find myself at a pause. What is more singular, I do not at present recollect hearing the question often asked, though surely it is a very natural one; and I never recollect hearing it answered, or even attempted to be answered. In general, people shelter themselves under metaphors, and while we hear poetry described as an utterance of the soul, an effusion of Divinity, or voice of nature, or in other terms equally elevated and obscure, we never attain anything like a definite explanation of the character which actually distinguishes it from prose.

I come, after some embarrassment, to the conclusion, that poetry is "the suggestion, by the imagination, of noble grounds for the noble emotions". I mean, by the noble emotions, those four principal sacred passions—Love, Veneration, Admiration, and Joy (this latter especially, if unselfish); and their opposites—Hatred, Indignation (or Scorn), Horror, and Grief,—this last, when unselfish, becoming Compassion. These passions in their various combinations constitute what is called "poetical feeling", when they are felt on noble grounds, that is, on great and true grounds. Indignation, for instance, is a poetical feeling, if excited by serious injury; but it is not a poetical feeling if entertained on being cheated out of a small sum of money. It is very possible the manner of the cheat may have been such as to justify considerable indignation; but the feeling is nevertheless not poetical unless the grounds of it be large as well as just. In like manner, energetic admiration may be excited in certain minds by a display of fireworks, or a street of handsome shops; but the feeling is not poetical, because the grounds of it are false, and therefore ignoble.

There is in reality nothing to deserve admiration either in the firing of packets of gunpowder, or in the display of the stocks of warehouses. But admiration excited by the budding of a flower is a poetical feeling, because it is impossible that this manifestation of spiritual power and vital beauty can ever be enough admired.

Farther, it is necessary to the existence of poetry that the grounds of these feelings should be *furnished by the imagination*. Poetical feeling, that is to say, mere noble emotion, is not poetry. It is happily inherent in all human nature deserving the name, and is found often to be purest in the least sophisticated. But the power of assembling, by *the help of the imagination*, such images as will excite these feelings, is the power of the poet or literally of the "Maker".

Now this power of exciting the emotions depends of course on the richness of the imagination, and on its choice of those images which, in combination, will be most effective, or, for the particular work to be done, most fit. And it is altogether impossible for a writer not endowed with invention to conceive what tools a true poet will make use of, or in what way he will apply them, or what unexpected results he will bring out by them; so that it is vain to say that the details of poetry ought to possess, or ever do possess, any *definite* character. Generally speaking, poetry runs into finer and more delicate details than prose; but the details are not poetical because they are more delicate, but because they are employed so as to bring out an affecting result. For instance, no one but a true poet would have thought of exciting our pity for a bereaved father by describing his way of locking the door of his house:

> Perhaps to himself at that moment he said,
> The key I must take, for my Ellen is dead;
> But of this in my ears not a word did he speak,
> And he went to the chase with a tear on his cheek.[1]

[1] Wordsworth: *The Childless Father*.

In like manner, in painting, it is altogether impossible to say beforehand what details a great painter may make poetical by his use of them to excite noble emotions: and we shall, therefore, find that a painting is to be classed in the great or inferior schools, not according to the kind of details which it represents, but according to the uses for which it employs them.

It is only farther to be noticed, that infinite confusion has been introduced into this subject by the careless and illogical custom of opposing painting to poetry, instead of regarding poetry as consisting in a noble use, whether of colours or words. Painting is properly to be opposed to *speaking* or *writing*, but not to *poetry*. Both painting and speaking are methods of expression. Poetry is the employment of either for the noblest purposes.

This question being thus far determined, we may proceed with our paper in the *Idler*.

It is very difficult to determine the exact degree of enthusiasm that the arts of painting and poetry may admit. There may, perhaps, be too great indulgence as well as too great a restraint of imagination; if the one produces incoherent monsters, the other produces what is full as bad, lifeless insipidity. An intimate knowledge of the passions, and good sense, but not common sense, must at last determine its limits. It has been thought, and I believe with reason, that Michael Angelo sometimes transgressed those limits; and, I think, I have seen figures of him of which it was very difficult to determine whether they were in the highest degree sublime or extremely ridiculous. Such faults may be said to be the ebullitions of genius; but at least he had this merit, that he never was insipid, and whatever passion his works may excite, they will always escape contempt.

What I have had under consideration is the sublimest style, particularly that of Michael Angelo, the Homer of painting. Other kinds may admit of this naturalness, which of the lowest kind is the chief merit; but in painting, as in poetry, the highest style has the least of common nature.

From this passage we gather three important indications of the supposed nature of the Great Style. That it is the work of men in a state of enthusiasm. That it is like the writing of Homer; and that it has as little as possible of "common nature" in it.

First, it is produced by men in a state of enthusiasm. That is, by men who feel *strongly* and *nobly*; for we do not call a strong feeling of envy, jealousy, or ambition, enthusiasm. That is, therefore, by men who feel poetically. This much we may admit, I think, with perfect safety. Great art is produced by men who feel acutely and nobly; and it is in some sort an expression of this personal feeling. We can easily conceive that there may be a sufficiently marked distinction between such art, and that which is produced by men who do not feel at all, but who reproduce, though ever so accurately, yet coldly, like human mirrors, the scenes which pass before their eyes.

Secondly, Great Art is like the writing of Homer, and this chiefly because it has little of "common nature" in it. We are not clearly informed what is meant by common nature in this passage. Homer seems to describe a great deal of what is common:—cookery, for instance, very carefully in all its processes.[1] I suppose the passage in the *Iliad* which, on the whole, has excited most admiration, is that which describes a wife's sorrow at parting from her husband, and a child's fright at its father's helmet;[2] and I hope, at least, the former feeling may be considered "common nature". But the true greatness of Homer's style is, doubtless, held by our author to consist in his imaginations of things not only uncommon but impossible (such as spirits in brazen armour, or monsters with heads of men and bodies of beasts), and in his occasional delineations of the human character and form in their utmost, or heroic, strength and beauty. We gather then, on the whole, that a

[1] *Iliad*, I, 463.   [2] *Iliad*, VI, 468.

painter in the Great Style must be enthusiastic, or full of
emotion, and must paint the human form in its utmost
strength and beauty, and perhaps certain impossible forms
besides, liable by persons not in an equally enthusiastic state
of mind to be looked upon as in some degree absurd. This
I presume to be Reynolds's meaning, and to be all that he
intends us to gather from his comparison of the Great Style
with the writings of Homer. But if that comparison be a
just one in all respects, surely two other corollaries ought
to be drawn from it, namely,—first, that these Heroic or
Impossible images are to be mingled with others very un-
heroic and very possible; and, secondly, that in the representation of the Heroic or Impossible forms, the greatest care
must be taken in *finishing the details*, so that a painter must
not be satisfied with painting well the countenance and
the body of his hero, but ought to spend the greatest part
of his time (as Homer the greatest number of verses) in
elaborating the scupltured pattern on his shield.

Modern Painters, vol. III, ch. i, pars. 11–18.

II. TESTS OF STYLE

First of all, putting the question of who writes or
speaks aside, do you, good reader, *know* good "style" when
you get it? Can you say, of half-a-dozen given lines taken
anywhere out of a novel, or poem, or play, That is good,
essentially, in style, or bad, essentially? and can you say why
such half-dozen lines are good, or bad?

I imagine that in most cases, the reply would be given
with hesitation; yet if you will give me a little patience, and
take some accurate pains, I can show you the main tests of
style in the space of a couple of pages.

I take two examples of absolutely perfect, and in manner
highest, i.e. kingly, and heroic, style: the first example in
expression of anger, the second of love.

(1) We are glad the Dauphin is so pleasant with us,
    His present, and your pains, we thank you for.
    When we have match'd our rackets to these balls,
    We will in France, by God's grace, play a set
    Shall strike his father's crown into the hazard.[1]

(2) My gracious Silence, hail!
    Wouldst thou have laughed, had I come coffin'd home
    That weep'st to see me triumph? Ah, my dear,
    Such eyes the widows in Corioli wear
    And mothers that lack sons.[2]

Let us note, point by point, the conditions of greatness common to both these passages, so opposite in temper.

(*A*) Absolute command over all passion, however intense; this the first-of-first conditions, (see the King's own sentence just before, "We are no tyrant, but a Christian King, Unto *whose grace* our passion is as subject As are our wretches fettered in our prisons"); and with this self-command, the supremely surveying grasp of every thought that is to be uttered, before its utterance; so that each may come in its exact place, time, and connection. The slightest hurry, the misplacing of a word, or the unnecessary accent on a syllable, would destroy the "style" in an instant.

(*B*) Choice of the fewest and simplest words that can be found in the compass of the language, to express the thing meant: these few words being also arranged in the most straightforward and intelligible way; allowing inversion only when the subject can be made primary without obscurity: thus, "his present, and your pains, we thank you for" is better than "we thank you for his present and your pains", because the Dauphin's gift is by courtesy put before the Ambassador's pains; but "when to these balls our rackets we have matched" would have spoiled the style in a moment, because—I was going to have said, ball and racket are of equal rank, and therefore only the natural order

[1] *Henry V*, I, 2.   [2] *Coriolanus*, II, I.

proper; but also here the natural order is the desired one, the English racket to have precedence of the French ball. In the fourth line the "in France" comes first, as announcing the most important resolution of action; the "by God's grace" next, as the only condition rendering resolution possible; the detail of issue follows with the strictest limit in the final word. The King does not say "danger", far less "dishonour", but "hazard" only; of *that* he is, humanly speaking, sure.

(*C*) Perfectly emphatic and clear utterance of the chosen words; slowly in the degree of their importance, with omission however of every word not absolutely required; and natural use of the familiar contractions of final dissyllable. Thus "play a set shall strike" is better than "play a set *that* shall strike", and "match'd" is kingly short—no necessity of metre could have excused "matched" instead. On the contrary, the first three words, "We are glad", would have been spoken by the king more slowly and fully than any other syllables in the whole passage, first pronouncing the kingly "we" at its proudest, and then the "are" as a continuous state, and then the "glad", as the exact contrary of what the ambassadors expected him to be.

(*D*) Absolute spontaneity in doing all this, easily and necessarily as the heart beats. The king *cannot* speak otherwise than he does—nor the hero. The words not merely come to them, but are compelled to them. Even lisping numbers "come", but mighty numbers are ordained, and inspired.

(*E*) Melody in the words, changeable with their passion, fitted to it exactly, and the utmost of which the language is capable—the melody in prose being Eolian and variable—in verse, nobler by submitting itself to stricter law.

(*F*) Utmost spiritual contents in the words; so that each carries not only its instant meaning, but a cloudy companionship of higher or darker meaning according to the

passion—nearly always indicated by metaphor: "play a set"—sometimes by abstraction—(thus in the second passage "silence" for silent one) sometimes by description instead of direct epithet ("coffined" for dead) but always indicative of there being more in the speaker's mind than he has said, or than he can say, full though his saying be. On the quantity of this attendant fulness depends the majesty of style; that is to say, virtually, on the quantity of contained thought in briefest words, such thought being primarily loving and true: and this the sum of all—that nothing can well be said, but with truth, nor beautifully, but by love.

These are the essential conditions of noble speech in prose and verse alike, but the adoption of the form of verse, and especially rimed verse, means the addition to all these qualities of one more; of music, that is to say, not Eolian merely, but Apolline; a construction or architecture of words fitted and befitting, under external laws of time and harmony.

When Byron says "rhyme is of the rude",[1] he means that Burns needs it,—while Henry the Fifth does not, nor Plato, nor Isaiah—yet in this need of it by the simple, it becomes all the more religious: and thus the loveliest pieces of Christian language are all in rime—the best of Dante, Chaucer, Douglas, Shakespeare, Spenser, and Sidney.

Fiction, Fair and Foul, pars. 64–68.

III. CLASSIC AND ROMANTIC

T H E difference which I have pointed out to you as existing between these great nations, exists also between two orders of intelligence among men, of which the one is usually called Classic, the other Romantic. Without entering into any

[1] *Island,* II, 5.

of the fine distinctions between these two sects, this broad
one is to be observed as constant: that the writers and
painters of the Classic school set down nothing but what is
known to be true, and set it down in the perfectest manner
possible in their way, and are thenceforward authorities
from whom there is no appeal. Romantic writers and
painters, on the contrary, express themselves under the impulse of passions which may indeed lead them to the discovery of new truths, or to the more delightful arrangement
or presentment of things already known: but their work,
however brilliant or lovely, remains imperfect, and without
authority. It is not possible, of course, to separate these two
orders of men trenchantly: a classic writer may sometimes,
whatever his care, admit an error, and a romantic one may
reach perfection through enthusiasm. But, practically, you
may separate the two for your study and your education;
and, during your youth, the business of us your masters is
to enforce on you the reading, for school work, only of
classical books; and to see that your minds are both informed
of the indisputable facts they contain, and accustomed to act
with the infallible accuracy of which they set the example.

Val D'Arno, par. 206.

The word "classic" when justly applied to a book, means
that it contains an unchanging truth, expressed as clearly
as it was possible for any of the men living at the time when
the book was written, to express it.

"Unchanging" or "eternal" truth, is that which relates
to constant,—or at least in our human experience constant,
—things; and which, therefore, though foolish men may
long lose sight of it, remains the same through all their
neglect, and is again recognized as inevitable and un-
alterable, when their fit of folly is past.

The books which in a beautiful manner, whether enig-

matic or direct, contain statements of such fact, are delighted in by all careful and honest readers; and the study of them is a necessary element in the education of wise and good men, in every age and country.

Every nation which has produced highly trained Magi, or wise men, has discerned, at the time when it most flourished, some part of the great system of universal truth, which it was then, and only then, in the condition to discern completely; and the books in which it recorded that part of truth remain established for ever; and cannot be superseded: so that the knowledge of mankind, though continually increasing, is built, pinnacle after pinnacle, on the foundation of these adamant stones of ancient soul. And it is the law of progressive human life that we shall not build in the air: but on the already high-storied temple of the thoughts of our ancestors; in the crannies and under the eaves of which we are meant, for the most part, to nest ourselves like swallows; though the stronger of us sometimes may bring, for increase of height, some small white stone, and in the stone a new name written. Which is indeed done, by those ordered to such masonry, without vainly attempting the review of all that has been known before; but never without modest submission to the scheme of the eternal wisdom; nor ever in any great degree, except by persons trained reverently in some large portion of the wisdom of the past.

Preface to the *Economist of Xenophon*, Pars. 1–2.

WOMEN IN LITERATURE

Note broadly in the outset, Shakespeare has no heroes;—
he has only heroines. There is not one entirely heroic
figure in all his plays, except the slight sketch of Henry the
Fifth, exaggerated for the purposes of the stage; and the
still slighter Valentine in *The Two Gentlemen of Verona*.
In his laboured and perfect plays you have no hero. Othello
would have been one, if his simplicity had not been so great
as to leave him the prey of every base practice round him;
but he is the only example even approximating to the heroic
type. Coriolanus—Cæsar—Antony, stand in flawed
strength, and fall by their vanities;—Hamlet is indolent,
and drowsily speculative; Romeo an impatient boy; the
Merchant of Venice languidly submissive to adverse fortune; Kent, in *King Lear*, is entirely noble at heart, but
too rough and unpolished to be of true use at the critical
time, and he sinks into the office of a servant only. Orlando,
no less noble, is yet the despairing toy of chance, followed,
comforted, saved by Rosalind. Whereas there is hardly a
play that has not a perfect woman in it, steadfast in grave
hope, and errorless purpose: Cordelia, Desdemona, Isabella,
Hermione, Imogen, Queen Katherine, Perdita, Sylvia,
Viola, Rosalind, Helena, and last, and perhaps loveliest,
Virgilia, are all faultless; conceived in the highest heroic
type of humanity.

Then observe, secondly,

The catastrophe of every play is caused always by the
folly or fault of a man; the redemption, if there be any, is
by the wisdom and virtue of a woman, and, failing that,
there is none. The catastrophe of King Lear is owing to
his own want of judgment, his impatient vanity, his misunderstanding of his children; the virtue of his one true
daughter would have saved him from all the injuries of the

others, unless he had cast her away from him; as it is, she all but saves him.

Of Othello I need not trace the tale;—nor the one weakness of his so mighty love; nor the inferiority of his perceptive intellect to that even of the second woman character in the play, the Emilia who dies in wild testimony against his error:—

> Oh, murderous coxcomb! What should such a fool
> Do with so good a wife?[1]

In *Romeo and Juliet*, the wise and brave stratagem of the wife is brought to ruinous issue by the reckless impatience of her husband. In *Winter's Tale*, and in *Cymbeline*, the happiness and existence of two princely households, lost through long years, and imperilled to the death by the folly and obstinacy of the husbands, are redeemed at last by the queenly patience and wisdom of the wives. In *Measure for Measure*, the foul injustice of the judges, and the foul cowardice of the brother, are opposed to the victorious truth and adamantine purity of a woman. In *Coriolanus*, the mother's counsel, acted upon in time, would have saved her son from all evil; his momentary forgetfulness of it is his ruin; her prayer, at last granted, saves him—not, indeed, from death, but from the curse of living as the destroyer of his country.

And what shall I say of Julia, constant against the fickleness of a lover who is a mere wicked child?—of Helena, against the petulance and insult of a careless youth?—of the patience of Hero, the passion of Beatrice, and the calmly devoted wisdom of the "unlessoned girl",[2] who appears among the helplessness, the blindness, and the vindictive passions of men, as a gentle angel, bringing courage and safety by her presence, and defeating the worst malignities of crime by what women are fancied most to fail in,—precision and accuracy of thought?

[1] *Othello*, V, 2, 236.
[2] Portia's description of herself: *Merchant of Venice*, III, 2, 159.

Observe, further, among all the principal figures in Shakespeare's plays, there is only one weak woman—Ophelia; and it is because she fails Hamlet at the critical moment, and is not, and cannot in her nature be, a guide to him when he needs her most, that all the bitter catastrophe follows. Finally, though there are three wicked women among the principal figures, Lady Macbeth, Regan, and Goneril, they are felt at once to be frightful exceptions to the ordinary laws of life; fatal in their influence also, in proportion to the power for good which they have abandoned.

Such, in broad light, is Shakespeare's testimony to the position and character of women in human life. He represents them as infallibly faithful and wise counsellors, —incorruptibly just and pure examples—strong always to sanctify, even when they cannot save.

Not as in any wise comparable in knowledge of the nature of man,—still less in his understanding of the causes and courses of fate,—but only as the writer who has given us the broadest view of the conditions and modes of ordinary thought in modern society, I ask you next to receive the witness of Walter Scott.

I put aside his merely romantic prose writings as of no value, and though the early romantic poetry is very beautiful, its testimony is of no weight, other than that of a boy's ideal. But his true works, studied from Scottish life, bear a true witness; and in the whole range of these, there are but three men who reach the heroic type—Dandie Dinmont, Rob Roy, and Claverhouse; of these, one is a border farmer; another a freebooter; the third a soldier in a bad cause. And these touch the ideal of heroism only in their courage and faith, together with a strong, but uncultivated, or mistakenly applied, intellectual power; while his younger men are the gentlemanly playthings of fantastic fortune, and only by aid (or accident) of that fortune, survive, not vanquish, the trials they involuntarily sustain. Of any disciplined, or con-

sistent character, earnest in a purpose wisely conceived, or
dealing with forms of hostile evil, definitely challenged and
resolutely subdued, there is no trace in his conceptions of
young men. Whereas in his imaginations of women,—in
the characters of Ellen Douglas, of Flora MacIvor, Rose
Bradwardine, Catherine Seyton, Diana Vernon, Lilias
Redgauntlet, Alice Bridgenorth, Alice Lee, and Jeanie
Deans,—with endless varieties of grace, tenderness, and
intellectual power, we find in all a quite infallible
sense of dignity and justice; a fearless, instant, and
untiring self-sacrifice, to even the appearance of duty, much
more to its real claims; and, finally, a patient wisdom of
deeply restrained affection, which does infinitely more than
protect its objects from a momentary error; it gradually
forms, animates, and exalts the characters of the unworthy
lovers, until, at the close of the tale, we are just able, and
no more, to take patience in hearing of their unmerited
success.

So that, in all cases, with Scott as with Shakespeare, it
is the woman who watches over, teaches, and guides the
youth; it is never, by any chance, the youth who watches
over, or educates, his mistress.

Next, take, though more briefly, graver testimony—
that of the great Italians and Greeks. You know well
the plan of Dante's great poem—that it is a love-poem to
his dead lady, a song of praise for her watch over his soul.
Stooping only to pity, never to love, she yet saves him from
destruction—saves him from hell. He is going eternally
astray in despair; she comes down from heaven to his help,
and throughout the ascents of Paradise is his teacher, in-
terpreting for him the most difficult truths, divine and
human; and leading him, with rebuke upon rebuke, from
star to star.

I do not insist upon Dante's conception; if I began I
could not cease: besides, you might think this a wild imagination of one poet's heart. So I will rather read to you a

few verses of the deliberate writing of a knight of Pisa to
his living lady, wholly characteristic of the feeling of all the
noblest men of the thirteenth, or early fourteenth century,
preserved among many other such records of knightly
honour and love, which Dante Rossetti has gathered for
us from among the early Italian poets.

> For lo! thy law is passed
> That this my love should manifestly be
>   To serve and honour thee:
> And so I do; and my delight is full,
> Accepted for the servant of thy rule.
>
> Without almost, I am all rapturous,
>   Since thus my will was set
>   To serve, thou flower of joy, thine excellence:
> Nor ever seems it anything could rouse
>   A pain or a regret,
>   But on thee dwells mine every thought and sense;
> Considering that from thee all virtues spread
>   As from a fountain head,—
> *That in thy gift is wisdom's best avail,*
>   *And honour without fail,*
> With whom each sovereign good dwells separate,
> Fulfilling the perfection of thy state.
>
>   Lady, since I conceived
> Thy pleasurable aspect in my heart,
>   *My life has been apart*
> *In shining brightness and the place of truth;*
>   Which till that time, good sooth,
> Groped among shadows in a darken'd place,
>   Where many hours and days
> It hardly ever had remember'd good.
>   But now my servitude
> Is thine, and I am full of joy and rest.
>   A man from a wild beast
> Thou madest me, since for thy love I lived.[1]

You may think perhaps a Greek knight would have had
a lower estimate of women than this Christian lover. His

[1] Pannuccio dal Bagno, Pisano. Vide Rossetti's *Dante and his
Circle*, p. 331.

spiritual subjection to them was indeed not so absolute; but as regards their own personal character, it was only because you could not have followed me so easily, that I did not take the Greek women instead of Shakespeare's; and instance, for chief ideal types of human beauty and faith, the simple mother's and wife's heart of Andromache; the divine, yet rejected wisdom of Cassandra; the playful kindness and simple princess-life of happy Nausicaa; the housewifely calm of that of Penelope, with its watch upon the sea; the ever patient, fearless, hopelessly devoted piety of the sister, and daughter, in Antigone; the bowing down of Iphigenia, lamb-like and silent; and, finally, the expectation of the resurrection, made clear to the soul of the Greeks in the return from her grave of that Alcestis, who, to save her husband, had passed calmly through the bitterness of death.

Now I could multiply witness upon witness of this kind upon you if I had time. I would take Chaucer, and show you why he wrote a Legend of Good Women; but no Legend of Good Men. I would take Spenser, and show you how all his fairy knights are sometimes deceived and sometimes vanquished; but the soul of Una is never darkened, and the spear of Britomart is never broken. Nay, I could go back into the mythical teaching of the most ancient times, and show you how the great people,—by one of whose princesses it was appointed that the Lawgiver of all the earth should be educated, rather than by his own kindred;—how that great Egyptian people, wisest then of nations, gave to their Spirit of Wisdom the form of a woman; and into her hand, for a symbol, the weaver's shuttle; and how the name and the form of that spirit, adopted, believed, and obeyed by the Greeks, became that Athena of the olive-helm, and cloudy shield, to faith in whom you owe, down to this date, whatever you hold most precious in art, in literature, or in types of national virtue.

Sesame and Lilies, lect. II, pars. 56–62.

ENIGMAS IN LITERATURE

It is a strange habit of wise humanity to speak in enigmas only, so that the highest truths and usefullest laws must be hunted for through whole picture-galleries of dreams, which to the vulgar seem dreams only. Thus Homer, the Greek tragedians, Plato, Dante, Chaucer, Shakespeare, and Goethe, have hidden all that is chiefly serviceable in their work, and in all the various literature they absorbed and re-embodied, under types which have rendered it quite useless to the multitude. What is worse, the two primal declarers of moral discovery, Homer and Plato, are partly at issue; for Plato's logical power quenched his imagination, and he became incapable of understanding the purely imaginative element either in poetry or painting: he therefore somewhat overrates the pure discipline of passionate art in song and music, and misses that of meditative art. There is, however, a deeper reason for his distrust of Homer. His love of justice, and reverently religious nature, made him dread, as death, every form of fallacy; but chiefly, fallacy respecting the world to come (his own myths being only symbolic exponents of a rational hope). We shall perhaps now every day discover more clearly how right Plato was in this, and feel ourselves more and more wonderstruck that men such as Homer and Dante (and, in an inferior sphere, Milton), not to speak of the great sculptors and painters of every age, have permitted themselves, though full of all nobleness and wisdom, to coin idle imaginations of the mysteries of eternity, and guide the faiths of the families of the earth by the courses of their own vague and visionary arts: while the indisputable truths of human life and duty, respecting which they all have but one voice, lie hidden behind these veils of phantasy, unsought, and often unsuspected.   *Munera Pulveris*, par. 87.

DANTE—THE *DIVINA COMMEDIA*

In reading Dante, this mode of reasoning from contraries is a great help, for his philosophy of the vices is the only one which admits of classification; his descriptions of virtue, while they include the ordinary formal divisions, are far too profound and extended to be brought under definition. Every line of the *Paradiso* is full of the most exquisite and spiritual expressions of Christian truth; and that poem is only less read than the *Inferno* because it requires far greater attention, and, perhaps, for its full enjoyment, a holier heart.

His system in the *Inferno* is briefly this. The whole nether world is divided into seven circles, deep within deep, in each of which, according to its depth, severer punishment is inflicted. These seven circles, reckoning them downwards, are thus allotted:

1. To those who have lived virtuously, but knew not Christ.
2. To Lust.
3. To Gluttony.
4. To Avarice and Extravagance.
5. To Anger and *Sorrow*.
6. To Heresy.
7. To Violence and Fraud.

This seventh circle is divided into two parts; of which the first, reserved for those who have been guilty of Violence, is again divided into three, apportioned severally to those who have committed, or desired to commit, violence against their neighbours, against themselves, or against God.

The lowest hell, reserved for the punishment of Fraud,

is itself divided into ten circles, wherein are severally punished the sins of,—

1. Betraying women.
2. Flattery.
3. Simony.
4. False prophecy.
5. Peculation.
6. Hypocrisy.
7. Theft.
8. False counsel.
9. Schism and Imposture.
10. Treachery to those who repose entire trust in the traitor.

There is, perhaps, nothing more notable in this most interesting system than the profound truth couched under the attachment of so terrible a penalty to sadness or sorrow. It is true that Idleness does not elsewhere appear in the scheme, and is evidently intended to be included in the guilt of sadness by the word "accidioso"; but the main meaning of the poet is to mark the duty of rejoicing in God, according both to St Paul's command, and Isaiah's promise, "Thou meetest him that rejoiceth and worketh righteousness." [1] I do not know words that might with more benefit be borne with us, and set in our hearts momentarily against the minor regrets and rebelliousnesses of life, than these simple ones:

Tristi fummo
Nel aer dolce, che del sol s' allegra,
Or ci attristiam, nella belletta negra.

We once were sad,
In the sweet air, made gladsome by the sun,
Now in these murky settlings are we sad.[2]   CARY.

The virtue usually opposed to this vice of sullenness is Alacritas, uniting the sense of activity and cheerfulness.

[1] *Isa.* lxiv, 5.   [2] *Inferno*, VII, 121.

Spenser has cheerfulness simply, in his description, never enough to be loved or praised, of the virtues of Womanhood; first feminineness or womanhood in speciality; then,—

> Next to her sate goodly Shamefastnesse,
> Ne ever durst her eyes from ground upreare,
> Ne ever once did looke up from her desse,*
> As if some blame of evill she did feare
> That in her cheekes made roses oft appeare:
> And her against sweet Cherefulnesse was placed,
> Whose eyes, like twinkling stars in evening cleare,
> Were deckt with smyles that all sad humours chaced.
>
> And next to her sate sober Modestie,
> Holding her hand upon her gentle hart;
> And her against, sate comely Curtesie,
> *That unto every person knew her part;*
> And her before was seated overthwart
> Soft Silence, and submisse Obedience,
> Both linckt together never to dispart.[1]

Another notable point in Dante's system is the intensity of uttermost punishment given to treason, the peculiar sin of Italy, and that to which, at this day, she attributes her own misery with her own lips. An Italian, questioned as to the causes of the failure of the campaign of 1848, always makes one answer, "We were betrayed"; and the most melancholy feature of the present state of Italy is principally this, that she does not see that, of all causes to which failure might be attributed, this is at once the most disgraceful, and the most hopeless. In fact, Dante seems to me to have written almost prophetically, for the instruction of modern Italy, and chiefly so in the sixth canto of the *Purgatorio*.

Hitherto we have been considering the system of the *Inferno* only. That of the *Purgatorio* is much simpler, it being divided into seven districts, in which the souls are severally purified from the sins of Pride, Envy, Wrath,

---

* "Desse", seat.
[1] *Faërie Queene*, IV, X, 50.

Indifference, Avarice, Gluttony, and Lust;[1] the poet thus implying in opposition, and describing in various instances, the seven virtues of Humility, Kindness,* Patience, Zeal, Poverty, Abstinence, and Chastity, as adjuncts of the Christian character, in which it may occasionally fail, while the essential group of the three theological and four cardinal virtues are represented as in direct attendance on the chariot of the Deity; and all the sins of Christians are in the seventeenth canto traced to the deficiency or aberration of Affection.

The system of Spenser is unfinished, and exceedingly complicated, the same vices and virtues occurring under different forms in different places, in order to show their different relations to each other. The peculiar superiority of his system is in its exquisite setting forth of Chastity under the figure of Britomart; not monkish chastity, but that of the purest Love. In completeness of personification no one can approach him; not even in Dante do I remember anything quite so great as the description of the Captain of the Lusts of the Flesh:

> As pale and wan as ashes was his looke;
> His body lean and meagre as a rake;
> And skin all withered like a dryed rooke;
> Thereto as cold and drery as a snake;
> That seemed to tremble evermore, and quake:
> *All in a canvas thin he was bedight,*
> *And girded with a belt of twisted brake:*
> Upon his head he wore an helmet light,
> Made of a dead mans skull.

* Usually called Charity: but this virtue in its full sense is one of the attendant spirits by the Throne; the Kindness here meant is Charity with a special object; or Friendship and Kindness, as opposed to Envy, which has always, in like manner, a special object. Hence the love of Orestes and Pylades is given as an instance of the virtue of Friendship; and the Virgin's, "They have no wine", at Cana, of general kindness and sympathy with others' pleasure.

[1] Vide Cantos x–xxv.

He rides upon a tiger, and in his hand is a bow, bent;

> And many arrows under his right side,
> Headed with flint, and fethers bloody dide.[1]

The horror and the truth of this are beyond everything that I know, out of the pages of Inspiration. Note the heading of the arrows with flint, because sharper and more subtle in the edge than steel, and because steel might consume away with rust, but flint not; and consider in the whole description how the wasting away of body and soul together, and the *coldness* of the heart, which unholy fire has consumed into ashes, and the loss of all power, and the kindling of all terrible impatience, and the implanting of thorny and inextricable griefs, are set forth by the various images, the belt of brake, the tiger steed, and the *light* helmet, girding the head with death.

Stones of Venice, vol. II, ch. viii, pars. 57–62.

---

[1] *Faërie Queene*, II, XI, 21.

SHAKESPEARE'S NAMES

O F Shakespeare's names I will afterwards speak at more length: they are curiously—often barbarously—much by Providence,—but assuredly not without Shakespeare's cunning purpose—mixed out of the various traditions he confusedly adopted, and languages which he imperfectly knew. Three of the clearest in meaning have been already noticed. Desdemona, "δυσδαιμονία", "miserable fortune", is also plain enough. Othello is, I believe, "the careful"; all the calamity of the tragedy arising from the single flaw and error in his magnificently collected strength. Ophelia, "serviceableness", the true lost wife of Hamlet, is marked as having a Greek name by that of her brother, Laertes; and its signification is once exquisitely alluded to in that brother's last word of her, where her gentle preciousness is opposed to the uselessness of the churlish clergy— "A *ministering* angel shall my sister be, when thou liest howling." Hamlet is, I believe, connected in some way with "homely", the entire event of the tragedy turning on betrayal of home duty. Hermione (ἕρμα), "pillar-like" (ἡ εἶδος ἔχε χρυσέης Ἀφροδίτης). Titania (τιτήνη), "the queen"; Benedict and Beatrice, "blessed and blessing"; Valentine and Proteus, enduring (or strong), (valens), and changeful. Iago and Iachimo have evidently the same root—probably the Spanish Iago, Jacob, "the supplanter". Leonatus, and other such names, are interpreted, or played with, in the plays themselves.   *Munera Pulveris*, par. 134.

DR JOHNSON

I HAVE said that had it not been for constant reading of the Bible, I might probably have taken Johnson for my model of English. To a useful extent I have always done so; in these first essays, partly because I could not help it, partly of set, and well-set purpose.

On our foreign journeys, it being of course desirable to keep the luggage as light as possible, my father had judged that four little volumes of Johnson—the *Idler* and the *Rambler*—did, under names wholly appropriate to the circumstances, contain more substantial literary nourishment than could be, from any other author, packed into so portable compass. And accordingly, in spare hours, and on wet days, the turns and returns of reiterated *Rambler* and iterated *Idler* fastened themselves in my ears and mind; nor was it possible for me, till long afterwards, to quit myself of Johnsonian symmetry and balance in sentences intended, either with swordsman's or paviour's blow, to cleave an enemy's crest, or drive down the oaken pile of a principle. I never for an instant compared Johnson to Scott, Pope, Byron, or any of the really great writers whom I loved. But I at once and for ever recognized in him a man entirely sincere, and infallibly wise in the view and estimate he gave of the common questions, business, and ways of the world. I valued his sentences not primarily because they were symmetrical, but because they were just, and clear; it is a method of judgment rarely used by the average public, who ask from an author always, in the first place, arguments in favour of their own opinions, in elegant terms; and are just as ready with their applause for a sentence of Macaulay's, which may have no more sense in it than a blot pinched between double paper, as to reject one of Johnson's, telling against their own prejudice,—though its symmetry be as of thunder answering from two horizons.

I hold it more than happy that, during those continent journeys, in which the vivid excitement of the greater part of the day left me glad to give spare half hours to the study of a thoughtful book, Johnson was the one author accessible to me. No other writer could have secured me, as he did, against all chance of being misled by my own sanguine and metaphysical temperament. He taught me carefully to measure life, and distrust fortune; and he secured me, by his adamantine common-sense, for ever, from being caught in the cobwebs of German metaphysics, or sloughed in the English drainage of them.

I open at this moment, the larger of the volumes of the *Idler* to which I owe so much. After turning over a few leaves, I chance on the closing sentence of No. 65; which transcribing, I may show the reader in sum what it taught me,—in words which, writing this account of myself, I conclusively obey:—

Of these learned men, let those who aspire to the same praise imitate the diligence, and avoid the scrupulosity. Let it always be remembered that life is short, that knowledge is endless, and that many doubts deserve not to be cleared. Let those whom nature and study have qualified to teach mankind, tell us what they have learned while they are yet able to tell it, and trust their reputation only to themselves.

It is impossible for me now to know how far my own honest desire for truth, and compassionate sense of what is instantly helpful to creatures who are every instant perishing, might have brought me, in their own time, to think and judge as Johnson thought and measured,—even had I never learned of him. He at least set me in the straight path from the beginning, and, whatever time I might waste in vain pleasure, or weak effort, he saved me for ever from false thoughts and futile speculations.

Praeterita, vol. I, pars. 251–252.

SIR WALTER SCOTT

I. INFLUENCE

OF the four great English tale-tellers whose dynasties have set or risen within my own memory—Miss Edgeworth, Scott, Dickens, and Thackeray—I find myself greatly at pause in conjecturing, however dimly, what essential good has been effected by them, though they all had the best intentions. Of the essential mischief done by them, there is, unhappily, no doubt whatever. Miss Edgeworth made her morality so impertinent that, since her time, it has only been with fear and trembling that any good novelist has ventured to show the slightest bias in favour of the Ten Commandments. Scott made his romance so ridiculous, that, since his day, one can't help fancying helmets were always pasteboard, and horses were always hobby. Dickens made everybody laugh, or cry, so that they could not go about their business till they had got their faces in wrinkles; and Thackeray settled like a meatfly on whatever one had got for dinner, and made one sick of it.

That, on the other hand, at least Miss Edgeworth and Scott have indeed some inevitable influence for good, I am the more disposed to think, because nobody now will read them. Dickens is said to have made people good-natured. If he did, I wonder what sort of natures they had before! Thackeray is similarly asserted to have chastised and repressed flunkeydom,—which it greatly puzzles me to hear, because, as far as I can see, there isn't a carriage now left in all the Row with anybody sitting inside it: the people who ought to have been in it are, every one, hanging on behind the carriage in front.

What good these writers have done, is therefore, to me, I repeat, extremely doubtful. But what good Scott has in him to do, I find no words full enough to tell. His ideal of honour in men and women is inbred, indisputable; fresh as the air of his mountains; firm as their rocks. His conception of purity in woman is even higher than Dante's; his reverence for the filial relation, as deep as Virgil's; his sympathy universal;—there is no rank or condition of men of which he has not shown the loveliest aspect; his code of moral principle is entirely defined, yet taught with a reserved subtlety like Nature's own, so that none but the most earnest readers perceive the intention: and his opinions on all practical subjects are final; the consummate decisions of accurate and inevitable common sense, tempered by the most graceful kindness.

Fors Clavigera, vol. II, letter XXXI.

II. LIFE

First, note these three great divisions—essentially those of all men's lives, but singularly separate in his,—the days of youth, of labour, and of death.

Youth is properly the forming time—that in which a man makes himself, or is made, what he is for ever to be. Then comes the time of labour, when, having become the best he can be, he does the best he can do. Then the time of death, which, in happy lives, is very short: but always a *time*. The ceasing to breathe is only the end of death.

He was fifty-four on the 15th August, 1825, and spoke his last words—"God bless you all",—on the 21st September, 1832: so ending seven years of death.

His youth, like the youth of all the greatest men, had been long, and rich in peace, and altogether accumulative

and crescent. I count it to end with that pain which you
see he remembers to his dying day, given him by—Lilias
Redgauntlet, in October, 1796. Whereon he sets himself
to his work, which goes on nobly for thirty years lapping
over a little into the death-time[1] (*Woodstock* showing
scarcely a trace of diminution of power).

Count, therefore, thus:—

Youth, twenty-five years	...	1771—1796.
Labour-time, thirty years	...	1796—1826.
Death-time, seven years	...	1825—1832.

Fors Clavigera, vol. II, letter XXXII.

III. CHARACTERISTICS

I THINK it probable that many readers may be surprised
at my calling Scott the great representative of the mind of
the age in literature. Those who can perceive the intense
penetrative depth of Wordsworth, and the exquisite finish
and melodious power of Tennyson, may be offended at
my placing in higher rank that poetry of careless glance,
and reckless rhyme, in which Scott poured out the fancies
of his youth; and those who are familiar with the subtle
analysis of the French novelists, or who have in anywise
submitted themselves to the influence of German philosophy, may be equally indignant at my ascribing a princi-
pality to Scott among the literary men of Europe, in an age
which has produced De Balzac and Goethe. I can only
crave the reader's patience, and his due consideration of
the following reasons for my doing so, together with those
advanced in the farther course of the work.

I believe the first test of a truly great man is his humility.

[1] The actual toil gone through by him is far greater during the
last years than before—in fact it is unceasing, and mortal; but I count
only as the true labour-time that which is healthy and fruitful.

I do not mean, by humility, doubt of his own power, or hesitation in speaking his opinions; but a right understanding of the relation between what *he* can do and say, and the rest of the world's sayings and doings. All great men not only know their business, but usually know that they know it; and are not only right in their main opinions, but they usually know that they are right in them; only, they do not think much of themselves on that account. Arnolfo knows he can build a good dome at Florence; Albert Dürer writes calmly to one who had found fault with his work, "It cannot be better done"; Sir Isaac Newton knows that he has worked out a problem or two that would have puzzled anybody else,—only they do not expect their fellow-men therefore to fall down and worship them; they have a curious under-sense of powerlessness, feeling that the greatness is not *in* them, but *through* them; that they could not do or be anything else than God made them. And they see something divine and God-made in every other man they meet, and are endlessly, foolishly, incredibly merciful.

Now, I find among the men of the present age, as far as I know them, this character in Scott and Turner preeminently; I am not sure if it is not in them alone. I do not find Scott talking about the dignity of literature, nor Turner about the dignity of painting. They do their work, feeling that they cannot well help it; the story must be told, and the effect put down; and if people like it, well and good; and, if not, the world will not be much the worse.

I believe a very different impression of their estimate of themselves and their doings will be received by anyone who reads the conversations of Wordsworth or Goethe. The *slightest* manifestation of jealousy or self-complacency is enough to mark a second-rate character of the intellect; and I fear that, especially in Goethe, such manifestations are neither few nor slight.

Connected with this general humility, is the total absence of affectation in these men,—that is to say, of any assumption of manner or behaviour in their work, in order to attract attention. Not but that they are mannerists both. Scott's verse is strongly mannered, and Turner's oil painting; but the manner of it necessitated by the feelings of the men, entirely natural to both, never exaggerated for the sake of show. I hardly know any other literary or pictorial work of the day which is not in some degree affected. I am afraid Wordsworth was often affected in his simplicity, and De Balzac in his finish. Many fine French writers are affected in their reserve, and full of sage tricks in placing of sentences. It is lucky if in German writers we ever find so much as a sentence without affectation.

Again: another very important, though not infallible, test of greatness is, as we have often said, the appearance of Ease with which the thing is done. It may be that, as with Dante and Leonardo, the finish given to the work effaces the evidence of ease; but where the ease is manifest, as in Scott, Turner, and Tintoret, and the thing done is very noble, it is a strong reason for placing the men above those who confessedly work with great pains. Scott writing his chapter or two before breakfast—not retouching; Turner finishing a whole drawing in a forenoon before he goes out to shoot (providing always the chapter and drawing be good), are instantly to be set above men who confessedly have spent a day over the work, and think the hours well spent if it has been a little mended between sunrise and sunset. Indeed, it is no use for men to think to appear great by working fast, dashing, and scrawling; the thing they do must be good and great, cost what time it may; but if it *be* so, and they have honestly and unaffectedly done it with *no effort*, it is probably a greater and better thing than the result of the hardest efforts of others.

Then, as touching the kind of work done by these two

men, the more I think of it I find this conclusion more impressed upon me,—that the greatest thing a human soul ever does in this world is to *see* something, and tell what it *saw* in a plain way. Hundreds of people can talk for one who can think, but thousands can think for one who can see. To see clearly is poetry, prophecy, and religion,—all in one.

Therefore, finding the world of Literature more or less divided into Thinkers and Seers, I believe we shall find also that the Seers are wholly the greater race of the two. A true Thinker, who has practical purpose in his thinking, and is sincere, as Plato, or Carlyle, or Helps, becomes in some sort a seer, and must be always of infinite use in his generation; but an affected Thinker, who supposes his thinking of any other importance than as it tends to work, is about the vainest kind of person that can be found in the occupied classes. Nay, I believe that metaphysicians and philosophers are, on the whole, the greatest troubles the world has got to deal with; and that while a tyrant or bad man is of some use in teaching people submission or indignation, and a thoroughly idle man is only harmful in setting an idle example, and communicating to other lazy people his own lazy misunderstandings, busy metaphysicians are always entangling *good* and *active* people, and weaving cobwebs among the finest wheels of the world's business; and are as much as possible, by all prudent persons, to be brushed out of their way, like spiders, and the meshed weed that has got into the Cambridgeshire canals, and other such impediments to barges and business. And if we thus clear the metaphysical element out of modern literature, we shall find its bulk amazingly diminished, and the claims of the remaining writers, or of those whom we have thinned by this abstraction of their straw stuffing, much more easily adjusted.*

* Observe, I do not speak thus of metaphysics because I have no pleasure in them. When I speak contemptuously of philology, it may

Again: the mass of sentimental literature, concerned with the analysis and description of emotion, headed by the poetry of Byron, is altogether of lower rank than the literature which merely describes what it saw. The true Seer always feels as intensely as any one else; but he does not much describe his feelings. He tells you whom he met, and what they said; leaves you to make out, from that, what they feel, and what he feels, but goes into little detail. And, generally speaking, pathetic writing and careful explanation of passion are quite easy, compared with this plain recording of what people said or did, or with the right invention of what they are likely to say and do; for this reason, that to invent a story, or admirably and thoroughly tell any part of a story, it is necessary to grasp the entire mind of every personage concerned in it, and know precisely how they would be affected by what happens; which to do requires a colossal intellect: but to describe a separate emotion delicately, it is only needed that one should feel it oneself; and thousands of people are capable of feeling this or that noble emotion, for one who is able to enter into all the feelings of somebody sitting on the other side of the table. Even, therefore, where this sentimental literature is first rate, as in passages of Byron, Tennyson, and Keats, it ought not to be ranked so high as the Creative; and though perfection, even in narrow fields, is perhaps as rare as in the wider, and it may be as long before we have another *In Memoriam* as another *Guy Mannering*, I unhesitatingly receive as a greater manifestation of power the right invention of a few sentences spoken by Pleydell and Mannering across their supper-table, than the most tender and passionate melodies of the self-examining verse.

be answered me, that I am a bad scholar; but I cannot be so answered touching metaphysics, for every one conversant with such subjects may see that I have strong inclination that way, which would, indeed have led me far astray long ago, if I had not learned also some use of my hands, eyes, and feet.

Having, therefore, cast metaphysical writers out of our way, and sentimental writers into the second rank, I do not think Scott's supremacy among those who remain will any more be doubtful; nor would it, perhaps, have been doubtful before, had it not been encumbered by innumerable faults and weaknesses. But it is pre-eminently in these faults and weaknesses that Scott is representative of the mind of his age; and because he is the greatest man born amongst us, and intended for the enduring type of us, all our principal faults must be laid on his shoulders, and he must bear down the dark marks to the latest ages; while the smaller men, who have some special work to do, perhaps not so much belonging to this age as leading out of it to the next, are often kept providentially quit of the encumbrances which they had not strength to sustain, and are much smoother and pleasanter to look at, in their way: only that is a smaller way.

Thus, the most startling fault of the age being its faithlessness, it is necessary that its greatest man should be faithless. Nothing is more notable or sorrowful in Scott's mind than its incapacity of steady belief in anything. He cannot even resolve hardily to believe in a ghost, or a water-spirit; always explains them away in an apologetic manner, not believing, all the while, even in his own explanation. He never can clearly ascertain whether there is anything behind the arras but rats; never draws sword, and thrusts at it for life or death; but goes on looking at it timidly, and saying, "it must be the wind". He is educated a Presbyterian, and remains one, because it is the most sensible thing he can do if he is to live in Edinburgh; but he thinks Romanism more picturesque, and profaneness more gentlemanly; does not see that anything affects human life but love, courage, and destiny; which are, indeed, not matters of faith at all, but of sight. Any gods but those are very misty in outline to him; and when the love is laid ghastly

in poor Charlotte's coffin;[1] and the courage is no more of use,—the pen having fallen from between the fingers; and destiny is sealing the scroll,—the God-light is dim in the tears that fall on it.

He is in all this the epitome of his epoch.

Again: as another notable weakness of the age is its habit of looking back, in a romantic and passionate idleness, to the past ages, not understanding them all the while, nor really desiring to understand them, so Scott gives up nearly the half of his intellectual power to a fond, yet purposeless, dreaming over the past, and spends half his literary labours in endeavours to revive it, not in reality, but on the stage of fiction; endeavours which were the best of the kind that modernism made, but still successful only so far as Scott put, under the old armour, the everlasting human nature which he knew; and totally unsuccessful, so far as concerned the painting of the armour itself, which he knew *not*. The excellence of Scott's work is precisely in proportion to the degree in which it is sketched from present nature. His familiar life is inimitable; his quiet scenes of introductory conversation, as the beginning of *Rob Roy* and *Redgauntlet*, and all his living Scotch characters, mean or noble, from Andrew Fairservice to Jeanie Deans, are simply right, and can never be bettered. But his romance and antiquarianism, his knighthood and monkery, are all false, and he knows them to be false; does not care to make them earnest; enjoys them for their strangeness, but laughs at his own antiquarianism, all through his own third novel, —with exquisite modesty indeed, but with total misunderstanding of the function of an Antiquary. He does not see how anything is to be got out of the past but confusion, old iron on drawing-room chairs, and serious inconvenience to Dr Heavysterne.

---

[1] Scott's wife, died 1826.

Again: more than any age that had preceded it, ours had been ignorant of the meaning of the word "Art". It had not a single fixed principle, and what unfixed principles it worked upon were all wrong. It was necessary that Scott should know nothing of art. He neither cared for painting nor sculpture, and was totally incapable of forming a judgment about them. He had some confused love of Gothic architecture, because it was dark, picturesque, old, and like nature; but could not tell the worst from the best, and built for himself perhaps the most incongruous and ugly pile that gentlemanly modernism ever designed; marking, in the most curious and subtle way, that mingling of reverence with irreverence which is so striking in the age; he reverences Melrose, yet casts one of its piscinas, puts a modern steel grate into it, and makes it his fireplace. Like all pure moderns, he supposes the Gothic barbarous, notwithstanding his love of it; admires, in an equally ignorant way, totally opposite styles; is delighted with the new town of Edinburgh; mistakes its dulness for purity of taste, and actually compares it, in its deathful formality of street, as contrasted with the rudeness of the old town, to Britomart taking off her armour.[1]

Again: as in reverence and irreverence, so in levity and melancholy, we saw that the spirit of the age was strangely interwoven. Therefore, also, it is necessary that Scott should be light, careless, unearnest, and yet eminently sorrowful. Throughout all his work there is no evidence of any purpose but to while away the hour. His life had no other object than the pleasure of the instant, and the establishing of a family name. All his thoughts were, in their outcome and end, less than nothing, and vanity. And yet, of all poetry that I know, none is so sorrowful as Scott's. Other great masters are pathetic in a resolute and predetermined way, when they choose; but, in their own minds, are evi-

[1] *Marmion*, Introd. to Canto v.

dently stern, or hopeful, or serene; never really melancholy. Even Byron is rather sulky and desperate than melancholy; Keats is sad because he is sickly; Shelley because he is impious; but Scott is inherently and consistently sad. Around all his power, and brightness, and enjoyment of eye and heart, the far-away Æolian knell is for ever sounding; there is not one of those loving or laughing glances of his but it is brighter for the film of tears; his mind is like one of his own hill rivers,—it is white, and flashes in the sun fairly, careless, as it seems, and hasty in its going, but

> Far beneath, where slow they creep
> From pool to eddy, dark and deep,
> Where alders moist, and willows weep,
>   You hear her streams repine.[1]

Life begins to pass from him very early; and while Homer sings cheerfully in his blindness, and Dante retains his courage, and rejoices in hope of Paradise, through all his exile, Scott, yet hardly past his youth, lies pensive in the sweet sunshine and among the harvest of his native hills.

> Blackford, on whose uncultured breast,
>   Among the broom, and thorn, and whin,
> A truant boy, I sought the nest,
> Or listed as I lay at rest,
>   While rose on breezes thin
> The murmur of the city crowd,
> And, from his steeple jangling loud,
>   St Giles's mingling din!
> Now, from the summit to the plain,
> Waves all the hill with yellow grain;
>   And on the landscape as I look,
> Nought do I see unchanged remain,
>   Save the rude cliffs and chiming brook;
> To me they make a heavy moan
> Of early friendships past and gone.[2]

Modern Painters, vol. III, ch. xvi, pars. 23–24.

[1] *Marmion*, IV, 10.   [2] *Marmion*, IV, 24.

IV. SCOTT AND NATURE

In consequence of his unselfishness and humility, Scott's enjoyment of nature is incomparably greater than that of any other poet I know. All the rest carry their cares to her, and begin maundering in her ears about their own affairs. Tennyson goes out on a furzy common, and sees it is calm autumn sunshine, but it gives him no pleasure. He only remembers that it is

> Dead calm in that noble breast
> Which heaves but with the heaving deep.[1]

He sees a thundercloud in the evening, and *would* have "doted and pored" on it, but cannot, for fear it should bring the ship bad weather. Keats drinks the beauty of nature violently; but has no more real sympathy with her than he has with a bottle of claret. His palate is fine; but he "bursts joy's grape against it",[2] gets nothing but misery, and a bitter taste of dregs, out of his desperate draught.

Byron and Shelley are nearly the same, only with less truth of perception, and even more troublesome selfishness. Wordsworth is more like Scott, and understands how to be happy, but yet cannot altogether rid himself of the sense that he is a philosopher, and ought always to be saying something wise. He has also a vague notion that Nature would not be able to get on well without Wordsworth; and finds a considerable part of his pleasure in looking at himself as well as at her. But with Scott the love is entirely humble and unselfish. "I, Scott, am nothing, and less than nothing; but these crags, and heaths, and clouds, how great they are, how lovely, how for ever to be beloved, only for their own silent, thoughtless sake!"

Modern Painters, vol. III, ch. xvi, par. 38.

[1] *In Memoriam*, xi.   [2] *Ode to Melancholy*.

V. LOVE IN NOVELS

It is to say little for the types of youth and maid which alone Scott felt it a joy to imagine, or thought it honourable to portray, that they act and feel in a sphere where they are never for an instant liable to any of the weaknesses which disturb the calm, or shake the resolution, of chastity and courage in a modern novel. Scott lived in a country and time, when, from highest to lowest, but chiefly in that dignified and nobly severe middle class to which he himself belonged, a habit of serene and stainless thought was as natural to the people as their mountain air. Women like Rose Bradwardine and Ailie Dinmont were the grace and guard of almost every household (God be praised that the race of them is not yet extinct, for all that Mall or Boulevard can do), and it has perhaps escaped the notice of even attentive readers that the comparatively uninteresting character of Sir Walter's heroes had always been studied among a class of youths who were simply incapable of doing anything seriously wrong; and could only be embarrassed by the consequences of their levity or imprudence.

But there is another difference in the woof of a Waverley novel from the cobweb of a modern one, which depends on Scott's larger view of human life. Marriage is by no means, in his conception of man and woman, the most important business of their existence; nor love the only reward to be proposed to their virtue or exertion. It is not in his reading of the laws of Providence a necessity that virtue should, either by love or any other external blessing, be rewarded at all; and marriage is in all cases thought of as a constituent of the happiness of life, but not as its only interest, still less its only aim. And upon analyzing with some care the motives of his principal stories, we shall often find that

the love in them is merely a light by which the sterner features of character are to be irradiated, and that the marriage of the hero is as subordinate to the main bent of the story as Henry the Fifth's courtship of Katherine is to the battle of Agincourt. Nay, the fortunes of the person who is nominally the subject of the tale are often little more than a background on which grander figures are to be drawn, and deeper fates forthshadowed. The judgments between the faith and chivalry of Scotland at Drumclog and Bothwell Bridge owe little of their interest in the mind of a sensible reader to the fact that the captain of the Popinjay is carried a prisoner to one battle, and returns a prisoner from the other: and Scott himself, while he watches the white sail that bears Queen Mary for the last time from her native land, very nearly forgets to finish his novel, or to tell us—and with small sense of any consolation to be had out of that minor circumstance,—that "Roland and Catherine were united, spite of their differing faiths".

Neither let it be thought for an instant that the slight, and sometimes scornful, glance with which Scott passes over scenes which a novelist of our own day would have analyzed with the airs of a philosopher, and painted with the curiosity of a gossip, indicates any absence in his heart of sympathy with the great and sacred elements of personal happiness. An era like ours, which has with diligence and ostentation swept its heart clear of all the passions once known as loyalty, patriotism, and piety, necessarily magnifies the apparent force of the one remaining sentiment which sighs through the barren chambers, or clings inextricably round the chasms of ruin; nor can it but regard with awe the unconquerable spirit which still tempts or betrays the sagacities of selfishness into error or frenzy which is believed to be love.

That Scott was never himself, in the sense of the phrase as employed by lovers of the Parisian school, "ivre d'amour",

may be admitted without prejudice to his sensibility, and
that he never knew "l'amor che move'l sol el' altre stelle",[1]
was the chief, though unrecognized, calamity of his deeply
chequered life. But the reader of honour and feeling will
not therefore suppose that the love which Miss Vernon
sacrifices, stooping for an instant from her horse, is of less
noble stamp, or less enduring faith, than that which troubles
and degrades the whole existence of Consuelo; or that the
affection of Jeanie Deans for the companion of her childhood, drawn like a field of soft blue heaven beyond the
cloudy wrack of her sorrow, is less fully in possession of her
soul than the hesitating and self-reproachful impulse under
which a modern heroine forgets herself in a boat,[2] or com-
promises herself in the cool of the evening.

Fiction, Fair and Foul, pars. 20–22.

VI. CHARACTERS

THERE is another, and a still more hidden method in
Scott's designing of story, in which, taking extreme pains,
he counts on much sympathy from the reader, and can
assuredly find none in a modern student. The moral purpose of the whole, which he asserted in the preface to the
first edition of *Waverley*, was involved always with the
minutest study of the effects of true and false religion on the
conduct;—which subject being always touched with his
utmost lightness of hand and stealthiness of art, and founded
on a knowledge of the Scotch character and the human
heart, such as no other living man possessed, his purpose
often escapes first observation as completely as the inner
feelings of living people do; and I am myself amazed, as
I take any single piece of his work up for examination, to

---

[1] *Paradiso*, last line.   [2] G. Eliot: *The Mill on the Floss*.

find how many of its points I had before missed or disregarded.

The groups of personages whose conduct in the Scott romance is definitely affected by religious conviction may be arranged broadly, as those of the actual world, under these following heads:—

(1) The lowest group consists of persons who, believing in the general truths of Evangelical religion, accommodate them to their passions, and are capable, by gradual increase in depravity, of any crime or violence. I am not going to include these in our present study. Trumbull, Trusty Tomkyns, Burley, are three of the principal types.

(2) The next rank above these consists of men who believe firmly and truly enough to be restrained from any conduct which they clearly recognize as criminal, but whose natural selfishness renders them incapable of understanding the morality of the Bible above a certain point; and whose imperfect powers of thought leave them liable in many directions to the warping of self-interest or of small temptations.

Fairservice. Blattergowl. Kettledrummle. Gifted Gilfillan.

(3) The third order consists of men naturally just and honest, but with little sympathy and much pride, in whom their religion, while in the depth of it supporting their best virtues, brings out on the surface all their worst faults, and makes them censorious, tiresome, and often fearfully mischievous.

Richie Moniplies. Davie Deans. Mause Headrigg.

(4) The enthusiastic type, leading to missionary effort, often to martyrdom.

Warden, in *Monastery*. Colonel Gardiner. Ephraim Macbriar. Joshua Geddes.

(5) Highest type, fulfilling daily duty; always gentle, entirely firm, the comfort and strength of all around them;

merciful to every human fault, and submissive without
anger to every human oppression.

Rachel Geddes. Jeanie Deans. Bessie Maclure, in *Old
Mortality*—the Queen of all.

Fiction, Fair and Foul, pars. 112–113.

VII. HISTORY

IT is strange to me, even now, on reflection—to find
how great the influence of this double ocean coast and
Cheviot mountain border was upon Scott's imagination;
and how salutary they were in withdrawing him from the
morbid German fancies which proved so fatal to Carlyle;
but there was this grand original difference between the
two, that, with Scott, his story-telling and singing were all
in the joyful admiration of that past with which he could
re-people the scenery he gave the working part of his day
to traverse, and all the sensibility of his soul to love; while
Carlyle's mind, fixed anxiously on the future, and besides
embarrassed by the practical pinching, as well as the un-
confessed shame, of poverty, saw and felt from his earliest
childhood nothing but the faultfulness and gloom of the
Present.

It has been impossible, hitherto, to make the modern
reader understand the vastness of Scott's true historical
knowledge, underneath its romantic colouring, nor the
concentration of it in the production of his eternally great
poems and romances. English ignorance of the Scottish
dialect is at present nearly total; nor can it be without very
earnest effort, that the melody of Scott's verse, or the
meaning of his dialogue, can ever again be estimated. He
must now be read with the care which we give to Chaucer;
but with the greater reward, that what is only a dream in

Chaucer, becomes to us, understood from Scott, a consummate historical morality and truth.

The first two of his great poems *The Lay of the Last Minstrel* and *Marmion*, are the re-animation of the Border legends, closing with the truest and grandest battle-piece that, so far as I know, exists in the whole compass of literature;—the absolutely fairest in justice to both contending nations, the absolutely most beautiful in its conceptions of both. And that the palm in that conception remains with the Scotch, through the sorrow of their defeat, is no more than accurate justice to the national character, which rose from the fraternal branches of the Douglas of Tantallon and the Douglas of Dunkeld. But,—between Tantallon and Dunkeld,—what moor or mountain is there over which the purple cloud of Scott's imagination has not wrapt its light, in those two great poems?—followed by the entirely heroic enchantment of *The Lady of the Lake*, dwelling on the highland virtue which gives the strength of clanship, and the Lowland honour of knighthood, founded on the Catholic religion. Then came the series of novels, in which, as I have stated elsewhere, those which dealt with the history of other nations, such as *Ivanhoe*, *Kenilworth*, *Woodstock*, *Quentin Durward*, *Peveril of the Peak*, *The Betrothed*, and *The Crusaders*, however attractive to the general world, were continually weak in fancy, and false in prejudice; but the literally Scotch novels, *Waverley*, *Guy Mannering*, *The Antiquary*, *Old Mortality*, *The Heart of Midlothian*, *The Abbot*, *Redgauntlet*, and *The Fortunes of Nigel* are, whatever the modern world may think of them, as faultless, throughout, as human work can be: and eternal examples of the ineffable art which is taught by the loveliest nature to her truest children.

Praeterita, vol. III, pars. 71–72.

BLAKE

You must have nearly all heard of, many must have seen, the singular paintings; some also may have read the poems, of William Blake. The impression that his drawings once made is fast, and justly, fading away, though they are not without noble merit. But his poems have much more than merit; they are written with absolute sincerity, with infinite tenderness, and, though in the manner of them diseased and wild, are in verity the words of a great and wise mind, disturbed, but not deceived, by its sickness; nay, partly exalted by it, and sometimes giving forth in fiery aphorism some of the most precious words of existing literature. One of these passages I will ask you to remember; it will often be serviceable to you—

> Doth the Eagle know what is in the pit,
> Or wilt thou go ask the Mole?[1]

It would be impossible to express to you in briefer terms the great truth that there is a different kind of knowledge good for every different creature, and that the glory of the higher creatures, is in ignorance of what is known to the lower.   *Eagle's Nest*, par. 21.

---

[1] Lines prefixed to *The Book of Thel*.

WORDSWORTH

WORDSWORTH's rank and scale among poets were determined by himself, in a single exclamation:

> What was the great Parnassus' self to thee,
> Mount Skiddaw?[1]

Answer his question faithfully, and you have the relation between the great masters of the Muse's teaching and the pleasant fingerer of his pastoral flute among the reeds of Rydal.

Wordsworth is simply a Westmoreland peasant, with considerably less shrewdness than most border Englishmen or Scotsmen inherit; and no sense of humour: but gifted (in this singularly) with vivid sense of natural beauty, and a pretty turn for reflections, not always acute, but, as far as they reach, medicinal to the fever of the restless and corrupted life around him. Water to parched lips may be better than Samian wine, but do not let us therefore confuse the qualities of wine and water. I much doubt there being many inglorious Miltons in our country churchyards; but I am very sure there are many Wordsworths resting there, who were inferior to the renowned one only in caring less to hear themselves talk.

With an honest and kindly heart, a stimulating egoism, a wholesome contentment in modest circumstances, and such sufficient ease, in that accepted state, as permitted the passing of a good deal of time in wishing that daisies could see the beauty of their own shadows,[2] and other such profitable mental exercises, Wordsworth has left us a series of studies of the graceful and happy shepherd life of our lake country, which to me personally, for one, are entirely

[1] "Pelion and Ossa flourish...."
[2] Vide Wordsworth's "So fair, so sweet...."

sweet and precious; but they are only so as the mirror of an existent reality in many ways more beautiful than its picture.

But the other day I went for an afternoon's rest into the cottage of one of our country people of old statesman class; cottage lying nearly midway between two village churches, but more conveniently for downhill walk towards one than the other. I found, as the good housewife made tea for me, that nevertheless she went up the hill to church. "Why do not you go to the nearer church?" I asked. "Don't you like the clergyman?" "Oh no, Sir", she answered, "it isn't that; but you know I couldn't leave my mother." "Your mother! she is buried at H— then?" "Yes, sir; and you know I couldn't go to church anywhere else."

That feelings such as these existed among the peasants, not of Cumberland only, but of all the tender earth that gives forth her fruit for the living, and receives her dead to peace, might perhaps have been, to our great and endless comfort, discovered before now, if Wordsworth had been content to tell us what he knew of his own villages and people, not as the leader of a new and only correct school of poetry, but simply as a country gentleman of sense and feeling, fond of primroses, kind to the parish children, and reverent of the spade with which Wilkinson had tilled his lands: and I am by no means sure that his influence on the stronger minds of his time was anywise hastened or extended by the spirit of tunefulness under whose guidance he discovered that heaven rhymed to seven, and Foy to boy.

Tuneful nevertheless at heart, and of the heavenly choir, I gladly and frankly acknowledge him; and our English literature enriched with a new and a singular virtue in the aerial purity and healthful rightness of his quiet song;— but *aerial* only,—not ethereal; and lowly in its privacy of light.

A measured mind, and calm; innocent, unrepentant; helpful to sinless creatures and scatheless, such of the flock as do not stray. Hopeful at least, if not faithful: content with intimations of immortality such as may be in skipping of lambs, and laughter of children—incurious to see in the hands the print of the Nails.

A gracious and constant mind; as the herbage of its native hills, fragrant and pure;—yet, to the sweep and the shadow, the stress and distress, of the greater souls of men, as the tufted thyme to the laurel wilderness of Tempe,— as the gleaming euphrasy to the dark branches of Dodona.

Fiction, Fair and Foul, pars. 50-52.

COLERIDGE

I LOVE Coleridge, and I believe I know nearly every line of both the *Ancient Mariner* and *Christabel*—not to speak of the *Three Graves* and the *Hymn in Chamouni*, and the *Dejection*, and I am very willing to allow that he has more imagination than Wordsworth, and more of the real poet. But after all Coleridge is nothing more than an intellectual opium-eater—a man of many crude though lovely thoughts—of confused though brilliant imagination, liable to much error—error even of the heart, very sensual in many of his ideas of pleasure— indolent to a degree, and evidently and always thinking without discipline; letting the fine brains which God gave him work themselves irregularly and without end or object—and carry him whither they will. Wordsworth has a grand, consistent, perfectly disciplined, all grasping intellect —for which nothing is too small, nothing too great, arranging everything in due relations, divinely pure in its

conceptions of pleasure, majestic in the equanimity of its benevolence—intense as white fire with chastised feeling. Coleridge may be the greater poet, but surely it admits of no question which is the greater *man*. Wordsworth often appears to want *energy* because he has so much *judgment*, and because he never enunciates any truth but with full views of many points which diminish the extent of its application, while Coleridge and others say more boldly what they see more partially. I believe Coleridge has very little moral influence on the world; his writings are those of a benevolent man in a fever. Wordsworth may be trusted as a guide in everything, he feels nothing but what we ought all to feel—what every mind in pure moral health *must* feel, he says nothing but what we all ought to believe— what all strong intellects *must* believe. He has written some things trifling, some verses which might be omitted—but none to be *regretted*.   Letter to Rev. W. L. Brown, 1843.

BYRON

NEITHER the force and precision, nor the rhythm, of Byron's language, were at all the central reasons for my taking him for master. Knowing the Song of Moses and the Sermon on the Mount by heart, and half the Apocalypse besides, I was in no need of tutorship either in the majesty or simplicity of English words; and for their logical arrangement, I had Byron's own master, Pope, since I could lisp. But the thing wholly new and precious to me in Byron was his measured and living *truth*—measured, as compared with Homer; and living, as compared with everybody else. My own inexorable measuring wand,—not enchanter's, but cloth-worker's and builder's,—reduced to mere in-

credibility all the statements of the poets usually called sublime. It was of no use for Homer to tell me that Pelion was put on the top of Ossa.[1] I knew perfectly well it wouldn't go on the top of Ossa. Of no use for Pope to tell me that trees where his mistress looked would crowd into a shade,[2] because I was satisfied that they would do nothing of the sort. Nay, the whole world, as it was described to me either by poetry or theology, was every hour becoming more and more shadowy and impossible. I rejoiced in all stories of Pallas and Venus, of Achilles and Aeneas, of Elijah and St John: but, without doubting in my heart that there were real spirits of wisdom and beauty, nor that there had been invincible heroes and inspired prophets, I felt already, with fatal and increasing sadness, that there was no clear utterance about any of them—that there were for *me* neither Goddess guides nor prophetic teachers; and that the poetical histories, whether of this world or the next, were to me as the words of Peter to the shut up disciples——"as idle tales; and they believed them not".[3]

But here at last I had found a man who spoke only of what he had seen, and known; and spoke without exaggeration, without mystery, without enmity, and without mercy. "That *is* so;—make what you will of it!" Shakespeare said the Alps voided their rheum on the valleys, which indeed is precisely true,—but it was told in a mythic manner, and with an unpleasant British bias to the nasty. But Byron, saying that "the glacier's cold and restless mass moves onward day by day",[4] said plainly what he saw and knew,—no more. So also, *Arabian Nights* had told me of thieves who lived in enchanted caves, and beauties who fought with genii in the air; but Byron told me of thieves with whom he had ridden on their own hills, and of the fair

---

[1] *Odyssey*, XI, 315.   [2] *Pastorals*, II, 74.
[3] Vide *Luke*, xxiv, 11.   [4] *Manfred*, I, I.

Persians or Greeks who lived and died under the very sun
that rose over my visible Norwood hills.

And in this narrow, but sure, truth, to Byron, as already
to me, it appeared that Love was a transient thing, and
Death a dreadful one. He did not attempt to console me
for Jessie's death, by saying she was happier in Heaven;
or for Charles's, by saying it was a Providential dispensation
to me on Earth. He did not tell me that war was a just price
for the glory of captains, or that the National command of
murder diminished its guilt. Of all things within range of
human thought he felt the facts, and discerned the natures
with accurate justice.

But even all this he might have done, and yet been no
master of mine, had not he sympathized with me in
reverent love of beauty, and indignant recoil from ugliness.
The witch of the Staubbach in her rainbow was a greatly
more pleasant vision than Shakespeare's, like a rat without
a tail, or Burns's, in her cutty sark.[1] The sea-king Conrad
had an immediate advantage with me over Coleridge's long,
lank, brown, and ancient, mariner; and whatever Pope
might have gracefully said, or honestly felt of Windsor
woods and streams, was mere tinkling cymbal to me, compared with Byron's love of Lachin-y-Gair.

I must pause here, in tracing the sources of his influence
over me, lest the reader should mistake the analysis which
I am now able to give them, for a description of the feelings
possible to me at fifteen. Most of these, however, were
assuredly within the knot of my unfolding mind—as the
saffron of the crocus yet beneath the earth; and Byron—
though he could not teach me to love mountains or sea
more than I did in childhood, first animated them for me
with the sense of real human nobleness and grief. He
taught me the meaning of Chillon and of Meillerie, and
bade me seek first in Venice—the ruined homes of Foscari
and Falier.

[1] *Manfred*, II, 2; *Macbeth*, I, 3; *Tam o' Shanter*.

And observe, the force with which he struck depended again on there being unquestionable reality of person in his stories, as of principle in his thoughts. Romance, enough and to spare, I had learnt from Scott—but his Lady of the Lake was as openly fictitious as his White Maid of Avenel: while Rogers was a mere dilettante, who felt no difference between landing "where Tell leaped ashore", or standing where "St Preux has stood". Even Shakespeare's Venice was visionary; and Portia as impossible as Miranda. But Byron told me of, and reanimated for me, the real people whose feet had worn the marble I trod on.

One word only, though it trenches on a future subject, I must permit myself about his rhythm. Its natural flow in almost prosaic simplicity and tranquillity interested me extremely, in opposition alike to the symmetrical clauses of Pope's logical metre, and to the balanced strophes of classic and Hebrew verse. But though I followed his manner instantly in what verses I wrote for my own amusement, my respect for the structural, as opposed to fluent, force of the classic measures, supported as it was partly by Byron's contempt for his own work, and, partly by my own architect's instinct for "the principle of the pyramid", made me long endeavour, in forming my prose style, to keep the cadences of Pope and Johnson for all serious statement.

Praeterita, vol. I, pars. 172–175.

If now, with the echo of these perfect verses in your mind,[1] you turn to Byron, and glance over, or recall to memory, enough of him to give means of exact comparison, you will, or should, recognize these following kinds of mischief in him. First, if any one offends him—as for instance Mr Southey, or Lord Elgin[2]—"his manners have not that repose that marks the caste",[3] etc. *This* defect in his Lord-

[1] Herrick: *Dirge for Jephthah's Daughter.*
[2] Vide: *Don Juan*, I, 222; X, 13; and *Curse of Minerva.*
[3] Tennyson: *Lady Clara Vere de Vere.*

ship's style, being myself scrupulously and even painfully reserved in the use of vituperative language, I need not say how deeply I deplore.

Secondly. In the best and most violet-bedded bits of his work there is yet, as compared with Elizabethan and earlier verse, a strange taint; and indefinable—evening flavour of Covent Garden, as it were;—not to say, escape of gas in the Strand. That is simply what it proclaims itself—London air. If he had lived all his life in Greenhead Ghyll, things would of course have been different. But it was his fate to come to town—modern town—like Michael's son; and modern London (and Venice) are answerable for the state of their drains, not Byron.

Thirdly. His melancholy is without any relief whatsoever; his jest sadder than his earnest; while, in Elizabethan work, all lament is full of hope, and all pain of balsam.

Of this evil he has himself told you the cause in a single line, prophetic of all things since and now. "Where *he* gazed, a gloom pervaded space." [1]

So that, for instance, while Mr Wordsworth, on a visit to town, being an exemplary early riser, could walk, felicitous, on Westminster Bridge, remarking how the city now did like a garment wear the beauty of the morning; Byron, rising somewhat later, contemplated only the garment which the beauty of the morning had by that time received for wear from the city: and again, while Mr Wordsworth, in irrepressible religious rapture, calls God to witness that the houses seem asleep, Byron, lame demon as he was, flying smoke-drifted, unroofs the houses at a glance, and sees what the mighty cockney heart of them contains in the still lying of it, and will stir up to purpose in the waking business of it,

> The sordor of civilization, mixed
> With all the savage which Man's fall hath fixed. [2]

[1] *Vision of Judgment*, 24.   [2] *Island*, II, 4.

Fourthly, with this steadiness of bitter melancholy, there is joined a sense of the material beauty, both of inanimate nature, the lower animals, and human beings, which in the iridescence, colour-depth, and morbid (I use the word deliberately) mystery and softness of it,—with other qualities indescribable by any single words, and only to be analysed by extreme care,—is found, to the full, only in five men that I know of in modern times: namely, Rousseau, Shelley, Byron, Turner, and myself,—differing totally and throughout the entire group of us, from the delight in clear-struck beauty of Angelico and the Trecentisti; and separated, much more singularly, from the cheerful joys of Chaucer, Shakespeare, and Scott, by its unaccountable affection for "Rokkes blak" [1] and other forms of terror and power, such as those of the ice-oceans, which to Shakespeare were only Alpine rheum; [2] and the Via Malas and Diabolic Bridges which Dante would have condemned none but lost souls to climb, or cross;—all this love of impending mountains, coiled thunder-clouds, and dangerous sea, being joined in us with a sulky, almost ferine, love of retreat in valleys of Charmettes, gulphs of Spezzia, ravines of Olympus, low lodgings in Chelsea, and close brushwood at Coniston.

And, lastly, also in the whole group of us, glows volcanic instinct of Astraean justice returning not to, but up out of, the earth, which will not at all suffer us to rest any more in Pope's serene "whatever is, is right" [3]; but holds, on the contrary, profound conviction that about ninety-nine hundredths of whatever at present is, is wrong: conviction making four of us, according to our several manners, leaders of revolution for the poor, and declarers of political doctrine monstrous to the ears of mercenary mankind; and driving the fifth, less sanguine, into mere painted-melody of lament over the fallacy of Hope and the implacableness of Fate.

---

[1] Chaucer: *Frankeleines Tale*.   [2] *Henry V*, III, 5.
[3] *Essay on Man*, Ep. I, last line.

In Byron the indignation, the sorrow, and the effort are joined to the death: and they are the parts of his nature (as of mine also in its feebler terms), which the selfishly comfortable public have, literally, no conception of whatever; and from which the piously sentimental public, offering up daily the pure oblation of divine tranquillity, shrink with anathema not unembittered by alarm.

Fiction, Fair and Foul, pars. 72–74.

DICKENS

Do you think you could tolerantly receive the opinion of a moderately and popularly wise man—such an one as Charles Dickens, for example? Have you ever considered seriously what *his* opinion was, about "Dependants" and "Menials"? He did not perhaps quite know what it was himself;—it needs wisdom of stronger make than his to be sure of what it *does* think. He would talk, in his moral passages, about Independence, and Self-dependence, and making one's way in the world, just like any hack of the *Eatanswill Independent*. But which of the people of his imagination, of his own true children, did he love and honour most? Who are your favourites in his books—as they have been his? Menials, it strikes me, many of them. Sam, Mark, Kit, Peggotty, Mary-my-dear,—even the poor little Marchioness! I don't think Dickens intended you to look upon any of them disrespectfully. Or going one grade higher in his society, Tom Pinch, Newman Noggs, Tim Linkinwater, Oliver Twist—how independent, all of them! Very nearly menial, in soul, if they chance on a good master; none of them brilliant in fortune, nor vigorous in action. Is not the entire testimony of Dickens, traced in its true force, that

no position is so *good* for men and women, none so likely
to bring out their best human character, as that of a de-
pendant, or menial? And yet with your supreme modern
logic, instead of enthusiastically concluding from his works
"let us all be servants", one would think the notion he put
in your heads was quite the other, "let us all be masters",
and that you understood his ideal of heroic English
character to be given in Mr Pecksniff or Sir Mulberry
Hawk!   *Fors Clavigera*, vol. II, letter XXVIII.

GEORGE ELIOT

ALL healthy and helpful literature sets simple bars between right and wrong; assumes the possibility, in men and
women, of having healthy minds in healthy bodies, and
loses no time in the diagnosis of fever or dyspepsia in either;
least of all in the particular kind of fever which signifies
the ungoverned excess of any appetite or passion. The
"dulness" which many modern readers inevitably feel, and
some modern blockheads think it creditable to allege, in
Scott, consists not a little in his absolute purity from every
loathsome element or excitement of the lower passions; so
that people who live habitually in Satyric or hircine conditions of thought find him as insipid as they would a picture
of Angelico's. The accurate and trenchant separation
between him and the common railroad-station novelist is
that, in his total method of conception, only lofty character is
worth describing at all; and it becomes interesting, not by
its faults, but by the difficulties and accidents of the fortune
through which it passes, while, in the railway novel,
interest is obtained with the vulgar reader for the vilest
character, because the author describes carefully to his

recognition the blotches, burrs and pimples in which the paltry nature resembles his own. *The Mill on the Floss* is perhaps the most striking instance extant of this study of cutaneous disease. There is not a single person in the book of the smallest importance to anybody in the world but themselves, or whose qualities deserved so much as a line of printer's type in their description. There is no girl alive, fairly clever, half educated, and unluckily related, whose life has not at least as much in it as Maggie's, to be described and to be pitied. Tom is a clumsy and cruel lout, with the making of better things in him (and the same may be said of nearly every Englishman at present smoking and elbowing his way through the ugly world his blunders have contributed to the making of); while the rest of the characters are simply the sweepings out of a Pentonville omnibus.

Fiction, Fair and Foul, par. 108.

DEFINITIONS & APHORISMS

A POET on canvas is exactly the same species of creature as a poet in song. (*Pre-Raphaelitism.*)

Poetry is the suggestion, by the imagination, of noble grounds for the noble emotions. (*M.P.* III.)

The object in all art is not to inform but to suggest, not to add to the knowledge but to kindle the imagination. He is the best poet who can by the fewest words touch the greatest number of secret chords of thought in his reader's own mind, and set them to work in their own way. (*Letters*, 1840–1850.)

There is no other definition of the beautiful, nor of any subject of delight to the aesthetic faculty, than that it is what one noble spirit has created, seen and felt by another of similar or equal nobility. (*Aratra Pentelici.*)

Sublimity is only another word for the effect of greatness on the feelings; greatness, whether of matter, space, power, virtue, or beauty. (*M.P.* I.)

Fine Art is that in which the hand, head, and heart of man go together. (*Two Paths.*)

Romance does not consist in the manner of representing or relating things, but in the kind of passions appealed to by the things related. The three romantic passions are those by which you are told, in Wordsworth's aphoristic line, that the soul of life is fed: "We live by Admiration, Hope, and Love". (*Art of England.*)

An artist is a person who has submitted to a law which it has been difficult to obey, that he may bestow a delight which it is gracious to bestow. (*Fors Clavigera*, III.)

Perfect taste is the faculty of receiving the greatest possible pleasure from those material sources which are attractive to our moral nature in its purity and perfection. (*M.P.* I.)

Good art always consists of two things. First, the observation of fact, secondly, the manifesting of human design and authority in the way that fact is told. (*Two Paths.*)

Literature does its duty, not in wasting our hours in political discussion, or in idle fiction; but in raising our fancy to the height of what may be noble, honest, and felicitous in actual life;—in giving us, though we may ourselves be poor and unknown, the companionship of the wisest fellow-spirits of every age and country,—and in aiding the communication of clear thoughts and faithful purposes, among distant nations. (*Eagle's Nest.*)

The value of books consists: First, in their power of preserving and communicating the knowledge of facts. Secondly, in their power of exciting vital or noble emotion and intellectual action. They have also the corresponding negative powers of disguising and effacing the memory of facts, and killing the noble emotions, or exciting base ones. (*Munera Pulveris.*)

Great nations write their autobiographies in three manuscripts:—the book of their deeds, the book of their words, and the book of their art. (*St Mark's Rest.*)

The entire purpose of a great thinker may be difficult to fathom, and we may be over and again more or less mistaken in guessing at his meaning; but the real, profound, nay, quite bottomless, and unredeemable mistake is the fool's thought—that he had no meaning. (*Two Paths.*)

There is only one way of seeing things, and that is, seeing the whole of them, without any choice, or more in-

tense perception of one point than another, owing to our special idiosyncrasies. (*Two Paths.*)

I have had but one steady aim in all that I have ever tried to teach, namely—to declare that whatever was great in human art was the expression of man's delight in God's work. (*Two Paths.*)

No great intellectual thing was ever done by great effort; a great thing can only be done by a great man, and he does it without effort. (*Pre-Raphaelitism.*)

Greatness can only be rightly estimated when minuteness is justly reverenced. (*M.P. v.*)

It is better that his work should be bold, than faultless; and better that it should be delightful, than discreet. (*Cambridge Address,* 1858.)

No great poet ever tells you that he saw anything finer than anyone ever saw before. Great poets try to describe what all men see, and to express what all men feel; if they cannot describe it they let it alone; and what they say, say "boldly" always, without advising their readers of that fact. (*Art of England.*)

In good composition every idea is presented in just that order, and with just that force, which will perfectly connect it with all the other thoughts in the work, and will illustrate the others as well as receive illustration from them; so that the entire chain of thoughts offered to the beholder's mind shall be received by him with as much delight and with as little effort as is possible. (*Two Paths.*)

What is the main lesson which, as far as we seek any in our classical reading, we gather for our youth from ancient history? Surely this—that simplicity of life, of language, of manners, gives strength to a nation; and that luxurious-

ness of life, subtlety of language, and smoothness of manners bring weakness and destruction on a nation. (*Cambridge Address*, 1858.)

A certain amount of art intellect is born annually in every nation, greater or less according to the nature and cultivation of the nation, or race of men; but a perfectly fixed quantity annually, not increasable by one grain. You may lose it, or you may gather it; you may let it lie loose in the ravine, and buried in the sands, or you may make kings' thrones of it, and overlay temple gates with it as you choose; but the best you can do with it is always merely sifting, melting, hammering, purifying,—never creating. (*A Joy for Ever.*)

The greatest men of any age, those who become its leaders when there is a great march to be begun, are indeed separated from the average intellects of their day by a distance which is immeasurable in any ordinary terms of wonder. (*Mornings in Florence.*)

There are many attractive qualities inconsistent with rightness—do not let us teach them,—let us be content to waive them. There are attractive qualities in Burns, and attractive qualities in Dickens, which neither of these writers would have possessed if the one had been educated, and the other had been studying higher nature than that of cockney London. (*Two Paths.*)

The dignity of a man depends wholly upon this harmony. If his task is above him he will be undignified in failure; if he is above it, he will be undignified in success. His own composure and nobleness must be according to the composure of his thought to his toil. (*Cestus of Aglaia.*)

Throughout the world, of the two abstract things, liberty and restraint, restraint is always the more honourable. (*Two Paths.*)

INDEXES

INDEX OF PROPER NAMES
AND CLASSICAL REFERENCES

In this Index the dark figures refer to the pages of this book.

ARISTOPHANES: Athenian writer of comedy (B.C. 448–288). 173

ARNOLFO (di Lapo): Florentine architect and sculptor (1232–1300). 249

ARTEMIS: daughter of Zeus, goddess of the moon and night, also of the forest and chase. 57

ARTHUR: *King John.* 53

ASTRAEAN JUSTICE: Astraea was the daughter of Zeus and Themis, and as such was identified with Dike, one of the goddesses of the Hours, who presided over legal order. In the tragic poets she is mentioned with the Erinyes, and as a relentless and stern divinity. 273

ATHENA: daughter of Zeus, generally regarded as the goddess of war, wise courage and victory. 172, 236, 269

—— had the aspect of Deiphobus. *Vide Iliad,* XXII, where Athena assumes the form of Hector's brother Deiphobus in order to encourage him to turn and meet Achilles. 56

ATRIDES: a patronymic from Atreus to denote his sons and descendants. Commonly denotes Agamemnon or Agamemnon and Menelaus (*Iliad,* I, 12). 54, 168

BEATRICE: Florentine lady idealised as the spirit of love by Dante in the *Divina Commedia.* 234

BEATRICE: *Much Ado About Nothing.* 232, 243

BELPHOEBE: Spenser, *Faerie Queene.* 181

BENEDICT: *Much Ado About Nothing.* 243

BÉRANGER: French poet (1780–1857). 194

BLATTERGOWL: Scott, *Antiquary.* 261

BODACH GLAS: Scott, *Waverley,* ch. LIX. 74

BOTTOM: *Midsummer Night's Dream.* 73

BRADWARDINE, Rose: Scott, *Waverley.* 234, 258

BRIDGENORTH, Alice: Scott, *Peveril of the Peak.* 234

BRITOMART: Spenser, *Faerie Queene.* 236, 241

BRUNDUSIUM, fountain of: a slip of the pen for Bandusia, a fountain near Venusia, addressed by Horace in *Odes,* III, 13. 74

BRUTUS: *Julius Caesar.* 74

BUCCLEUCH: Scott, *Lay of the Last Minstrel,* Canto III. 73

BULICAME: hot sulphur spring near Viterbo (Campagna), *Inferno,* XIV, 79. 178

BURLEY: Scott, *Old Mortality.* 261

CALYPSO: Ulysses dwells at Ogygia for seven years with the nymph Calypso, who promises him immortality if he will be her husband. He refuses, and Hermes is eventually sent by Zeus to order Calypso to release him. 55, 166

CANACE: Chaucer, *Squire's Tale.* 181

287 INDEX OF PROPER NAMES

SCAMANDER: the god of the river Scamander in Troas attacked
Achilles who was helped by Hephaestus. The god of fire dried
up the waters of the river, whereupon Scamander begged for
respite (*Iliad*, XXI, 212–260). 168
SCYLLA: a terrible monster of the sea dwelling on a rock between
Italy and Sicily. 55
SELENE: goddess of the moon, daughter of Hyperion. 57
SEYTON, Catherine: Scott, *The Abbot*. 234
SHYLOCK: *Merchant of Venice*. 198, 231
SILVIA: *Two Gentlemen of Verona*. 181, 231
SLENDER: *Merry Wives of Windsor*. 199
SOPHOCLES: Greek tragedian (B.C. 495–405). 180, 183
SPEZZIA: Genoa. Shelley drowned, 1822. 211, 273
STEWART, Dugald: Scottish philosopher (1753–1828). 102

TELEMACHUS: son of Ulysses and Penelope. 168
TEMPE: beautiful valley of Thessaly, ancient Greece. 267
TEREIAN MOUNT: a mountain of Mysia, probably near Cyzicus
(*Iliad*, II, 829). 172
THETIS: mother of Achilles. 182
TINTORET: Italian painter (1518–1594). 250
TITANIA: *Midsummer Night's Dream*. 243
TOBY: *Twelfth Night*. 199
TOMKYNS: Scott, *Woodstock*. 261
TOUCHSTONE: *As You Like It*. 199
TRUMBULL: Scott, *Redgauntlet*. 261
TULLYVEOLAN: Scott, *Waverley*. 68
TURNER, J. M. W.: British painter (1775–1851). 249, 273
TYBALT: *Romeo and Juliet*. 74

UGOLINO: Italian soldier, imprisoned and starved to death at Pisa
(Dante, *Inferno*, XXXIII, 30). 187
ULYSSES: hero of Homer's *Odyssey*. 54, 168–172
—— untying winds. The sailors of Ulysses untied the bag containing
the unfavourable winds, which he had been given by Æolus.
They were then driven back from their course. 54
UNA: Spenser, *Faerie Queene*. 236

VALENTINE: *Two Gentlemen of Verona*. 243
VERNON, Diana: Scott, *Rob Roy*. 234, 260
VEVAY: town on Lake of Geneva. 184
VIGNE, Casimir de la: French poet (1793–1843). 154
VIOLA: *Twelfth Night*. 231
VIRGILIA: *Coriolanus*. 105, 231

WESTERN, Squire: Fielding, *Tom Jones*. 68
WHITE LADY: Scott, *The Monastery*. 74
WHITE MAID OF AVENEL: Scott, *The Monastery*. 271

SUBJECT INDEX

Other names will be found in the Index of Proper Names.